The English Language Tea[...]
Global Civil Society

How can English language teachers contribute to peace locally and globally?

English language teachers and learners are located in the *global civil society*—an international network of civil organizations and NGOs related to human rights, the environment, and sustainable peace. English, with its special role as an international language, is a major tool for communication within this network.

On the local level, many teachers are interested in promoting reconciliation and sustainable peace, but often they do not know how to do so. This book provides information, analysis, and techniques to help teachers around the world take action toward this goal.

Balancing, in a readable and accessible way, the global and the local, core and periphery, cultural diffusion and resistance, theory and practice, pessimism and optimism, outsider and insider perspectives, the expert role and the apprentice role, and prescriptive and elicitive methods, it offers an alternative to literature about critical applied linguistics, globalization, and peace education that is simply too complex and wordy to spread easily from theoretician to the classroom teacher.

Engaging, informative, provocative, and highly readable, this book is a welcome resource for English language teacher trainers, pre-service teachers, practicing classroom teachers, and Peace Corps workers around the world.

Barbara M. Birch is a Professor in the Department of Linguistics at California State University, Fresno. She has taught EFL in Spain, Ecuador, and Pakistan, conducted inservice workshops for Peace Corps volunteers in Macedonia, and worked with English teacher trainers in Ulaanbaatar, Mongolia.

ESL & Applied Linguistics Professional Series
Eli Hinkel, Series Editor

Visit www.routledge.com/education for additional information on titles in the ESL & Applied Linguistics Professional Series

The English Language Teacher in Global Civil Society

Barbara M. Birch

California State University, Fresno

Routledge
Taylor & Francis Group

NEW YORK AND LONDON

First published 2009
by Routledge
270 Madison Ave, New York, NY 10016

Simultaneously published in the UK
by Routledge
2 Park Square, Milton Park, Abingdon, Oxon OX14 4RN

Routledge is an imprint of the Taylor & Francis Group, an informa business

© 2009 Taylor & Francis

Typeset in Sabon by
Keystroke, 28 High Street, Tettenhall, Wolverhampton
Printed and bound in the United States of America on acid-free paper by
Walsworth Publishing Company, Marceline, MO

Library of Congress Cataloging in Publication Data
Birch, Barbara M.
The English language teacher in global civil society / Barbara M. Birch.
p. cm. – (ESL & applied linguistics professional series)
1. English language–Study and teaching–Foreign speakers. 2. English
teachers. 3. Globalization. I. Title.
PE1128.A2B498 2009
428.2'4–dc22
2008047707

ISBN10: 0–415–99448–9 (hbk)
ISBN10: 0–415–99449–7 (pbk)
ISBN10: 0–203–87804–3 (ebk)

ISBN13: 978–0–415–99448–4 (hbk)
ISBN13: 978–0–415–99449–1 (pbk)
ISBN13: 978–0–203–87804–0 (ebk)

Contents

Where the mind is without fear and the head is held high
Where knowledge is free
Where the world has not been broken up into fragments
By narrow domestic walls
Where words come out from the depth of truth
Where tireless striving stretches its arms towards perfection
Where the clear stream of reason has not lost its way
Into the dreary desert sand of dead habit
Where the mind is led forward by thee
Into ever-widening thought and action
Into that heaven of freedom, my Father, let my country awake.

(Thakur, 1917:27–28)

Preface

This book is about how English language teachers can contribute to peace locally and globally. English language teachers and learners are located in the *global civil society*—an international network of civil organizations and NGOs related to human rights, the environment, and sustainable peace. English, with its special role as an international language, is a major tool for communication within this network. English language teachers and learners can play an important role in conflict transformation and reconciliation in deeply divided or diverse societies. Their classrooms can be important focal points for change. On the local level, many teachers are interested in promoting reconciliation and sustainable peace, but often they do not know how to do so. By providing information, analysis, and techniques, this book helps teachers around the world take action toward this goal by

- synthesizing threads from many fields and topics into a coherent and empowering argument for the activist role teachers can take to promote social change;
- covering issues in critical applied linguistics, approaches and methodologies in ESL/EFL, global and local curricular issues, and specific skill areas like reading, writing, and speaking; and
- balancing, in a readable and accessible way, the global and the local, core and periphery, cultural diffusion and resistance, theory and practice, pessimism and optimism, outsider and insider perspectives, the expert role and the apprentice role, and prescriptive and elicitive methods, offering an alternative to literature about critical applied linguistics, globalization, and peace education that is simply too complex and wordy to spread easily from theoretician to the classroom teacher.

The book is organized in three sections.

Part I: The English Language Teacher in Global Civil Society

English language teachers and learners are located in an international network of civil organizations related to human rights, environmental protection and sustainable peace, called *global civil society*. Its culture, called *global civic culture*, is based on notions of global citizenship as spelled out in the Earth Charter, and its lingua franca is English. Global citizenship involves notions of self-identity in relationship to others and species identity. I suggest a new goal for English language teachers: global citizenship.

Part II: The English Language Teacher in Local Civil Society

What is global is also local. I characterize local uncivil societies as well as a new paradigm for peacemaking as both universal and particular responsibilities of local citizens. Although teachers are often interested in promoting reconciliation and sustainable peace, they often do not know how to do so. English teachers and learners can take advantage of their position in both a global and a local network of relationships to import outsider and discover insider mechanisms to promote justice and environmental safety, and to address hatred and fear. English language teachers and learners are currently underutilized resources in conflict transformation and reconciliation in deeply divided or diverse societies. Classrooms can be important focal points for transition to a preferred future.

Part III: The English Language Teacher and Pedagogies of Transition

Pedagogies of transition are meant to move participants through conscientization and conflict to relationship through dialogue in conflict transformation, tolerance, remembrance, reconciliation, and forgiveness.

The central premises of this volume are:

- The network of English language teachers, as part of global civil society, is a global resource for sustainable peace.
- English language teachers can understand the local causes of conflict and violence and discover ways to transform it.
- Teachers and learners can imagine preferred future and work towards it together through pedagogies of transition.
- The pedagogies of transition repair relationships through conflict transformation, tolerance, remembrance, reconciliation, and forgiveness.

My hope is that this book will be widely used as a resource and course text for English language teacher trainers, pre-service teachers, and practicing classroom teachers around the world.

Acknowledgments

I did not write this book alone. I am grateful to my husband, Jim, for his constant help and encouragement. Thanks are due also to my neighbors who gave me feedback on portions of an earlier manuscript, my colleagues at California State University, Fresno, who taught me a lot about peace and conflict, and all the English language teachers and students I have met in Spain, Ecuador, the United States, Pakistan, Macedonia, and Mongolia, from whom I have learned so much. I am indebted to Naomi Silverman and Eli Hinkel for their trust and vision. I acknowledge the creative people at Earth Charter International and the Great Transitions Network for permissions to borrow from their websites. I also thank the many inspirational authors who took my thoughts to new places.

Part I

The English Language Teacher in Global Civil Society

Chapter 1

The Big Picture

Taking up Poster's (1989) terms, critical applied linguistics is an approach to language-related questions that springs from an assumption that we live amid a world of pain and that applied linguistics may have an important role in either the production of or the alleviation of some of that pain. But, it is also a view that insists not merely on the alleviation of pain but also the possibility of change.

(Pennycook, 2001: 7)

Here Pennycook challenges applied linguists to examine the social and cultural contexts of their work, and to see the "big picture". He asks applied linguists to be accountable for their contributions to that big picture. For instance, do their definitions of language minimize or empower speakers? Do theories of language learning belittle or respect the diverse capacities of the human mind? Do observations about language learners disparage or dignify their process and outcome? Does language learning transform or maintain the status quo?

English language teachers are applied linguists, so big-picture questions are relevant to us. In fact, big-picture questions are of special relevance to us because the context of our work is global. The more successful we are, the more our work carries a hint of cultural imperialism. No pedagogy is politically or socially neutral; no learning or lack of learning is without economic and cultural repercussions for society or for individuals. And yet we do not address such issues enough among ourselves or with our students. Too often, like horses with blinders on, we ignore events outside our classrooms and their potential to enhance or hinder learning.

There's more. Like everyone else, English language teachers have entered the twenty-first century with an increased sense of insecurity. We see that terrorism, the war against terror, and local wars and conflicts increasingly target innocent bystanders—that is, us and our families, friends, and colleagues across the globe. We cannot breathe our air, drink our water, or eat our produce without wondering how it might harm us in the long run. Global warming threatens to affect our lives and livelihoods and those of our children and grandchildren. The high cost of oil is making life difficult almost everywhere. Poverty and destitution continue to affect the health, education, and well-being of whole segments of our societies.

In the face of this, when we set our pedagogical sights on correct pronunciation, grammar, and vocabulary, we fall far short of meeting Pennycook's challenge. When we restrict our teacherly attention to sanitized speech functions, facile interactions, and simplistic intercultural communication, we fail to imagine realistic alternatives to our status quo. We waste our strategic positions and power to educate for a peaceful and sustainable world.

There is no neutrality. Teachers can either "cooperate in their own marginalization by seeing themselves as 'language teachers' with no connection to such social and political issues" or we can accept that, "like it or not, English teachers stand at the very heart of the most crucial educational, cultural, and political issues of our time" (Gee, 1994:190). My purpose is to make a case that English language teachers are at the center of important sociocultural networks, and that we have a special role we can play in current events. We can use our unique positions and agencies to inform the goals around which our pedagogy rotates. Rather than communicative competence or some such, I legitimize a new goal for our pedagogy: global citizenship.

Overview

In Part I of this book I make the case that there is a new force in the world, global civil society, and that along with it there is a new global civic culture emerging from latency into actuality. Globalization is creating a number of new "imagined communities" to be discussed in this book. In Part II of the book, I look at some ideas about a transition from the status quo to an image of "preferred futures" with synergy and morality. I argue that teachers are strategically placed to understand violence and interfere with it through education. Each chapter in Parts I and II begins with a general treatment of a topic and concludes with a section highlighting its relevance to English language teachers. My thinking is that pedagogy is agency, that teachers can be powerful agents of change if they so choose because of their positions in sociocultural networks. In Part III, I focus on one area of preferred futures out of many possible areas: building the foundations for sustainable peace. I present several pedagogies of transition designed to restore relationships and reciprocity.

Terminology

Chapter 1 is an introductory look at the context of our work: various forms of globalization, the spread of English, and language ideologies.

Chapter 2 is about the development of global civil society, its relationship to other global players, and some of its prominent organizations. *Global civil society* refers to a large network of civil organizations like Human Rights Watch and Amnesty International. Chapter 3 describes *global civic culture* as a pro-human and pro-social fusion of the good parts of many human cultures. *Civic* refers to the rights and responsibilities of civilians towards each other in a sociopolitical relationship. Global civic culture is not native to any existing human culture but is adopted by an imagined community of global civilians. *Global civilians* are those who work in global civil society (not in government, religious, or military institutions) and, more broadly, those who endorse the principles of the Earth Charter.

Chapter 4 introduces a second imagined global community, *global citizens*, and what makes them cosmopolitan. I use the term *cosmopolitan* in its original sense of "citizen of the world" and not in its debased sense of a sophisticated, glamorous, or worldly person. Global citizens have a mindset that allows them to commit to the rights and responsibilities of a global sociopolitical relationship: world citizenship, over and above, or in addition to, other affiliations. These two global communities are not exclusive of each other but rather overlap. Global civilians may or may not be global citizens. Global citizens may or may not be global civilians.

Derivation and Definition

- Nouns

  - *Civilian*: a person who is not a member of a military, government, or religious institution; a person actively following the pursuits of civil life.
  - *Citizen*: a member of a unit of political organization, who owes allegiance to the unit and to others within the unit, has duties and responsibilities towards the unit and others in the unit, and is entitled to protection, rights, and privileges from the unit and from others in the unit.
  - *Civility*: pro-human and pro-social communication and behavior; declarative and procedural knowledge of nonviolent norms of communication and behavior.
  - *Citizenship*: the legitimate relationship of duties, responsibilities, protection, rights, and privileges among people within a unit.

- Adjectives

  - *Civil*: pertaining to a public sphere that is not military or police, church, or government; as the root word of "civilize," socialized in nonviolent communication and behavior.

- *Civic*: pertaining to the duties, responsibilities, rights, protection, and privileges of citizens and noncitizens within a unit, including oversight and knowledge of the rules and laws.
- *Uncivil*: pertaining to societies with little or no public or other sphere to counterbalance government, military, and religion; also said of societies characterized by violence; pertaining to people who do not recognize or fulfill the relationship of citizenship, or to people who flout norms of nonviolent communication and behavior.

- Verb

  - *Civilize*: formerly, to bring out of barbarism and an uneducated state, to elevate in social and private life, to teach to be more "advanced"; currently, to bring into synergy through education, socialization, and rule of law.

Part II focuses on the specific area of sustainable peace as an image of our preferred futures and on what English language teachers can accomplish in their local (un)civil societies. Robertson (1992) coined a new word for a new concept, *glocalization*, a blend of globalization and localization. It refers to the interdependence of the local with the global and the global with the local, a social and psychological place with both creative and chaotic tension. Chapter 5 is an attempt to picture what a sustainable world at peace might look like when local societies have *synergy*, the outpouring of positive energy when people combine their agencies, and *morality*, a sense of relationship with others that balances self-interest with other-interest. Chapter 6 deals with violence and what psychologists tell us about why people collaborate with those who urge them to kill.

In Chapter 7, I discuss postmodern ideas of peacebuilding—for instance, that we cannot rely on political structures like nation-states, ideologies, military might, or politicians to create a peaceful world. Instead, we civilians build it ourselves through our connections with others when we become *pro-social capitalists*, another imagined community, investing in synergy. Chapter 8 deals with the sociopolitical and economic goals of educational systems and their nonalignment with goals of earth sustainability, global citizenship, or sustainable peace. I conclude the chapter with some ideas for one learning area within Education for Sustainability Development (ESD). Focusing my attention on sustainable peacebuilding, I suggest that English language teachers help people repair or create relationships by making spaces for pro-social dialogue in their classrooms.

Part III is about (re)connecting for a preferred future as a goal for global citizenship, and deals with *nonviolent communicative competence*, the ability to use language in a way that benefits individuals in a social relationship (Birch, 1994). Chapter 9 is about post-method conflict transformation and Chapter 10 is about increasing post-racist tolerance. Chapter 11 is about remembering the past to let go of it. Chapter 12 is about the potential for reconciliation in divided societies. Chapter 13 is the riskiest topic of all: forgiveness. In each chapter, classroom participants are invited to explore the creative and chaotic tension involved with learning about, in, and through conflict.

For each topic, I make prescriptive and elicitive suggestions. *Prescriptive* suggestions are top-down and outside-in in the sense that they may not be indigenous. They are additive norms of nonviolent communication; that is, they are meant, if necessary, to transform communication patterns to facilitate relationship-building. *Elicitive* suggestions are intended to help teachers create or discover, from the discourse genres of local cultures, additional norms of nonviolent communication that percolate from the bottom up and the inside out to global civic culture ("lobalization") so that they become resources for us all.

Problematizing Prescription

At this point let me say that there is some resistance to normative prescriptive discourse about language in applied linguistics. Linguists take great care to say that they describe language, rather than prescribe certain usages as better, or proscribe certain usages as inferior. Throughout the book, I will attempt to make the case that some of the resistance to prescribing in our field is attributable to so-called individualist or even egocentric ways of relating to others. In the spirit of Pennycook's (2001) critical applied linguistics, I problematize that attitude. I am not talking about prejudice about dialect difference, grammar rules or pronunciation norms (Birch, 2004). I am instead looking at appropriating both inside and outside cultural resources for nonviolent communication. I believe that it is the teacher's function (from the perspective of global society) to teach socially responsible language to learners.

Kramsch and Thorne (2002:99) credit Bakhtin with a distinction between *genre*, the stock of conventions of communication available in a culture, and *style*, the communicative choices that individuals make from the available stock. Some types of "verbal hygiene" (Cameron, 1995) are affronts to human dignity because, imposed for nefarious purposes, individual stylistic choice is negated. Forcing people to greet others with a "Heil Hitler" under penalty of punishment (and the like) is antisocial, violent and coercive, but prescription which adds to the pro-social and nonviolent stock of genres in a culture is positive. When people value relationship and collective welfare, they voluntarily modify their communicative style towards civil norms to aid in connecting and reconnecting. Classroom participants may need to learn new norms of communication as expected civil behavior in the classroom. In any case, Martusewicz (2001:18) makes the point that dynamic and critical education like the nonviolent dialogue we are talking about "ensures that predictability and prescription, and thus control of the outcome of teaching, will always be, strictly speaking, impossible." Thus, ultimately, teachers can only influence genre and style; resistance is always possible.

Globalization

Globalization, as we might expect, is a huge and controversial topic. Very generally speaking, *globalization* refers to the expanding interdependence or interconnectedness among people, institutions, and organizations across the globe and the repercussions of that interdependence. Globalization is amoral, neither good nor bad. However, what humans choose to do within it or how their actions affect others can be judged as positive or negative, moral or immoral. In this book I will argue that some aspects of globalization are positive and moral.

Globalization has already had a profound effect on our idea of knowledge, broadening our ideas of what it is, who has it, where it is produced, how and why. In this section, I discuss only a few aspects that are relevant to English language teachers. I look at globalization as an economic system, as a process of diffusion, and as a relationship among global civilians. Although I highlight certain aspects of globalization separately, they are inherently interdependent.

A Transnational System

Globalization is a loose and unorganized but effective system which connects individuals around the world in social, business, economic, political, and technological networks. One aspect of globalization might be called a transnational economic system. Because it operates at the corporate level with the assistance of national and international governmental organizations (IGOs) like the World Bank, it is considered top-down. For some, this system has a positive impact on the world because of possible increased employment and potentially lowered prices on materials and goods. For others, the transnational economic system has had a predominantly negative impact on the people of the world. For instance, Keane calls this aspect of globalization "turbo-capitalism."

> Turbo-capitalism is a species of private enterprise driven by the desire for emancipation from taxation restrictions, trade union intransigence, government interference, and all other external restrictions upon the free movement of capital in search of profits . . . For the first time ever, modern capitalist firms have unlimited grazing rights.
> (Keane, 2001:29)

Such transnational corporations operate above any laws to exploit people and the environment in order to increase their sales and profits. Indeed, some people call them "neo-liberal," using the term liberal in its sense of greatest freedom from restriction, or even "predatory" (Falk, 1999). In their greed, transnational corporations do not respect human rights, cultural diversity, sustainable development, or ecological concerns. To its detractors, predatory globalization is nothing more than the new face of imperialism with the permission of the World Bank and the World Trade Organization. From their perspective, rich countries continue to abuse and take advantage of less developed countries.

Some transnational corporations engage in what they call global corporate citizenship, philanthropic programs intended to improve their tarnished image as social and economic exploiters and polluters. Collins (1994) discussed the global corporate citizenship of the Body Shop; Stabile (2000) analyzed Nike's. Advertising and media campaigns promote these attempts at "image management" to persuade consumers to overlook sweatshops, human trafficking, child slavery, and environmental degradation. But international corporations do not simply exploit; they also spread cultural values like consumerism and materialism.

Cultural Diffusion

Globalization also refers to cultural diffusion, processes by which concepts and products spread from one culture to another. Cultural diffusion is nothing new. The history of humankind is a history of the spread of ideas, knowledge, and artifacts through trade, conquest, and borrowing. Cultural concepts like writing systems, religions, literatures, goods, and technologies have oozed across borders in many directions from such centers as China, England, India, Japan, Russia, Saudi Arabia, and the United States to distant people and places.

Diffusion can have positive, negative, or neutral repercussions if you look back from our vantage point. The diffusion of numbers and mathematics from India and Arabia to Europe was positive. The diffusion of feng shui, anime, and sudoku from Asia to the US and Europe was neutral (in my opinion). The diffusion of slavery by Europeans from Africa to America was negative, except for the important fact that it has made America a more ethnically and culturally interesting place. It is clear that some diffusion has both positive and negative results. The spread of writing allowed knowledge to be stored in books, but it also caused oral traditions to deteriorate in some cultures.

The difference between cultural diffusion in the past and nowadays resides in the sheer amount of diffusion taking place, its multidirectionality, and its speed. Globalization means cultural diffusion on a massive, complicated, and very rapid scale. It is unclear at this point what will ultimately be seen as positive, neutral, or negative from a future vantage point. The English language teacher has a part to play in this.

Cultural diffusion can add, replace, subtract, or fuse. These diffusional processes are not exclusive of each other. Instead, they interact with each other uniquely in each case of diffusion. An additive process can become replacive over time or it can become fusional or, with enough motivation, societies can resist and interrupt a replacive process. An *additive* process is when a concept or product is added to a second culture; for instance, when food fads catch on across the globe, or, more seriously, when the latest weaponry is bought and sold by arms dealers to armies. The added thing or concept may displace local things and concepts, but it doesn't drive them out completely. Additive cultural diffusion is the process by which the inventory of communicative genres available in a culture increases.

A *replacive* process is when a local concept or product is replaced, or largely replaced, by an outside concept or idea. When international rule of law, transparency in government, or parliamentary procedure travels from established democracies to new democracies, it is intended to replace some local ways of doing things, like bribery or coercion (although local ways may not disappear completely). If the local way of doing things ultimately disappears altogether, then a replacive process can also be called a *subtractive* process. The prohibition against headhunting has caused that activity to be subtracted from the culture of the indigenous people of the Oriente in Ecuador, but they have replaced human heads with animal heads so as not to lose their headshrinking technology.

A *fusional* process is one in which the outside influence fuses with the inside to create a hybrid. For instance, local democracies fuse norms of parliamentary procedure to local decision-making processes like consensus or reliance on kin or tribal authorities. Ultimately, fusion can lead to subtraction as well, if the original "pure" idea or thing ceases to exist. Fusion is also an important concept for human identity; there may be "hybrid" identities that are fusions of several ethnicities, generating questions about how such identities are related to their source ethnicities.

There are also different attitudes towards cultural diffusion. Some people have a positive but rather simplistic or uncritical attitude towards global cultural diffusion. This attitude, called *globalism*, means embracing additive, replacive, subtractive, and fusional processes as enlightened progress. Globalists advocate a superficial form of multiculturalism. That is, they accept changes to their culture in the name of "progress," but they do not necessarily know how to accept other people or other cultures. They do not critically evaluate the positive or negative effects of cultural diffusion. There are also those who oppose cultural diffusion unthinkingly because they see it as domination. Others choose to resist diffusion selectively; they adopt a reflectively critical, rational, and evaluative stance.

If people have a strong aversion to outside concepts and things, they may feel the need to defend their own culture and society. Moderate defensiveness may lead people to reject diffusion in order to maintain their own culture or societal norms. Intense defensiveness is often associated with religious *fundamentalism* (zealous adherence to conservative religious beliefs), political *chauvinism* (blind patriotism or devotion to nationalism, historical traditions, or military might), or *ethnocentrism* (irrational beliefs in the superiority of one's race or ethnic group over others). Fundamentalism, chauvinism, and ethnocentrism are sometimes associated with violence towards others who are different.

Global Civil Society

Globalization is also a bottom-up egalitarian, pro-social, and pro-human relationship among the people of the world in a network of global organizations. *Pro-social* refers to attitudes and behaviors benefiting others in a societal relationship and environmental context. *Pro-human* refers to attitudes and behaviors benefiting the self, individuals, groups, and the human species. Early examples of global pro-social and pro-human organizations had to do with women's suffrage or the abolition of slavery; they crossed the Atlantic back and forth between Europe and America in the nineteenth and early twentieth centuries. Later, after the excessive violence in Europe and Asia in the twentieth century, the United Nations came into being. One of its first acts, in 1948, was to encode a set of universal values for the welfare of all humans.

The United Nations Universal Declaration of Human Rights (UNUDHR) proclaimed civil rights for everyone in the world. It was the first statement of human rights and freedoms incorporating the input of many nations and their values through the parliamentary process in the United Nations. It declared genocide and other crimes against humanity illegal, but it did not have the legal force of a treaty or a convention among nations. It was to be diffused through education and by legislation at the national and international levels. The UNUDHR preamble states:

Now, Therefore THE GENERAL ASSEMBLY proclaims THIS UNIVERSAL DECLARATION OF HUMAN RIGHTS as a common standard of achievement for all peoples and all nations, to the end that every individual and every organ of society, keeping this Declaration constantly in mind, shall strive by teaching and education to promote respect for these rights and freedoms and by progressive measures, national and international, to secure their universal and effective recognition and observance, both among the peoples of Member States themselves and among the peoples of territories under their jurisdiction.

(United Nations Universal Declaration of Human Rights, 1948)

Despite the intentions of its writers, the UNUDHR is still a latent universal at present. It has not stopped genocide from happening, but it established a universal standard of behavior, an ethical norm for everyone to adhere to. A latent universal is real, but it is emergent, not actual. Human rights as a universal value will emerge into actuality through cultural diffusion "by teaching and education" and through "progressive measures." Diffusion of this document has continued for sixty years and has led to a number of other treaties and documents, like the Earth Charter, discussed further in Chapter 3.

With the growth and spread of human rights, a global civil society has sprung up. Global civil society is the conglomerate of institutions separate from nation-states, markets, and organized religions, and including non-governmental organizations (NGOs), non-profit organizations, educational institutions, charities, grassroots people's movements, trade unions, environmental groups, service clubs, policy institutions, groups of faith, and the independent media. In general, they attempt to oppose the negative aspects of turbo-capitalism as well as mitigate national and regional social, political, and environmental problems.

Despite this, it is important to note that global civil society is dependent on transnational economic enterprises for its existence. Of particular importance are communication networks and media conglomerates that create a public sphere within which much of global civil society operates. Cell-phone companies and internet providers allow global civilians to work together across boundaries of time and space. Satellite television news carries pictures of famines and wars into the world's houses, apartments, huts, gers, and tents.

> Hailed by media narratives that probe the wider world in tones of (ironic) intimacy, the members of global civil society become a bit less parochial, a bit more cosmopolitan. Global publics are taught lessons in the art of flexible citizenship: they learn that the boundaries between native and foreigner are blurred and that they have become a touch more footloose. They learn to distance themselves from themselves; they discover that there are different temporal rhythms, other places, other problems, other ways to live. They are invited to question their own dogmas, even to extend ordinary standards of civility—courtesy, politeness, respect—to others whom they will never meet. . . . Global public spheres centred on ground-breaking media events like Live Aid can even be spaces of fun in which millions taste something of the joy of acting publicly with and against others for some defined common purpose. Global publics, like the recent UN-sponsored multimedia event "A World Freed of Violence Against Women," can also highlight cruelty; and global publics can also be sites of disaster, spaces in

which millions taste unjust outcomes, bitter defeat, and the tragedy of ruined lives.

(Keane, 2001:43)

Keane highlights the main features of global civil society and global civilians. The boundaries between cultural insider and outsider are blurred for them. Global civilians are not parochial, they have flexible allegiances, and they can distance themselves from their own culture in order to question conventions. They create a space for global publics to learn *critical consciousness*, the capacity to evaluate information independently rather than simply adopting group or authority opinions (Staub, 2003:505). They demonstrate for the global public what it means to have *critical loyalty*, a commitment to the welfare of their own people balanced with a commitment to universal principles, instead of blind loyalty to a policy or course of action adopted by the group at a particular time which may conflict with universal principles (Staub, 2003:506).

The extract also spotlights how the transnational corporate world and the global civil world rely on communication networks and media. And communication networks and the media are parasitic on corporations, national governments, and civil society. Global communication and information transfer take advantage of and encourage linguistic homogeneity. Linguistic spread started many millennia ago, and continued in colonial and imperial times. The list of imperial languages once included Latin, Greek, Turkish, French, Spanish, Russian, German, Chinese, and others, but now it has mostly narrowed to one.

Global English

There can be no denying that English is currently the major lingua franca around the world. In some cases, English was additive, learned as a foreign or second language by choice. Sometimes English was imposed, but people resisted the loss of their first language(s) and became bilinguals or multilinguals. In other cases, especially where the native population was weakened by conquest or when there were relatively few speakers, English was forced on a people who were unable to resist. These last cases are subtractive because the speakers and the world lost their language and culture.

But the diffusion of English has also been fusional. Within the UK there are different varieties of English, and outside there are also many established varieties of English. In these different varieties English has fused with elements from local or other immigrant languages in complicated ways that I cannot discuss here. Additive, replacive, and fusional processes have made the notion of English native speaker versus non-native speaker largely irrelevant. Now, the term *expert speaker* is used to describe people who are fluent in English. By taking away the native versus non-native dichotomy, people attempt to erase a sociocultural and linguistic boundary.

Although it will be many years before we can discern whether the diffusion of English is ultimately more positive than negative or otherwise in the long run, people adopt different attitudes with respect to the repercussions and potential repercussions of the global diffusion of English. For instance, some see English as a means to an end. Is it a means to promote turbo-capitalism, making the people of the world better consumers of merchandise? Is learning English a path to cultural imperialism or a tool to resist imperialism? Or is it one tool among many to diffuse the values of human rights?

English Imperialism

Imperialism is the ancient idea that one nation or people can increase its security and comfort by acquiring power over and taking advantage of other nations and people. The imperial nation takes resources, land, food, products, and people from the vanquished nations. It usually seeks to impose its culture, religion, and language on the subordinate nations and people in the empire. Nowadays, global cultural and economic hegemony (i.e. the ability to control) is replacing nationalistic political hegemony.

By analogy, the idea that language should spread without regard for the status of other languages is called *linguistic imperialism* (Phillipson, 1992). In its strongest form, as part of a colonialist agenda, English was meant to replace other languages, and no economic, pedagogical, or social support was offered for other languages. The end, assimilation, justified the means, sometimes draconian measures of cultural and linguistic repression, such as removal of children from their rightful homes to be educated in English-speaking boarding schools. English imperialism sought to use English to "civilize" (in the former sense of the word) the colonies and assimilate them to English culture and society.

In a lesser form of linguistic imperialism, English is simply added to the list of official languages spoken in the area. In any case, even in this view, English is just one of the means for English-speaking cultures to dominate other cultures politically and economically. English imperialists generally do not feel that they need to learn any other languages because everyone will eventually know English. For them, their status as monolinguals is normal, and bilingualism and multilingualism are abnormal. Rather than feeling disabled when venturing out of their countries, they expect others to accommodate to their ignorance.

English imperialists also maintain the inherent primacy of native speakers over non-native speakers. They believe that English belongs to certain countries and peoples and, although others borrow it, they can never own it. To them, the accepted standard varieties of English are more correct or acceptable than other nonstandard or foreign varieties. Furthermore, English language instruction is big business; in some cases part of turbo-capitalism. Between huge textbook publishers and language schools, English teaching around the world is profitable. Gray (2002) has an excellent analysis of the global textbooks and the diffusion of consumerism and materialism through an international English that assumes wealth, leisure, and individualism as values.

Knowledge of English inevitably affects people's socioeconomic status because knowledge creates a have/have not dichotomy among them. People in many parts of the world attempt to surmount personal, social, and economic obstacles like caste, religion, or gender by learning English and taking part in predatory globalization. Nevertheless, with this kind of instrumental motivation (what's in it for me?), sometimes very little benefit derived from English learning returns to the local community.

Language with an Agenda

Agnieszka Tennant (2002) notes that language teaching is a way for outsiders to integrate normally into a culture, whereby they can spread political or religious ideas:

> I was one of many young Poles wooed by God in the world's most popular and powerful language. Eager to wake from a communism-induced malaise, my generation (born in the 1970s) studied English hungrily. Soon after the Iron Curtain lifted in 1989, we abandoned the foreign, yet eerily familiar, Russian language (mandatory classes attempted to indoctrinate us with readings that idolized Lenin and Stalin). Instead, we took up the tongue, it seemed, of Liberty herself: the sensuous, many-idiomed, supple English . . . Teaching English may well be the 21st century's most promising way to take the gospel to the world. It's the globalized world's equivalent of a cup of water for the thirsty . . . Start an evangelical church in Poland, and no one will come. Start an English school, and you'll make many friends.

This demonstrates that language study can be in aid of political indoc-trination or religious proselytizing. Language can be strategic and emblematic of life choices (Birch, 1995). It can be used as a weapon. I have so far not mentioned another important globalized network, one that is, at least in part, a defensive reaction to predatory globalization, turbo-capitalism, and military power. It is the globalization of terror. Among other things, the use of terror is a complicated reaction to perceived cultural, religious, and territorial imperialism. (To say that it is perceived does not imply that it is not real. See the above quote and also Pennycook

and Makoni, 2005.) The reaction to such threats, in the extreme, is fundamentalism, chauvinism, and ethnocentrism.

In the globalization of terror, a frequent justification given by Islamist
leaders for teaching and learning English is "Learn the language of your
enemy!" The 9/11 hijackers had studied in English-speaking countries and
spoke fluent English (Karmani, 2005). In reaction to the globalization of
terror, the USA has stepped up instruction in so-called strategic languages
like Persian and Arabic, in a kind of escalation of the linguistic war.

English is also important as a means to gain access to international
media conglomerates to foment plans for war. Hartley (2003:127)
describes this vividly in his book about his journalistic work with Reuters
in Africa.

> "What do you need to start a guerrilla war?" my friend Buchizya once
> asked the Marxist Congolese rebel leader Laurent-Desire Kabila.
>
> "Ten thousand dollars and a satellite phone," replied Kabila. "You
> use the dollars to recruit enough fighters to raid the local police station
> for their guns. The phone you use to call the world's press after the
> attack."

Of course, my purpose in writing this book is transparent. I combine
language learning with learning about global citizenship, global civil
society, and sustainable peace. The overt agenda is to help English language teachers see themselves as agents envisioning and teaching for
preferred futures for their localities. Rahman (2005:133), after discussing
the inequities of English, socioeconomic class, and economic and political
exclusion in Pakistan, concludes:

> English should be taught in a just manner (i.e. to all students) through
> texts that expose students to the values of peace, tolerance, and respect
> for rights. These concepts may have been articulated in their present
> form in Western democracies but they are of universal application. If
> English is useful in disseminating them then that is an aspect of it which
> should be valued. In short, instead of allowing English to become a
> source of class and ideological conflict, it can be made into a source of
> empowerment and humanitarian improvement for all in Pakistan.

English Ecology

Global civil society is compatible with another attitude towards language, commonly called *English ecology* (Pennycook, 1994). In this
approach, people view language as one of many resources that cultures and
societies have at their disposal. English language learning is meant to be
additive; a tool is added to the toolbox without taking away any others.
Multilingualism is the norm because most people grow up bilingual or

trilingual. Those unfortunate people who are monolingual do well to learn a second and third language. This is because language is a connection between people; it is a way for them to integrate with each other as equals. It is also a tool for communication; and the more tools, the more communication.

The term "glocalization" applies to language in the following way. As English spreads, each region appropriates it and makes it its own. Faruqi (1986) claims English for Islam; there is a drive to accommodate English and English instruction to Islamic traditions, as shown by some of the materials on the TESOL Islamia website (www.tesolislamia.org). We see and hear differences between Indian, Nigerian, Sri Lankan, and Japanese English, but no matter. "We shouldn't have to apologize for using 'Japanese English.' The notion that English belongs to the Americans or the Britons is very narrow-minded. English is now the language of the world" (Suzuki, cited in Hadley, 2004).

English is a big tent, accepting "turning turtle" or "overturning," and "sleeping policeman" or "speed bump." From the ecological point of view, a globally diverse English gains when new words, concepts, and expressions flow up from the grassroots, creating a juxtaposition of numerous glocalized variants. The meeting point, however, must maintain some degree of comprehensibility. What may become the common ground is a dialect consisting of around 2,000 of the most common words, substituting Latinate verbs for compound verbs like "put off" or "get on with," and avoiding idiomatic expressions. This dialect has been called *Basic English*, intended to be an international second language, or, more recently, *Offshore English* (Werth, 2008). Basic English is a limited goal, an entry point for English learners.

The Worldliness of English

Pennycook (1994:71) uses the term *worldliness of English* to refer to the idea that English is both globally general and locally specific. It emphasizes both the global position of English and its glocalization, its locality in many cities, villages, and rural parts of the world. English is part of a colonial legacy but is appropriated by former colonialists and colonials for resistance and social change, such as using the term "expert speaker" to rub away current distinctions between native and non-native speakers. In this sense, language is performative and dynamic; it does not just reflect culture and society, but has the power to evoke a change in society or culture. English is both changing the world and being changed by the world. The change is not limited to syntactic or lexical changes but includes the idea of how "acts of language use always imply a position within a social order, a cultural politics, a struggle over different representations of the self and other" (Pennycook, 1994:34).

The worldliness of English is "a term intended to refer to the material existence of English in the world, its spread around the world, its worldly character as a result of being so widely used in the world, and its position not only as reflective but also as constitutive of worldly affairs" Pennycook (1994:36). To be constitutive as well as reflective means a number of things. First, language is a way for people, including English language teachers, to exercise their agency. Words legitimize, so language is social action. Second, language is a way for people to imagine and therefore transition to preferred futures. For example, Pennycook introduced a new meaning for the word "worldliness," a meaning which points to people's use of English in a deep way that balances respect for the diversity of other cultures and languages with universal concern and responsibility. Third, local English language teachers contribute to the worldliness of English by encouraging code-switching and borrowing from resource languages into English, constituting change.

"Worldly English" contrasts with simplistic notions of English as an International Language (EIL): that English is simply a way for people to communicate with each other and that things will magically turn out well. It is a way to resist English that assumes values like consumerism and materialism. Instead, the worldliness of English has a potential linkage to global citizenship, to the dialogue for sustainable peacebuilding.

> I want to conclude, then, on a certain note of optimism here and suggest a role for the English language classroom in the world that makes it not the poor cousin to other classes that it so often seems to be, but rather a key site in global cultural production. Counter-discourses formulated through English and the articulation of insurgent knowledges and cultural practices in English offer alternative possibilities to the colonizers and post-colonizers, challenging and changing the cultures and discourse that dominate the world. In some sense, then, the English language classroom, along with other sites of cultural production and political opposition, could become a key site for the renewal of both local and global forms of culture and knowledge. I shall close this book here on this optimistic note, in the hope that critical English language educators may be able to use the concept of worldliness I have been developing here and engage in a critical, transformative and listening critical pedagogy through English.
>
> (Pennycook, 1994:326)

Learning is Agency

In most cultures, teachers have certain traditional forms of authority over learners, some of which they use and some of which they may not be aware of. Naturally, there is cultural and individual variation in the power that teachers have, but even in egalitarian cultures teachers often have more authority than they are aware of. A major criticism of many student-centered or participatory learning methods is that they assume that the teacher and the student are equal when, in fact, they are not. They do not transfer from more egalitarian cultures to more hierarchical cultures because of the authority structures in place.

But this book is not about authority over others, but about learning as agency with diverse others in global cultural production. Martusewicz (2001:2) examines education as a something that "gets made *between* teachers and learners in all kinds of different contexts." Education is a "generative force . . . all possible kinds of ideas, beliefs, interpretations, and meanings are generated [with] *difference* as its fuel." To her, to become educated "requires not only an attention to questions regarding the welfare of self and others, but also a willingness to confront and shift one's own habits, practices, and beliefs for that purpose . . . education demands a willingness to judge, to choose between all possibilities for the well-being of one's self and community. Education must be framed by the decisive confrontation with issues of social and ecological justice." As the starting point for education as global cultural production and confrontation, then, we need to understand the relationship between self and community, because that is the basis for understanding ethics.

The Self

Cultures have traditionally been described as either collectivist or individualist, but the apparent dichotomy is false because individuals within cultures vary greatly in their self-definitions and their orientations towards others. The basis for individualist and collectivist cultures rests on differing concepts of the self. At the most personal level, humans have a basic self-concept, at the very least, that each is a physical entity existing in a physical space. Humans have a sense of a *private self* with internal thoughts and feelings others cannot know. Some people view this internal self as a soul or ego but the religious or psychological connotation of each of those words is problematic. Egocentricity, for example, is often related to ideas of narcissism, fear, threat, arrogance, and selfishness. For this reason, Hinduism and Buddhism teach that the private ego is a delusion. The Japanese word *jibun*, for self, is often taken to mean one's share of the shared life space (Markus and Kitayama, 1991:228).

At any rate, the private self, however it is construed, relates to others in a local sociocultural network through a *public self or selves*. Markus and Kitayama (1991) summarized a number of studies that find cultural differences in public self-concept, especially how the public self relates to the private self and to other people. Psychologists discuss two such public self-concepts which are differentiated from each other by their sense of attachment to or detachment from others. One view is that the private self and public self are unified into a self-concept of a unique individual with attributes and motivations that remain constant over time and situation. This *independent self* is associated with individualist cultures, although there is a lot of individual variation in any culture. The other view is that the private self is associated with several public selves, each one a part of a sociocultural network of relationships like family, work, or social groupings. Each public self is highly focused on other people within the relationship. This *interdependent self* is generally associated with Asian, African, and Latin American cultures, and many Western women as well.

For the independent self, internal emotions, feelings, and goals are the motivations for voice and agency: this is called self-interest. The expectation is that people will say what is on their mind and reveal private thoughts, valued as *honesty*. A high value is also placed on autonomy from others and *integrity*, or consistency of values and behavior throughout various situations. This makes the independent public self rather context-free. Independent people tend to project their own feelings on others or attribute some quality to others. *Projection* means that people believe that others share their emotions. If they are happy, they think others are happy. If they are angry, they assume others are angry too. *Attribution* means that people interpret others' behaviors in terms of internal qualities like generosity or stinginess instead of simply noting the behavior. An independent person might say, "He's stingy." An interdependent person might say, "He doesn't like to spend money." Kitayama and Uchida (2004:155) note that independents "often fail to give proper weight to significant contextual information in drawing a judgment about a focal person." Thus, to the applied linguist, it seems that honesty and integrity in speech counterbalance the tendency to project and attribute feelings and qualities onto the other, facilitating communication.

The interdependent public self, on the other hand, is more context-sensitive. People are motivated to fit inside relationships, and to fulfill or create obligations with others. People's actions are performed with reference to others in the network and their abilities, judgments, and personality characteristics are context-dependent. People's private selves are not revealed; instead, agency is controlled and regulated and voice may be indirect. Autonomy is not valued as much as collective *welfare*, sympathetic *concern* for others, and in-group *cooperation*. An important concept for interdependent agency is *reciprocity*. Markus and Kitayama (1991:229) put it this way:

> Yet in many cases, responsive and cooperative actions are exercised only when there is a reasonable assurance of the "good-intentions"

of others, namely their commitment to continue to engage in reciprocal interactions and mutual support. Clearly, interdependent selves do not attend to the needs, desires, and goals of all others. Attention to others is not indiscriminate; it is highly selective and will be most characteristic of relationships with "in-group" members . . . Given the importance of others in constructing reality and regulating behavior, the in-group–out-group distinction is a vital one for interdependent selves, and the subjective boundary of one's in-group may tend to be narrower for interdependent selves than for the independent selves.

An important ability that interdependent people learn in childhood is *empathy*. Their need to be cooperative and successful in their networks obliges them to take the role of the other, to read the other's mind, while at the same time concealing their private thoughts so as to avoid conflict. Thus, empathy for others and personal concealment or indirectness in speech counterbalance each other. An applied linguist sees a paradox here: if interpersonal understanding is the goal, would a judicious amount of empathy for others combined with a touch of revelation and directness not be more efficient, at least in intercultural conversations? Is it possible that pro-social nonviolent communication would result from a combination of independent and interdependent behaviors? In any case, the connection between self, voice, and agency is a crucial one.

The Collective

Whether they are individualist or collectivist, people in sociocultural networks, both inside and outside the classroom, use their agency with others. I call this agency *pro-social capital*, as a way of appropriating economic value-laden terms for social relationships among people. People's pro-social capital comes from their investment in creating and sustaining reciprocal relationships between the self and others. The more "pro-social capitalists" invest in relationships, the more return they and their society get. As pro-social capitalists, English language teachers and learners use language and language instruction for social transformation and they also contribute to the worldliness of English by appropriating local norms into English.

Each of the sections "Learning is Agency" in the first seven chapters will explore different kinds of pro-social pedagogical agency as potential sources of learning for English language teachers and their students. Many of them involve different aspects of nonviolent communicative competence. Among the pedagogical powers I will be discussing are legitimization, global cultural consciousness, metacultural awareness, complex thinking, moral development, and critical thinking.

Chapter 2

Global Civil Society

> Global civil society, for the activists, therefore, is about "civilizing" or democratizing globalization, about the process through which groups, movements and individuals can demand a global rule of law, global justice, and global empowerment. Global civil society does, of course, in my own version, include those who are opposed to globalization and those who do not see the need for regulation. Thus, my version of global civil society is based on the belief that a genuinely free conversation, a rational critical dialogue, will favor the "civilizing" option.
>
> (Kaldor, 2003:12)

In her book *Global Civil Society: An Answer to War*, Kaldor discusses the civil or public part of local society and culture, separate from military, religious, and governmental organizations. Local civil societies seem to have emerged in more individualist cultures, perhaps because civil associations strengthen the sociocultural fabric which might otherwise be fragmented. The functions of local civil society in collectivist cultures may take other forms; there may not be as much of a vacuum for civil society to occupy.

Nevertheless, local civil society has gone global, which Kaldor believes might be a way to deal with conflict nonviolently. She includes within global civil society individuals who oppose turbo-capitalism as well as those who do not. She argues that global civil society is an alternative physical and temporal "space" where people can discuss globalization and monitor it and shape it. In this dialogue space, individuals temper the power of the corporate transnational system, the ideology of national or regional forces (governmental, military, social), and the influence of organized religions. In her view, the dialogue leads to a more participatory or "civilizing" distribution of power to benefit peoples and societies.

For instance, when disputants discuss their concerns in a context where violence and fear are simply not options, as in global society, their vexing questions may bring about viable alternatives to war. Similarly, environmental organizations hold forums where people can criticize destructive policies and decisions and argue for economic boycotts. Health organizations give news of risks and information about dangers. They use the media to mobilize assistance even when national governments remain unresponsive. Local civil rights groups use pressure from outside groups to increase their participation in their own internal national processes; this is called the "boomerang effect."

The organizations of the global civil society together build an international culture of altruism, with a pro-social and pro-human agenda of human rights, environmental protection, health and education, and sustainable development. However, as was noted in Chapter 1, global civil society relies on globalized communication, technology, and information conglomerates. It also depends increasingly on funding from national governments. Northern European NGOs receive 50 to 90 percent of their funding from governments, because the latter have realized the important work that NGOs can do that they cannot (Kriegman, 2006).

There are some organizations, like the United Nations and the United States Peace Corps, on the fringes of the global civil society because they are associated with and supported by the governments of nation-states. There are also some faith-based groups connected to the global civil society, like Pax Christi Netherlands (a Christian human rights group) and the Tikkun Community (an organization of Jews, Christians, Muslims, Hindus, and Buddhists who support healing and reconciliation in Israel and Palestine). With his Nobel Peace Prize money, the Dalai Lama of Tibet established the Foundation for Universal Responsibility to support personal and social change towards nonviolence, coexistence, gender equity, and peace. These groups are associations of people of faith which might receive support from organized religious hierarchies, but they themselves are separate from organized religious structures. Global civil organizations maintain their autonomy from governments, religions, and transnational corporations. (Websites for all of these organizations and all others mentioned in the book can be found in the bibliography.)

Global Civil Organizations

Internally, global civil society is the network of national and transnational non-profit, non-governmental associations dedicated to social, economic, or political change based on sustainability, human rights, social justice, and environmental protection. Keane (2001:23) likens global civil society to a "dynamic biosphere" or

> the thickening and stretching of networks of socio-economic institutions across borders to all four corners of the earth, such that the

peaceful or "civil" effects of these non-governmental networks are felt everywhere, here and there, far and wide, to and from local areas, through wider regions to the planetary level itself.

Human Rights Watch (HRW)

Formerly known as Helsinki Rights Watch, HRW is a world-wide non-governmental organization that was founded in 1978 to monitor compliance with the Helsinki Accords in Soviet Bloc countries. HRW researchers now investigate human rights abuses in all regions of the world and draw media attention to pressure abusive governments. It lobbies the United Nations, the European Union, the United States, and other nations around the world to change policies. To maintain scrupulous independence, HRW does not accept support from any government or government-funded agency. It is composed of 150 lawyers, journalists, academics, and country experts of many nationalities and diverse backgrounds, aided by many volunteers around the world, and has worked with other organizations to achieve a treaty banning child soldiers and landmines, as well as to provide evidence for the Yugoslav and Rwanda war crimes tribunals.

Peace Brigades International (PBI)

Since 1981, PBI has been an organization committed to applying nonviolent methods to conflicts to bring about peace and justice. It believes that violence begets more violence and therefore sustainable peacebuilding can only be founded on democracy, human rights, and social change through nonviolent means. It uses a cooperative structure of decision-making in which relationships and processes are as important as outcomes. PBI volunteers protect noncombatants through their physical presence. They also observe and report what is happening during international conflicts. PBI is non-partisan; volunteers attempt to keep an open mind about the issues, report objectively, and stay non-judgmental.

Inter-Parliamentary Union (IPU)

Like the United Nations, the IPU operates at the fringe between government and the global civil society because it is supported by individual member parliaments. This international organization of parliaments of sovereign states was founded in 1889, making it one of the oldest international organizations and the first permanent site of multilateral political negotiations. Since its beginning, the IPU has promoted peace through international arbitration. It is one of the groups credited with founding the UN and the Permanent Court of Arbitration in The Hague. Between

1901 and 1927, eight Nobel Prizes for Peace went to leaders of the IPU. It has six domains of interest: representative democracy; human rights and humanitarian law; international peace and security; sustainable development; education, science, and culture; and women in politics. To promote democracy, the IPU sets standards and guidelines for elections, strengthens representative institutions by offering technical assistance, protects members of parliament and their human rights, and advocates greater representation of women in parliaments.

Médecins Sans Frontières (MSF)

Founded in 1971, MSF (or Doctors Without Borders) provides medical and emergency aid to victims of war, epidemics, and natural or man-made disasters. It also serves those who are excluded from healthcare in more than 70 countries. MSF is an international network of doctors, nurses, logistics, water, and sanitation experts, and other professionals working with 22,500 locally hired staff members. It oversees healthcare, rehabilitates and runs clinics, performs surgery, battles epidemics, carries out vaccinations, operates feeding centers for malnourished children, and offers mental healthcare. MSF also constructs wells, dispenses clean drinking water, and provides shelter materials like blankets and plastic sheeting. It treats infectious diseases such as tuberculosis, sleeping sickness, and HIV/AIDS, and provides medical and psychological care to marginalized groups like street children.

Greenpeace

In 1971, a small team of activists sailed from Vancouver, Canada, to Amchitka, an island off the west coast of Alaska. Their mission was to bear witness to the nuclear testing conducted there by the United States. The boat was stopped and sent back but the activists succeeded in drawing media attention to the testing in a sensitive area. Now Greenpeace is an international organization involved in stopping climate change and nuclear threats, protecting forests, oceans, and whales, and opposing genetic engineering and pollution. Headquartered in Amsterdam, Greenpeace now has 2.8 million supporters around the world, and offices in 41 countries. It accepts donations only from individuals or receives grants from foundations. It is committed to using nonviolent means to bring media attention to environmental crimes committed by governments and corporations. Its methods are designed to promote open and informed debate about issues that others ignore.

Global Reporting Initiative (GRI)

Sustainable development is the economic development of land and businesses and the social development of communities in a way that does not prejudice the environment or the future. When the hidden costs of degrading the environment are factored in, the true effects of development can be determined. In 1997, the non-profit Center for Education and Research in Environmental Strategies (CERES) started the GRI as a way to measure and report on the sustainability of various types of development. The GRI vision is that organizations should issue an annual economic, environmental, and social performance report just as they issue financial reports. The reports would provide data establishing which organizations are promoting sustainability. This could constitute a basis for achieving greater accountability. To date, more than 1,000 organizations in sixty countries have used the GRI Reporting Framework. GRI cooperates with the United Nations to provide a forum for research and discussion on sustainable development.

Servicio Paz y Justicia (SERPAJ)

Service Peace and Justice is a Latin American Christian social organization with a mission to promote solidarity and nonviolence and the construction of a society based on human rights. Since 1974, it has opposed institutionalized violence, poverty, and oppression. Adolfo Pérez Esquivel, Nobel Prize winner in 1980, was one of the founders of SERPAJ, and its coordinator between 1974 and 1986. The goal of SERPAJ is the creation of pluralist participatory societies with justice, freedom, rights, and peace for men and women. Its methods are consciousness-raising, organization, multi-sector networking, and building solidarity. It has offices in Bolivia, Brazil, Chile, Costa Rica, Ecuador, Mexico, Nicaragua, Panama, Paraguay, and Uruguay.

Wikimedia Foundation

Created in 2001, the Wikimedia Foundation is an international non-profit organization with the goal of encouraging the development and distribution of free multilingual content so that all people will have access to knowledge in their own language, provided they have access to a computer and the internet. Its best-known product, Wikipedia, is a multilingual free-content encyclopedia written by volunteers. It is already one of the most visited websites on the internet and appears in more than 30 languages. The connection between Wikipedia and pro-human, pro-social associations can be seen in this file on "peace":

World peace is seen as a consequence of local self-determined behaviors which inhibit the institutionalization of power and subsequent violence. The solution is not so much based on an agreed agenda, let alone investment in higher authority whether divine or political, but rather a self-organized network of mutual-supporting mechanisms whose emergent phenomenon is a sustainable politico-economic social fabric. Such a realization can only be brought about through a shared thought experiment by all participating subjectivities, inclusive of diversity, and is similar in significant ways to the formation and maintenance of this wikipedia.

(Wikimedia, 2006)

This defines world peace not as a "thing" but as a glocalized pro-human and pro-social network of people in relationships that support sustainable peacebuilding. The goal of providing free and relatively accessible information created by the people for the people in their own language is laudable. It remains to be seen what impact projects like Wikipedia will have on global education and communication.

The Global Compact

Global civil society is a viable medium through which glocalization occurs. In an attempt to organize even further and mitigate the perhaps inevitable effect of turbo-capitalism, the United Nations has issued a Global Compact to encourage corporations, labor unions, business associations, and global civil society to work together. Organizations and businesses that join the Global Compact make a commitment not to repeat the mistakes of colonialism and imperialism by observing universal values of human rights, labor standards, the environment, and anticorruption in business. They agree to promote responsible global citizenship with the goal of a sustainable and inclusive global economy. However, an online search of the participants revealed that, although there are many business associations, labor unions, and NGOs, no transnational corporation belongs to the Global Compact as yet. We see a picture emerging of an ever-expanding, loose network of civil organizations working with the United Nations, some parts of national governments, faith groups, and (maybe some day) responsible corporations with the aim of sustainable peacebuilding. This positive globalization may be an answer to war.

The Development of Global Civil Society

Kaldor traces the growth of this activist planetary biosphere from small civilian associations within democratic societies, like the movements for the abolition of slavery in England and the United States. She cites an early description of civil society by de Tocqueville, who observed democracy in the United States in 1831.

> As soon as several inhabitants of the United States have taken up an opinion or a feeling they wish to promote in the world, they look for mutual assistance; and as soon as they have found one another out, they combine. From that moment they are no longer isolated men, but a power seen from afar, whose actions serve for example and whose language is listened to.
>
> (de Tocqueville, cited in Kaldor, 2003:20)

Civil societies start with awareness, when people become aware of a problem, envision an alternative reality, and dedicate themselves to alleviating the problem. Then, they organize and use the power of cooperation to accomplish a worthy project that benefits themselves, society, and others. Free associations have been viewed as necessary to balance the effects of potentially greedy commerce and tyrannical government. It is within civil society that associations of people legitimize social change through persuasion. The associations in civil society are civilizing in that they increase participation and address social injustices and health problems by advocating legislation and systematic social change.

Human Rights

Free associations of individuals have always been involved with civil and political rights. In fact, the idea of civil and political rights began in the Western world when the King of England agreed to demands made by a small association of nobles in 1100. Later, another king made concessions to the rights of Members of Parliament (another association, though not civil) in the Magna Carta, and constitutional law was born. In response to free associations in the eighteenth and nineteenth centuries, various constitutions and declarations in Europe and America increased the rights, first, of white male property owners, then, of white males. Finally, suffrage, abolitionist, and civil rights movements increased the rights of people who had been excluded: people of color and females. In 1948 the United Nations Universal Declaration of Human Rights came into being.

Then, in 1975, the Helsinki Accord was ratified by major nation-states in Europe, the Union of Soviet Socialist Republics and the US. The accord ensured that the political status quo, especially the oppressive Soviet sovereignty over Eastern Europe, would continue unchallenged by Western powers. At first, it seemed a major victory for the Soviet Union and a defeat for freedom, but it led to a decrease in tensions between the USSR and the Western capitalist nations. A side-effect of the accord was that world attention focused on the oppressive power of an imperialistic entity over the citizens of its Eastern European satellite states. The accord included two fairly predictable and innocuous clauses about respect for human rights and self-determination. These clauses forged a link between an emergent global civil society and local civil societies demanding human rights in Poland, Hungary, and Czechoslovakia.

Post-Totalitarian Followership

Many people credit the human rights clauses, as much as economics or politics, with the peaceful breakdown of the Eastern Bloc. As Adam Michnik, a Polish writer and activist, puts it,

> On the other hand, it was the time of Détente, the time of the Helsinki Agreement, part of which was a so-called third basket—a basket of human rights. And this basket, which in the eyes of our Communist leaders was just a decoration without any importance, became for us, opposition people, an instrument in trying to loosen the tight corset of Communist dictatorship. What used to be closely guarded internal matters of every Communist regime became a subject of international monitoring, and international institutions—like the Helsinki Watch, which were then created, and gained huge importance monitoring repression of human rights in Communist countries.
>
> (Michnik, 1999, cited in Kaldor, 2003:55)

As early as 1976, Michnik and others called for the creation of spaces for freedom within the oppressive status quo in Poland. Since the totalitarian government was a fact of life and efforts to change government from within were inevitably suppressed violently, as in the Hungarian uprising of 1956, the only alternative for opposition movements was to speak directly to the independent public to influence their behavior. Michnik called this new awareness "post-totalitarian".

> Why post-totalitarian? Because power is still totalitarian, whereas society isn't any more; it is already anti-totalitarian, it rebels and sets up its own independent institutions, which lead to something we could call civil society, in Tocqueville's sense. This is what we tried to build: civil society.
>
> (Michnik, 1998, cited in Kaldor, 2003:55)

This new positive energetic awareness was directed at people, not governments. It transformed the *followership* since the leadership wouldn't change. In other words, since the leaders refused to budge, the followers could transform the power structures only by ceasing to follow. The concept of followership is going to be an important one throughout this book.

There was a flowering of civic activity in Eastern Europe, including the Workers' Defense Committee, which was a precursor to Solidarity, the Polish labor union which arose in the 1980s. Helsinki Rights Watch was formed in 1978 as a world-wide non-governmental organization to monitor compliance with the Helsinki Accords in Soviet Bloc countries. This international support from a global civil organization (and from Western democratic governments) contributed to the peaceful fall of the communist governments in Eastern Europe. Ironically, by taking totalitarianism as a given, civilians were able to defeat it by working cooperatively around it and creating spaces for their pro-social and pro-human dialogues. In addition, in those countries that developed civil societies, when the governments did fall, there was something to take their place besides a vacuum. In those countries where there was less civil activity, such as Yugoslavia and Romania, the transition to freedom was more difficult.

International Movements

The union of local civil societies claiming human rights in Eastern Europe in the 1970s and the newly forming global civil groups was just one of a number of trends. People were losing faith in their governments and there was increasing distrust. The years before, during, and after the Second World War demonstrated that the leaders of so-called civilized nation-states (the USSR and its allied states, Germany and its allies, Spain, Japan, the US, China, and others) willingly compromised and sacrificed the welfare of their people for the sake of ideology or to increase or maintain their own or their nation's political and military hegemony. Ever more concerned people all over the globe questioned the need for war and nuclear weapons; at first, these groups were localized, but over time they transcended national boundaries. Similarly, beginning in the 1960s, many people united in opposition to social inequalities, demanding the end of discrimination in the US and of apartheid in South Africa. Since then, across the globe, grassroots civil movements have formed to demand civil and political rights, environmental protection, sustainable development, healthcare, education, and more.

Critiques of Global Civil Society

At present, global civil society may be humanity's best effort to bring the latent universality of the Universal Declaration of Human Rights into actuality, but it is important not to overlook its problems and limitations.

Eurocentrism

The concept of civil society—that is, the space between the market, government, and religion that people have chosen to fill with associations—is a product of the way Western people organize themselves. To some critics, the idea of a global civil society is alien to their culture, and not necessarily positive. They justifiably resent being on the receiving end of global civilian efforts, just as some North Americans, Australians, and Europeans sometimes resent cultural change that comes through immigration.

The concept of civil society may not spread too easily to other cultures and civilizations, where there may be no "empty" public space to be filled. In many places, people do not have a history of associating in the same way; their society organizes itself in different ways. Their associations may be hometown, clan, or kinship groups, age-sets such as elders, men's or women's groups, tribes, trades or guilds, or social classes. Lewis (2002), after considering the relevance of civil society to various African contexts such as Nigeria, Tanzania, Tunisia, and Uganda, makes the point that it is the function of civil society as a concept and not necessarily the form that is relevant to Africa. Indigenous gender groups, age-sets, or tribal organizations may serve to mitigate the power of religion, government, the military, or business interests. They too are going global. The Russian Association of Indigenous Peoples of the North, Siberia, and Far East (RAIPON) is an organization of 41 indigenous groups formed to protect human and cultural rights, defend legal interests, and solve environmental and economic problems.

Unequal Distribution

Global civil society is currently dominated by Northern and Western organizations designed to support or foment indigenous local efforts at improvement. It reinforces the dichotomy between the outsider expert and the insider consumers of expertise and defeats the purpose of bottom-up localized empowerment. Some areas of the globe with intractable problems hardly see any benefits of global civil society because they are squashed between turbo-capitalism and the violence of defensive nation-states like Russia or the United States. Keane cites an interview with a Tunisian professor when he says:

> Still others—many Muslims say—are made to feel that the enormous potential of global civil society to expand dialogue among civilizations, to "affirm differences through communication" is being choked to death by the combined forces of global markets and military might, manifested for instance in the violent repression of the Palestinians by the dangerous alliance between the United States and Israel.
>
> (Keane, 2001:38)

Agendas and Goals

Organizations in global civil society sometimes seek to change conditions rather than structures or systems. *Conditional goals* are short-term improvements that affect the conditions of specific people but do not lead to long-term changes that benefit communities. There is an old saying, for all its condescension and sexism: "Give a man a fish; you have fed him for today. Teach a man to fish; you have fed him for a lifetime (provided his water source is not polluted)." The former (outsider gives hungry people food) addresses a condition with a reaction. The latter (outsider-expert teaches people how to catch food) addresses a structure, empowering individuals through education.

For instance, some activists in labor disputes seek higher wages and better working conditions for exploited factory or agricultural workers. The multinational corporations co-opt the dispute; they neutralize it by giving in to demands for a small increment in wages and slightly better working conditions. When the immediate demands are met, the activists leave. The workers are really little better off in the long run, because they changed their conditions but did not change their situation. They are still being exploited, with little participation in the immense profits the corporation earns. If they formed a collective bargaining unit to engage in ongoing negotiations with the corporation, their situation would change. What's more, the social, political, and economic system in which they find themselves would change. I suggest an addition to the saying above: "Support people starting a fishing cooperative and they and their children will feed themselves for generations to come (assuming they do not overfish)."

Some NGOs invest in helping destitute people improve their lives by giving them livestock. That is a *structural goal*. Ultimately, however, what makes the most difference to the poor and uneducated is for their countries to be relieved of their crushing debts to the World Bank and the International Monetary Fund. That is a *systemic goal*. Countries that have achieved debt relief have been able to invest in education and health services for their people and to stimulate their economies.

The question of the agenda for global civil society comes down to either reaction or proaction. Lipschutz (2005:761) notes that the countries affected by a terrible tsunami had limited capacity to respond to the disaster, and within a few days international organizations had mobilized to help. However, they did not work to change the structure of the economy or the system of politics that most directly led to poverty and risk in the first place. With natural disasters like hurricanes, tsunamis, earthquakes, and volcanic eruptions, it is impossible to protect everyone. However, it is possible to be proactive about prevention or mitigation before the tragedy rather than reactive about aid after the tragedy. It is often the poorest people who live, work, and study in low-lying ramshackle buildings that are most vulnerable to weather conditions or earthquakes. Global civil society has been criticized as being focused on conditions rather than structures and systems, and on being reactive rather than proactive.

Ideals

Despite the fact that global civil society has a largely coherent pro-social and pro-human agenda (as we shall see in the next chapter), there are still important conflicts. The goals of global civil society may conflict with local morality or norms, or the goals of some organizations may oppose each other. Environmental goals often conflict with the goals of labor unions. Kriegman (2006:13) notes that gender equity movements are devoted to changing the status of women, but that goal often conflicts with indigenous and religious traditions. Women are sometimes referred to as the "fourth world," the worst off within the "third world" developing nations.

Strategies

Organizations in global civil society advocate nonviolent means of change. However, nonviolent methods take time and they seem slow and passive to activists with little patience. To some, boycotts and think tanks, white papers and media events get bogged down in a "paralysis of analysis" and never get to the heart of the matter. When so-called peaceful demonstrations get ugly, some are appalled but others consider such violent conflict an inevitable part of social and cultural change. It also draws more media attention.

In fact, global civil society is largely powerless in the face of violence. The threat of nuclear attack by nation-states or by terrorist groups still looms over humanity. Global civil society, with some exceptions, retreats to safe ground far away when civil strife or ethnic wars break out. Some organizations, like Peace Brigades International, sponsor global civilians who intentionally get in the way of combatants and attempt to create safe public spaces for dialogue. However, unless and until huge numbers of people are willing to risk their lives as voluntary civilian peacebuilders, that strategy is of limited effectiveness. The only defense at present may be creating a dialogue space in a public sphere to voice, attend to, and acknowledge issues. Kaldor (2003) suggests that global civil society needs some kind of army, like peacekeeping troops, but this misses an important point. It may be the case that global civil society will ultimately be more effective in preventing future violence through proactive sustainability strategies like education.

Arrogance

At times the organizations and individuals in global civil society are not self-reflexive; they simply assume that they are correct. They do not examine their relationship with big global players like the United States, the European Union, the World Bank, the International Monetary Fund, and the World Trade Organization. Some organizations may be compromised by donors like the World Bank and therefore cannot answer accusations of imperialism (Moore, 2007). Sometimes decision-making or the financial situation is non-transparent. It is unclear who the NGO is accountable to: its members, its board of directors, or its donors. In fact, global civil society is self-organizing and, therefore, it suffers from a lack of leadership or direction. That is why some people, like Kriegman (2006), advocate some kind of world government.

Elitism

The vast majority of people in the world are too poor and uneducated to access phones or the internet. To the disadvantaged, turbo-capitalism looks good in that it provides immediate jobs and opportunities at least for some. To them, the desperation and struggle of their daily lives make a mockery of the lives lived by most global civilians and the middle-class people who support them from Japan, the United States, or Europe. Because of this disparity, global civil society could be called elitist. Yet the label does not stick very easily. Elitism is the belief by some people that they are entitled to special treatment or to be in control because of their superiority in intelligence, status, or resources. When global civilians of Peace Brigades International or Greenpeace risk their lives as human shields or to prevent pollution, they are deliberately taking themselves out of their elite, and therefore safe, status. When human rights abuse investigators spend their time digging up mass graves and identifying corpses, it is hard to call them elitist.

Further, psychologists like Staub (2003:63) note that if people have their basic needs fulfilled as children and young adults, they have the preconditions for altruism. If they have enjoyed positive connections to family and community, they value people and have empathy. If they themselves are secure and have a good self-concept, they are more open to the needs of others. If people are raised to feel effective, they are more prone to act on empathy and caring. "A realistic understanding of the world, when it is at least moderately benevolent, also makes it more likely that people will express caring and empathy in action." It could be argued that, with very notable exceptions of altruistic people emerging from difficult life experiences like poverty and deprivation, neglect, lack of opportunity, and war, people from relatively stable and comfortable backgrounds have the psychic and economic wherewithal to create civil society. Thus, this kind of "elitism" may simply be necessary.

Finally, to call global civilians elitist is to lose sight of the genuinely high-status power brokers in the world, the wealthy trendsetters, cultural leaders, entertainers, corporate tycoons, and politicos who travel around the world in their private jets. They wield power because of their exalted positions in international organizations or corporations and their vast financial takings from popular culture or artistic fame (Rothkopf, 2008).

Learning is Agency

Legitimacy is a primary concept in social and political psychology. It is possible for political systems to perpetuate themselves through force and coercion, but such systems are inherently unsustainable. Therefore, leaders need to persuade people to support the status quo by producing an aura of legitimacy for themselves. People think a system is *legitimate* if it is in accord with the norms, values, beliefs, practices, and procedures accepted by a group (Zelditch, 2001:33). Systems perceived as legitimate are sustainable because people are less likely to resist them.

Legitimacy

Legitimacy is the collective product of many individuals' psychologies, so it must be created and recreated constantly through language and media. Educational systems are an important way that social and political systems create and perpetuate the language, myths, rituals, and ideologies that legitimize the status quo. However, civilians are not passive accepters of ideology. Instead, education systems are also where initially "illegitimate" language and ideas, like civil rights, anti-war thinking, recycling, or anti-smoking movements, surface. As the transformative movements achieve legitimacy in their own right, their validation by peers or by accepted authorities appropriates emergent language, values, norms, beliefs, practices, and procedures so that they are available in the culture. Once they are available as alternative legitimacies, there is pressure on the original system to change and motivation for transition to a new way.

English language teachers have the power to continue to legitimize the status quo, to legitimize the status quo selectively, to legitimize transitions, or to delegitimize aspects of society and culture through their choice and innovation of language and themes. There is a connection between the idea of the worldliness of English and legitimization. For example, the term "expert speaker" delegitimizes the distinction between native speaker and non-native speaker and legitimizes a more egalitarian concept based on language expertise. This chapter legitimizes a latent *imagined community* of global civilians and a global conglomerate of civil society with a pro-social and pro-human agenda. Other chapters will legitimize other imagined communities.

An Imagined Community

Global civil society is an "outside" community of altruistic global civilians in relationships with others in sociocultural networks. The community opposes the spread of rampant consumerism, economic exploitation, human rights violations, and environmental degradation. It opposes war and the globalization of terror because it supports nonviolent ways of dealing with conflicts. Its linkages have the potential to cut across divisive national, ethnic, religious, caste, and class boundaries. The community uses English and other languages as tools to accomplish its mission. Its communication networks reinforce shared attitudes and behaviors, allowing global protests against unilateral "media event" warfare, intertribal genocide, or terrorism.

To build the social, cultural, political, and economic framework for sustainable peace, global civilians use their agencies to cooperate with others. They do not rely on governments or others to fix things. They refuse to be passive followers of the status quo. Recall that in Eastern Europe, the totalitarian leadership was a given, so the only thing that could change was the followership. The author of the Wikipedia article cited earlier recognized that sustainable peace is not going to come from the outside-in or top-down but must be built bottom-up and inside-out by communities of followers who cooperate to create a thick and dense sociocultural network with mechanisms that transform violence into dialogue. It is only in and through such relationships that enough cooperative power can be generated for such a crucial transition. English language teachers can legitimize an image of a glocalized community of people at work for preferred local futures.

Motivation

It is well known that language learning is facilitated when learners are motivated to learn. There are, of course, different types of motivation, but one type is called *integrative motivation*, when language learners learn a language because they want to feel part of the community of speakers or writers of that language. At this point in time, many English learners may not want to integrate to what they perceive as American, British, Australian, or Canadian culture. They feel ambivalent about absorbing a culture that is decadent or antipathetic to them. However, language learners may be attracted to an international altruistic community of global civilians in global civil society. If they can see a latent English-speaking multilingual and multicultural community with which they want to integrate by willing consent, without leaving their own culture behind, it may facilitate their language learning.

With *instrumental motivation* language learners want to acquire language skills as a resource for doing something. It may be that they want to get a better job, emigrate or travel, or go into business. They may want to use English altruistically to resolve local or global problems or conflicts through working in NGOs or trade unions. Feuerverger (2001:76) in her book *Oasis of Dreams: Teaching and Learning Peace in a Jewish-Palestinian Village in Israel*, puts it this way:

> On this point there is no dissension between Jew and Palestinian anywhere in Israel. Its cultural imperialism is accepted by both sides, like it or not. Israelis are pragmatists: there is wholehearted agreement in this vision: English is neither yours nor mine; it is what we all need to succeed. English transcends the conflict, the cultural borders, the animosity. English is the world. English is freedom. English is power. English opens the doors for all of us.

Thus, English is an important glocalized resource for people. As a resource, it should be equitably distributed among people in a society. Teachers should be aware of and work to delegitimize the have/have not split between people who know English and people who do not. In some countries, English learning is the domain only of wealthy or elite people, or only of men. It may be forbidden to teach English in national or state schools (even if English is an official language of the country) so as to exclude some people from participation. Teachers can advocate that English and other literacies should be accessible to all members of society.

Chapter 3

Global Civic Culture

Whether based on religious or secular-humanist beliefs, there are people in all countries who feel allegiance to a community that in one sense does not exist—the community of humankind. It is this allegiance that we are calling species identity. The community of humankind is a country without borders, with no capital city and with only one law—to avoid doing harm to any fellow human beings. However, one cannot feel allegiance to an abstraction. That is where the concept of civic culture comes in. It can only become operational through a set of common understandings developed on the basis of interaction in all the ways we have been describing in these chapters: between governments, in the United Nations, and between people across national borders. We have to enter into more social interaction and become more consciously linked across national borders, to give substance to that civic culture.

(Boulding, 1990:65–6)

Global civil society is not only a set of non-governmental organizations in a global network and it is not just a community of global civilians. It is a community with a civic culture. The word "civic" refers to the rights and responsibilities of civilians to each other and to the group in a societal and cultural relationship. Thus *global civic culture* refers to a global culture of rights and responsibilities of humans towards humanity and the earth.

Species Identity

The quote from Boulding is complicated. *Species identity* is a relationship of affiliation with others at the personal level of experience, with a connection to both a local and a global collective experience of identity with humanity. The personal, the local, and the global levels of species identity are connected to each other by an *ethic*, which is a set of common values that guide moral behavior in relationships.

The Personal

First, Boulding talks about individuals all over the world who wish to do no harm to others out of personal convictions, either religious or philosophical. Perhaps they feel affiliated with humanity because they respect human consciousness, capacity to suffer and love, search for meaning in life, or they sense their position in a sociocultural fabric. Boulding calls this relationship of affiliation *species identity*, which is not the same as what has been called speciesism. *Speciesism* is a preference for the human species to the disadvantage of other species and is used as a justification for destruction of animal life and habitat. Rather, species identity is internal to the human collective, and does not preclude identification with other species as well.

Species identity is similar to *cosmopolitanism*, an ancient Greek concept that there is a single moral community that all humans belong to, over and above communities related to personality, family, ethnicity, or nationality. The image associated with cosmopolitanism is that of the individual in the center of concentric rings. The first concentric ring is the family, the second is the local community, and so on, out to the last ring, which is humanity. The image suggests drawing the outermost ring into the center, towards the individual (Nussbaum, 1996). The same idea has been attributed to Kong Zi (Confucius) and it is compatible with ahimsa in Hinduism and dharma in Buddhism, although these latter concepts are often associated with identification with or respect for all sentient beings, not just humanity.

Appiah (2006:xv) points out that cosmopolitanism has two equal sides. We have obligations to others of our species (universal concern) and we have much to learn from others if we respect cultural and linguistic diversity (respect for legitimate difference). These two ideals are in a creative tension with each other. For instance, if people go too far towards respect for diversity, they may fall into superficial relativism. *Relativism* is the attitude that there is no way to judge morality because values are relative to cultures. They may believe that they must like everything about others. The ethic of species identity says that not all behaviors are acceptable. On the other hand, if people have universal concern without respect for differences, they may project their own cultural norms onto others and fall into superficiality that way.

The challenge is for people to feel affiliation, or identity, even with those who oppose or harm them: the stranger, the infidel, the oppressor. Species identity is more than a reverence for humankind in the abstract; it is a reverence for human creatures with all their flaws and frailties. It is a commitment to maintaining a relationship with humans no matter how diverse and incomprehensible they might be. For cosmopolitanism to be more than elitist superficiality, it must be rooted in a moral ethic that combines the universal with the diverse.

Species identity is the basis for the statements of human reciprocity that occur in all of the major religions and philosophies of the world in one form or other: "Do unto others as they would have you do unto them." Reciprocity applies to all humanity, not just members of one's family, clique, or local community. It takes both affiliation and empathy in order to understand what other people want, and thus it combines Appiah's two strands of universal concern and respect for differences. It is only by taking another's perspective that one can truly do no harm to others. And yet the capacity to take another's perspective is the crux of the primary perceptual and conceptual difference of self-concept among humans in cultures and societies.

The Local Collective

Recall the earlier discussion about different kinds of self-identity and how they relate to sociocultural networks as either mainly independent or mainly interdependent (Markus and Kitayama, 1991). Collectivist cultures have sociocultural networks of interdependent individuals who derive their motivations and duties from their positions within relationships. They are willing to subordinate their own interests in favor of others in their group or their group itself because it makes them happy to achieve group goals. They interpret people's behavior as either maintaining or disrupting the social order. In individualist cultures, the sociocultural networks are formed of independent individuals with varying degrees of autonomy. Their motivations and duties derive from their own needs and goals, and their happiness is related to how they achieve their own goals. They tend to attribute motivations to others and judge behaviors in those terms, or they interpret behaviors in light of the effects the behaviors might have for themselves.

It is interesting that there is no shortage of war, violence, and oppression among people of either individualist or collective cultures. Addressing this idea, Staub (2003:354–5) distinguishes between two types of interdependent self-identity: embedded and connected. *Embedded individuals* are so enmeshed in their sociocultural network that they cannot oppose, resist, or even speak out against their group. They cannot separate themselves from their group or its identity; they are *sociocentric*. *Connected individuals* have a strong relationship with their group as part of their identity, but they have also learned to separate themselves so that they can take a more objective perspective on their group's culture and behavior.

Staub hypothesizes that both embedded individuals and intensely autonomous or egocentric individuals might tend to be blindly patriotic and therefore more susceptible to war propaganda and agitation. Embedded interdependent individuals derive feelings of security from their national identity and so give it their uncritical loyalty. Janowitz (1985)

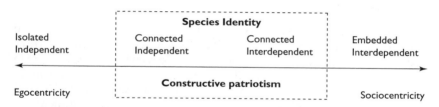

Figure 3.1 Species identity, constructive patriotism, independence, and interdependence on a continuum of egocentricity (self-orientation) and sociocentricity (group-orientation)

proposes that individualism in the United States and its lack of community cause people to feel lonely and isolated, so they use great patriotism to feel connection and grounding. (Sports fanatic rivalry and religious cult behavior also come to mind in this regard.) In contrast, connected inter-dependent and independent individuals are more likely to be *constructive patriots* who love their country and people but can question practices of their group that contradict human welfare.

For species identity, as shown in Figure 3.1, independent people need to perceive and value connection and relationships with others. They need to be aware of their place in a large sociocultural network that they need to fit into, at times perhaps sacrificing some autonomy in order to connect. They need to develop empathy for others' perspectives, not projection, attribution, or interpretation. For species identity, interdependent people need to enlarge the scope of their networks to include the outsider, and ease psychological barriers between themselves and others. They need to develop, perhaps, a little autonomy while maintaining connection. This topic, the paradox of marginality and connection, will come up again in future chapters; it is an important one.

The Global Collective

And at the global level of experience, individuals with species identity share a global ethic underlying global civic culture. Global civic culture is latent; it is the emerging culture of an imagined community of global civilians and others who support them. The ethic defines what *global citizenship* means: the rights and responsibilities that citizens have towards others within a global sociopolitical relationship. Global citizenship is pro-human and pro-social: the good of the individual is balanced by the good of the collective and vice versa. The ethic is the Earth Charter, the complete text of which can be found in the Appendix at the end of this book.

The Earth Charter

The Earth Charter is a vision of a sustainable world that can be traced back to the UN Charter in 1945. The UN Charter originally set three major goals for itself: to ensure peace and world security, to secure human rights, and to foster cooperation for social and economic development. In 1972, environmental protection was added as a fourth goal. The UN Charter created the United Nations; the Earth Charter is creating a new planetary culture. There isn't the space here for a lengthy critical analysis of the Earth Charter, so instead I would like to focus attention on two main areas of contrast between the Universal Declaration of Human Rights and the Earth Charter.

First, the provenance could not be more different. The UNUDHR was drafted, approved, and proclaimed by representatives of nations belonging to the UN in 1948. The Earth Charter was drafted by consensus between 1987 and 2000 in the most intentionally collaborative and consultative dialogue in history (Vilela and Corcoran, 2005). The dialogue involved numerous meetings among thousands of men, women, and organizations from all continents, faith groups, and ethnicities. Since its writing, the Earth Charter has been endorsed by over 2,000 organizations and millions of people around the world.

Second, there is no power inherent in the UNUDHR. Instead, the values it legitimizes are to be extended by education and by international and national legislation enacted by nations and the territories under the jurisdiction of those nations. Thus, the UNUDHR assumes a hierarchical world of nation-states and colonies, and people under the control of national and colonialist governments. In contrast, the language of the Preamble to the Earth Charter legitimizes a "we" as the unified voice of a species, an imagined community locating ourselves at a transitional time in history, a crossroads that will determine our common destiny. "We" recognize our relationships of family, community, humanity, nature, and our home planet. To move together towards the promise of the future, "we" must join together to create a sustainable society with principles based on right relationships with each other and with the earth.

The power of the Earth Charter is located in human agency that moves around and between national governments and settles in relationships; it assumes a global civil society and a global culture of environmental protection, human rights, justice, and peace. The power of the Earth Charter comes from our reciprocal sense of responsibility to each other and to humans of the future. The charter is an ethic of morality for the world that balances the interests of the individual and the collective. The phrases contained in the section "The Way Forward" could not be more different from the legalese of the UNUDHR.

The Earth Charter is a holistic vision of local and global partnerships of individuals, families, organizations, and communities from the arts, sciences, religions, educational institutions, media, businesses, non-governmental organizations, and governments committed to the United Nations and to obligations under existing and newly formed peace, economic, and environmental agreements. It ends with a plea: "Let ours be a time remembered for the awakening of a new reverence for life, the firm resolve to achieve sustainability, the quickening of the struggle for justice and peace, and the joyful celebration of life."

Global Civic Culture

Dower (2005:178) sees the Earth Charter and global citizenship as complementary. The charter is the content of the global ethic, and the global citizenship of its endorsers is the form of the global ethic, its "motivating sense." In other words, the Earth Charter is the set of common understandings that motivate and guide the relationships of the pro-human and pro-social culture of global citizenship. It is the "what" of global civic culture, and global civil society is "how" global civic culture moves from latency to actuality. Global civic culture rests on the moral content of the Earth Charter and defines the form as the sum of global civilian activities in global civil society, the UN, green corporations, sympathetic national governments, and the like. In some important ways, global civic culture is different from what we normally think of as culture.

Altruism

Ordinarily, when people think of culture, they think of a fixed system of beliefs, traditions, values, and behaviors of a group of people in a society in the context of an environment. Nevertheless, humans create dynamic and constantly changing cultures through at least three components: artifacts, values (including beliefs and traditions), and behaviors. The components of culture are interrelated with each other and with the environment. For example, if people need clothing (artifacts) and esteem cleanliness (value), they wash their clothes (behavior). They invent (behavior) washing implements (artifacts) to be more efficient if time (value) is important to them. If people do not need clothing, they may not wear much of it except for modesty (value). The purpose of culture, vague and shapeless as it may be, is to organize people, their values, artifacts, and behaviors so that they can interact in a society within an environment; but, for many people, their culture is largely unconscious and inconsistent.

Culture is learned by transmission from humans to other humans. Because it is learned and not innate, it is changeable and dynamic. That is why cultural diffusion exists wherever diverse cultures come into contact with each other. Most of the time, there are inconsistencies among the components of culture. People say their culture values children and childhood, yet child abuse or slavery is a more or less secretly tolerated behavior. People pay lip service to valuing women and their freedom, but they do nothing to prevent domestic violence against them. People believe that their culture promotes the ideal of equality among people, but they turn a blind eye to prejudice and privilege because they want to maintain the status quo. People believe they are peace-loving, yet they own semi-automatic guns designed to kill people. Cultures also clash with their environment, leading to habitat destruction, global warming, and pollution.

In general, cultures tolerate a great deal of dysfunction; they permit conditions, situations, structures, and systems that benefit neither the individual nor the society, like violent conflict, poverty, inadequate health-care, and poor education. I call this aspect of culture *dysergy* because it is the opposite of synergy, the outpouring of energy when actions and structures benefit both individuals and groups. And despite the appearance that there is political or social leadership in conventional cultures, in fact they are adrift without a rudder. There is no consensus about where it is going, if anywhere. Pennycook (2001:127) laments, "A problem with broad critical analysis is that it is often fundamentally pessimistic: We live in a patriarchal, homophobic, racist world increasingly governed by the interests of multinational business. This is a useful understanding of the world, but we also need to be able to believe in some alternative."

Global civic culture is different from regular cultures because it is altruistic; that is, it legitimizes only pro-human and pro-social values, artifacts, and behavior. In its altruism, it is conscious, consistent, and goal-oriented. It is conscious because global civilians have articulated their values in the Earth Charter. There is a consensus about most of the values and behaviors and they are consistent with species identity.

Global civic culture is consistent because artifacts and behaviors are in accord with the values; weapons, landmines, and arms-dealing are incon-sistent. Global civilians turn the principles of the Earth Charter into international treaties and conventions, national policies and laws, and education for change. They apply pressure on those governments or com-panies that flout the principles. With the Earth Charter as its heart, global civic culture is goal-directed in its altruism. The goal is that personally, locally, and globally, we continue to find "our way toward becoming and being local and global human communities characterized by respect, dignity, fairness, cooperation, and the nonviolent resolution of conflict" (Lederach, 2005:24). To do this, it will be necessary to draw upon resources from many cultures.

A Cultura Franca

Global civic culture is certainly not North American, Australian, British, or European. It is not Chinese, Japanese, or Indian. It is not African or indigenous Australian. It is not South American or Polynesian. It is not any known culture on the planet. It is a fusion of the perspectives and knowledge of many cultures and native to no one culture. It combines the best of independence and interdependence. But right now it needs people to imagine it from latency to actuality.

I think of global civic culture as a *cultura franca*, making an analogy with the term "lingua franca." A *lingua franca* is a common language used among a group of people whose first languages are different. It evolves in a situation where people of various languages come into contact with each other and need to communicate for work, trade, or cooperation. People do not forget their native languages; they add a new language to facilitate communication. There are three types of lingua franca. First, an existing natural language like English, French, or Chinese can become a lingua franca if enough people learn it as a second language. Second, a lingua franca like Esperanto can be invented by one person or a committee. Third, a lingua franca like Tok Pisin can evolve naturally from a mixture of words and phrases taken from all of the languages in the contact situation.

This third sense forms the analogy with cultura franca, because global civic culture, as Boulding (1990) envisions it, draws together the threads of the peaceful aspects of many cultures: the Beloved Community of Martin Luther King, the Eightfold Path of Buddhism, the Golden Rule in its various versions, biblical and Q'uranic teachings, Hindu nonviolence, the Earth Charter, and other spiritual and philosophical traditions. These traditions have features held in common, although they also have differences to lend. It is not cultural imperialism if one culture does not dominate others. Diverse people share a cultura franca but it is additive to their personal, social, and ethnic cultures (and may conflict with them).

Multicultural Resources

At present, global civic culture is a *pidgin* cultura franca. It is incomplete, not native anywhere. It may be too heavily Eurocentric. It urgently needs, to borrow a metaphor from the field of language policy, *corpus planning*. Corpus planning refers to efforts to increase or expand the vocabulary in certain fields like technology or science. When Hebrew was revitalized as a living language, it needed new vocabulary to bring it into the present. Similarly, global civic culture requires an elaboration of values, emotions, skills, responsible agency, behaviors, and pro-social communicative strategies.

In terms of values, many societies value peaceful cooperation and obligation to others. Miller, Bersoff, and Harwood (1990) found that feelings of moral obligation to others are far stronger among Indians than among Americans. Indians think responsiveness to the needs of others is an important moral obligation. I found the same to be true in Pakistan, where our bearer risked his life to rescue our daughters when the bombs from an arsenal fell on Islamabad and Rawalpindi in 1988. The Japanese concept of *wa* is the harmonious ebb and flow of an interpersonal relationship (Markus and Kitayama, 1991:228).

In many African and Asian cultures, generosity, hospitality, and sharing with others are of great importance, to the point of significant self-sacrifice. Geertz (1974) identifies such concepts in Bali and Morocco. Central Asian nomadic tribes place a high value on simple living, hospitality, generosity, and making maximum use of scarce resources. Many cultures value compassion, equanimity, and nonviolence and teach methods of training the mind away from destructive emotions and towards positive ones. Buddhist mind-training methods based on the Four Noble Truths literally change the way the mind functions. The West perfects its medication; the East meditation.

Global civic culture is open to adding or subtracting emotions. Japanese *amae* is defined as "the sense of, or the accompanying hope for, being lovingly cared for and [it] involves depending on and presuming another's indulgence" (Markus and Kitayama, 1991:237). *Amae* is to be in a reciprocal, interdependent relation with another where one feels complete freedom. According to Markus and Kitayama, anthropologists challenge the universality of emotions like anger and aggression. For instance, early anthropologists found little evidence of anger among Tahitians:

> It is not that these people [Tahitians] have learned to inhibit or suppress their "real" anger but that they have learned the importance of attending to others, considering others, and being gentle in all situations, and as a consequence, very little anger is elicited. In other words, the social reality is construed and actually constructed in such a way that it does not lend itself to the strong experience, let alone the outburst, of negative ego-focused emotions such as anger.
>
> (Markus and Kitayama, 1991:236)

For behavioral resources, Boulding (2000:92) highlights the important in-group conflict-suppressing and conflict-resolving skills acquired through childrearing practices by the Inuit of the Canadian north, the Mbuti of Zaire, the Zuni of the United States, and the Arapesh of New Guinea. She says they "set a high value on nonaggression and noncompetitiveness and therefore handle conflict in a variety of nonviolent means." Similarly, there are communicative norms of behavior, like the Chinese concept of *jen*, a person's capability to interact with fellow human beings in a sincere, polite, and decent fashion (Hsu, 1985).

Another cultural resource for pro-social communication, *right speech*, is part of the Eightfold Path for Buddhists, a moral code or philosophy to follow to be free from suffering. Buddha taught that right speech has five characteristics: honesty, gentleness, "profitability," kindness, and timeliness. Profitability is communication that neither creates division nor contributes to dissension in a society or group. Buddha suggested that people examine their motives before, during, and after speaking to make sure they are pure and of good will (Birch, 2006). Some cultures use ritual silence as a way to detach from conflict so that people can reflect.

Additive Cultural Fusion

The pidgin cultura franca is an example of cultural fusion, where the scattered peaceful bits from around the world fuse together into a global culture that people learn as a second or third culture with which they are comfortable. It is not Western, Eastern, Northern, or Southern, but a blend or convergence of all of them. Global civic culture looks to peace heroes like Gandhi, Martin Luther King, Nelson Mandela, the Dalai Lama, and that unknown Chinese student in Tiananmen Square.

For a few generations, the cultura franca will be additive. So, for many, the attitudes, behaviors, and procedures of the cultura franca are learned as adults, as people become cosmopolitan or as they sicken of war, death, and environmental destruction. They do not forget their home cultures, but they converge their actions towards a common pro-social and pro-human ground. They adopt the cultura franca in order to enjoy communication and cooperation when people come from various home cultures. For instance, although people have different paternalistic or egalitarian attitudes towards women in their home cultures, women in global civic culture have the same status as men, because that is a human right and a goal of the Earth Charter. In the global cultura franca, men and women are treated fairly and have equal opportunities.

Similarly, many people in a home culture like the United States pay only lip service to peace and justice, but peace and justice are universal values in the global civic culture. People from a racist or classist home culture often profess tolerance but practice discrimination, but the global cultura franca is tolerant and works for equality for all. Likewise, global civic culture values inclusive participation in decision-making as part of the culture of peace. Although people's home culture may not be very participatory, the cultura franca encourages participation and enacts it through local versions of parliamentary procedure, voting, democracy, and consensus. Pidgin languages often become creolized if they acquire native speakers who truly flesh out their grammar and lexicon. Global civic culture could, in the same way, become "creolized" if it became native to groups of people.

Global civic culture is another strand of globalization. The cultura franca is global in that it is a grassroots bottom-up phenomenon culminating in the Earth Charter principles. But global civic culture also trickles down to the local unless resisted. Where local culture is dysergic and conflicts with the global, it may undergo transition, or voluntary change. Ill health may be replaced by good health. Poverty may be subtracted, and education may be added. Further, traditional notions of self-identification within a culture may change. Highly autonomous people may acquire empathy for others and begin to see themselves as interdependent with others. Embedded people may begin to see that their group affiliations are changeable; therefore, they feel connected but detached. At the intersection of the global and the local there is potential for transition.

Bottom-up Cultural Realism

But structural and systemic cultural transitions are best when they occur from the bottom up and inside out and not from the top down or outside in. Once initiated, they can be supported from the top and outside, as in the case of the Eastern European movements, but the need and motivation for change should come from inside the local collective. Women's or men's circumcision must be eradicated by the very people who practice it, if they feel that it is unjust or cruel. Violent gangs must be disbanded by the neighborhoods affected by those gangs. Women's rights must be demanded by the very women who feel they are being marginalized or repressed, if that is what they feel.

My Libyan women students once educated me about the advantages of their arranged marriages over American dating customs, as a form of resistance to the superficial textbook materials; they were perfectly satisfied and felt no loss of freedom. At the time, I was a frazzled single-mother graduate student barely making ends meet, so who was I to argue with them about freedom? When they asked me, "Who is taking care of you?" I saw the value of interdependence and the drawbacks of autonomy.

Globalization is changing our notions of culture and our hypotheses about how societies and individuals handle cultural diversity. One hypothesis is *assimilation*, when a nondominant group chooses or is forced to adopt or accommodate to the characteristics of a dominant group (the melting-pot metaphor). Another is *cultural pluralism*, when boundaries between the diverse groups are maintained and respected within a citizenship relation (the salad-bowl metaphor). The third is *cultural hybridity*, when the meeting of two cultures results in a third culture that is neither one nor the other but a fusion of both (the tofu-burrito metaphor).

After describing and critiquing these hypotheses in his book *Cultural Globalization and Language Education*, Kumaravadivelu notes that a major criticism of existing theories of intercultural interaction is that none has succeeded in addressing the grave social inequalities and injustices that exist when there is unsymmetrical contact between a dominant and a nondominant group. He posits another hypothesis, which he calls *cultural realism*, because it is based on a realistic view of the global modern world:

> The premise of cultural realism is based on a simple and straightforward proposition that globalization, with its incessant and increased flow of people, goods, and ideas across the world, is creating a novel "web of interlocution" that is effectively challenging the traditional notions of identity formation of an individual or a nation.
>
> (Kumaravadivelu, 2008: 165)

Global civic culture is based on cultural realism; Kumaravadivelu's global "web of interlocution" both requires and contributes to Boulding's "set of common understandings developed on the basis of interaction." Globalization is transforming our ideas of identity, affiliation, and culture.

Learning is Agency

To deal with the realities of globalization, Kumaravadivelu proposes that individuals develop *global cultural consciousness*, a critical and reflective approach to evaluating one's own and other cultures to select the best features, allowing one to stay rooted in a home culture but adopting aspects of other cultures.

> What lies behind my lived experience, and that of a multitude of others, is a complex process of creating critical cultural consciousness through constant and continual self-reflection. What guides us in such critical self-reflection is our inherited culture derived from the time-tested traditions of the cultural community into which each of us is born. Our learned knowledge and lived experiences of other cultural discourse domains not only expand our cultural horizon but also clarify and solidify our individual inherited cultural heritage. This critical self-reflection helps us to identify and understand what is good and bad about our own culture, and what is good and bad about other cultures. In other words, in understanding other cultures, we understand our own culture better; in understanding our own, we understand other cultures better. This is the hallmark of an individual's complex cultural growth.
>
> (Kumaravadivelu, 2008:5–6)

Kumaravadivelu suggests that classroom participants use critical reflection and ethnography—that is, close attention to culture and society through interview, observation, and study. He proposes that the goal of culture learning is cultural transition because it requires participants to assess, among other things, personal identity, collective identities, society and culture, and stereotypes. He notes that "difficult and sometimes disturbing dialogues can bring about a change of basic attitudes toward one's own culture and toward others" (Kumaravadivelu, 2008:181). It is through global cultural consciousness that Kumaravadivelu proposes people become aware of and address social injustice and inequity.

Kumaravadivelu's (2008:505–6) critical cultural consciousness is similar to psychologist Staub's concepts of critical consciousness and critical loyalty. Recall that critical consciousness is the capacity to evaluate information independently rather than simply adopting group or authority opinions. Critical loyalty is a commitment to balance local welfare with universal welfare, instead of loyalty to group policies despite conflict with universal principles. It means that people balance their good with the good of other people in the world, leading to constructive patriotism, and therefore adds another dimension to global cultural consciousness, the dimension of species identity.

Culture learning is not limited to comparisons between existing human cultures but must bring in universal principles and human cultures that could come into being in the future. The Earth Charter can be used as material for classroom learning themes and the basis for comparison with local culture. Classroom participants might ask themselves what peaceful aspects of their culture they could contribute to global civic culture. Global cultural consciousness, critical consciousness, and critical loyalty are important agencies to use in creating the cultura franca.

Trigger Events

Complex cultural growth often comes about from what might be called *trigger events*, events that show a contrast or paradox that heightens awareness of cultural differences and similarities. The conversation with my Libyan students, described earlier, was a trigger event for me. Another experience had happened in Ecuador years earlier. While living through the floods of El Niño in 1983, I whined to my former father-in-law, saying, "How can you stand this rain and flooding? It happens every few years." He answered very calmly, knowing my origins in Wisconsin, "We feel that way about freezing and snow. They happen every year." This was more than just a conversation for me. I had a number of realizations in a split second. Snow is as bad as flooding (or worse). People get used to their own reality so they do not see it. People get used to their environment so it seems natural. As an affluent people, most Wisconsinites are simply more able to deal with snow and cold and control its effects.

Another trigger event happened when I was a young teaching assistant for the first class of "mainland Chinese" students to come to my university in the early 1980s. In a discussion we came upon a paradox of morality: in the USA abortion was viewed as immoral but was tolerated, while the pornographic industry was generally overlooked. In prudish China, abortion was mandatory after one child, while pornography was illegal and seemed highly immoral to my students. It seems to me that besides ethnography and critical reflection, culture learning should take advantage of intercultural trigger events that involve contradiction and paradox.

Marginality and Connection

Teachers support local languages and learners who feel a sense of loss at the curtailment of their language or culture. "When English becomes the first choice as a second language, when it is the language in which so much is written and in which so much of the visual media occur, it is constantly pushing other languages out of the way, curtailing their usage in both qualitative and quantitative terms" (Pennycook, 1994:14). Speaking of how language encodes tradition and tradition shapes his identity and his moral code, Kazmi (1997:11) says.

> As more and more attention is given to English, the first language is marginalized. The marginalization of my mother tongue creates a temporal tension in my being-in-the-world—a tension which is the result of the power differential between the two languages . . . It, to put it simply, breaks the continuity between my past and my present. My past is my tradition and the tradition of my community/society . . . To withdraw or abandon the language through which tradition speaks is to render tradition mute . . . As a result of the break, I feel somewhat removed from my tradition and hence less capable of drawing support and getting guidance from it.

In this respect, Pennycook cites the term *deculturalization* and quotes Lee Kuan Yew, writing for a newspaper in 1978:

> A person who gets deculturalized—and I nearly was, so I know the danger—loses his self-confidence. He suffers from a sense of deprivation. For optimum performance, a man must know himself and the world. He must know where he stands. I may speak the English language better than the Chinese language because I learnt English early in life. But I will never be an Englishman in a thousand generations and I have not got the Western value system inside; mine is an

Eastern value system. Nevertheless I use Western concepts, Western words because I understand them. But I also have a different system in my mind.

(Pennycook, 1994:247)

Pennycook explores two possiblities. One is that by learning a neutral, "cultureless" English instead of a "cultured" first language, people could end up with no culture at all, a kind of "desembodied, deculturalized boat adrift on the sea of pragmatism" (Pennycook, 1994:247). This is the fear that marginality will leave people in paralyzing moral relativity. The other possibility is that by learning a "cultured" English instead of a first language, people are forced to acquire the non-native culture associated with English. But this quote also highlights some people's ability, because of cultural consciousness, to decouple culture, language, identity, and values. Lee Kuan Yew seems resilient in the face of linguistic and cultural globalization because he remains attached to his self-chosen values while using different linguistic codes. Some people choose the values they believe in and have different languages and cultures as resources to encode them. The worldliness of English also suggests that English and global civic culture can add values from other cultures as well as appropriate the words and conversational strategies used to express them.

Chapter 4

Global Citizens

There is a new kind of man in the world, and there are more of that kind than is commonly recognized. He is a national citizen with international intuitions, conscious of the age that is past and aware of the one now in being, aware of the radical differences between the two, willing to accept the lack of precedents, willing to work on the problems of the future as a labor of love, unrewarded by governments, academies, prizes, and position. He forms part of an invisible world community of . . . citizens who see the world whole and feel at one with all its parts.

(Taylor, 1969:52)

In 1969, Taylor expressed his admiration for a new kind of person, motivated by species identity, comfortable with diversity, and willing to work altruistically for change. In the quaint sexist language of the time, such "men" were able to "see the world whole and feel at one with all its parts." Perhaps the concept of the world citizen or cosmopolitan which had been around for millennia in many cultures had gone into hiding in the West and only became more apparent in the postcolonial world. Perhaps it was only in the latter half of the twentieth century, after the horrors of the Second World War and during the chill of the Cold War, that the growing numbers of such people allowed them to be imagined as a community.

Because such people joined forces to halt nuclear escalation and pollution, and to increase civil rights through civil societies, cultural commentators like Taylor took notice. He was seeing what had been latent becoming actual. He became aware of a growing community that transcended national boundaries. But Taylor noticed that these people had other characteristics as well. They were conscious of the past and the present. They were able to work without precedents, imagining a different future, and devoting themselves altruistically to the problems of the time. They had critical loyalty to their country, balancing local welfare with universal welfare. It is not a stretch to describe them as having global cultural consciousness. They felt a commitment to other people within a global sociopolitical relationship, with the rights and responsibilities of citizenship that such a relationship entails. The people Taylor described were not commonplace. To see how different they were, we must look once again at the conundrum of self-identity.

The Paradox of Identity and Affiliation

Davies, in her book *Education and Conflict*, talks about a paradox of identity. The paradox is that when people feel a secure self-identity, they tend to be less aggressive towards others, but when they define themselves essentially in terms of their affiliations of faith, ethnicity, or nationality, these can be important causes of conflict (Davies, 2004:212). A sense of personal identity and connection to a social group are both important. Identity is what exists behind and underneath people's affiliations of sex, social roles, skin color, nationality, religion, profession, social class, and caste. It is not the same as ego or self-esteem.

As we have seen before, everyone has a sense of a basic self separate from others and different from physical space. It is the part of us designated by the pronoun "I" and the part that responds when someone says, "you." The concept of self is shaped by cultural and social experiences. Markus and Kitayama (1991) made the point that in individualist cultures, the people's self-identity tends to be highly elaborate and differentiated from others, while in collectivist cultures, people's knowledge about others is generally more elaborated and distinctive than knowledge about the self.

Nevertheless, in all cultures, people also have multiple culturally and personally created affiliations that are important to them and that constrain their conceptual and perceptual world. Among others, they are affiliated with families and clans, faith groups, ethnic groups, ability groups, gender groups, and working groups. Affiliations are what make people feel that they belong, that they have a home somewhere in an interlocking social fabric. In the past, people considered their affiliations as fixed identities, but in the present, some people are beginning to think that affiliations are constructed and can be deconstructed. The abled become disabled. The disabled become abled. The heterosexual realizes that she is bisexual. The Catholic becomes a Jew. A man becomes a woman. A Turk becomes a German. A student becomes a teacher. In addition, for many people, their sense of an identity as a parent, employee, or son or daughter, or their relationship with animals and nature can change over time.

Affiliations carry a lot of socially and culturally determined expectations with them that constrain an individual's behavior. As expected, people from collectivist cultures tend to be more sensitive and responsive to the expectations of others. But the conceptual and perceptual constraints that affiliations place on people within a culture can be a prison if people cannot step outside them. The sense of belonging to one group and not another often rather arbitrarily divides people into social categories that include some people and exclude others. When these collective categories are stereotypes, they form a conceptual and perceptual trap.

Kitayama and Uchida (2004:155) point to evidence that independent people are better able than interdependent people to discount stereotypes because they are better at ignoring contextual information. Interdependents, on the other hand, incorporate contextual information, including stereotypes, which they use to make judgments about people. However, independents fall prey to projection and attribution more than interdependents. For species identity, the ability to drop stereotypes and expectations is necessary, but it is also crucial to attend to others with empathy and avoid projection and attribution. It seems that there might be something different from the connected self-identities so far described.

Multicultural Identity

> Multicultural man is the person who is intellectually and emotionally committed to the fundamental unity of all human beings while at the same time he recognizes, legitimizes, accepts, and appreciates the fundamental differences that lie between people from different cultures. This new kind of man cannot be defined by the languages he speaks, the countries he has visited, or the number of international contacts he has made. Nor is he defined by his profession, his place of residence, or his cognitive sophistication. Instead, multicultural man is recognized by the configuration of his outlooks and world views, by the way he remains open to the outlooks and world views, by the way he remains open to the imminence of experience.
>
> (Adler, 1976:36)

In the 1970s, Adler used the term "multicultural man" to describe what he thought was a third kind of psychological self-identity that was neither the independent self nor the interdependent self. It was a *multicultural identity*, a fusion of East and West, as shown hypothetically in Figure 4.1. Multicultural people have adaptable and flexible self-concepts that are always in a state of transition in response to experiences and life experiments. Their self-concepts have indefinite boundaries, perhaps more permeable and open, and they are dynamic, not static. They can distance themselves from their own culture and evaluate it, with global cultural consciousness and critical loyalty. Multicultural people adopt other perspectives as they go from place to place and culture to culture. Like interdependent people, they adapt to different values and behaviors in any given situation. Nevertheless, they retain some kind of internal moral anchor rooted in the altruism of their culture and/or a common moral

	Global Citizenship			
Isolated Independent	Connected Independent	Multicultural Identity	Connected Interdependent	Embedded Interdependent
Egocentricity		Global Citizen		Sociocentricity

Figure 4.1 A hypothetical global citizen with a multicultural identity and/or a cognitive style integrating independence and interdependence, on a continuum of egocentricity and sociocentricity

code as expressed in the Earth Charter. Multicultural people avoid the pitfalls of relativity by holding fast to moral anchors, which they have found through reflecting critically on their identity and culture.

Intercultural Comfort Zones

In 1991, Bennett published a description of stages of sensitivity to intercultural differences. Although unsure about how well these stages travel around the globe, I nonetheless believe they are important in understanding the notion of multicultural identity (and in a later chapter, awareness of prejudice). Here I have adapted them and called them *intercultural comfort zones*. These comfort zones are not rigid and exclusive. People's comfort with other cultures and with intercultural encounters depends on with whom they are in contact, their emotional state, or their situation. People may be in denial about differently gendered cultures ("women and men are the same"), defensive about their own culture ("my culture is the best"), and accepting of some other cultures ("they're different but they're cute"). Some people occupy the same range of comfort zones throughout their lives, while others move through and into different zones because of the positive or negative trigger experiences that they have, and their ability to reflect on those experiences critically. These comfort zones are related to multicultural identity.

Denial

Denial is a comfort zone where people have little awareness of culture and potential cultural difference. They may not have an abstract concept of culture at all. They might belong to an isolated homogeneous group where they didn't learn how to perceive and understand cultural differences. To them, cultural isolation is normal; their own culture is as imperceptible to them as is the air. Their culture is the only way the world is. I was in this comfort zone as a small child. I grew up in rural Wisconsin where the only diversity was between Catholics (them) and Protestants (us) in my community. I did not see "culture" until I came into contact with Spanish-speaking migrant families through a Catholic friend. I thought they had an attractive culture and ethnicity; I didn't.

People who wish to stay in denial avoid culturally diverse experiences. They do not want to travel outside their comfort zone. Bennett (1991) says that when they talk about others, they use broad terms like "foreigner" or "oriental." They may be well meaning but ignorant about others, or they may negatively stereotype groups of people. According to Bennett, people in denial sometimes dehumanize others outside their own group; they perceive other groups as less than or not human and sometimes become genocidal.

Defense

People in defense live in a world of them versus others. They are more culturally aware than people in denial because they recognize cultural difference, but they dislike or denigrate variation. The greater the difference they see, the more negatively they evaluate it. Their home culture is considered the highest stage of cultural development, and other cultures and people are open for proselytizing and imperialism. People with a defensive attitude also protect their world view from change by exaggerating the positive aspects of their home culture compared to other cultures. If someone makes a neutral or positive statement about another culture to them, the remark is taken as an attack on their home culture. For example, a positive comment that women cooperate with each other may be taken by a culturally defensive male as a put-down of men. Conversely, a positive comment about men focusing single-mindedly on a task may be taken as a put-down of women by a culturally defensive female.

Defense has long been the majority attitude in the West (i.e. worldwide colonialism and imperialism, ethnic cleansing, the settlement of the Americas and Australia), but in this postcolonial world, defense itself is on the defensive. That explains why some defensive people feel besieged and try to protect their status, prestige, and identity from others. They are extremely vocal when given the opportunity. In the extreme, defensive people favor segregation and nationalism, and support backlash actions like racial supremacy, hate, or terrorist groups. In an unusual turnaround, there is a complete reversal of defense. In this attitudinal space, the other culture is viewed as superior and the home culture is disrespected. Classic examples are the volunteers, missionaries, or immigrants who "go native" and do not want to have anything to do with their compatriots. They love the other culture and its people as superior to their own.

Minimization

In this comfort zone, people are culturally aware and accept superficial cultural differences, like food, clothing, or "exotic" customs. They tend to overestimate how sensitive they are to cultural difference. They are fond of saying that all human beings are the same under the skin and have the same values. Sometimes the similarity involves people in relationship to the divine. People with this attitude are not bad. The problem is that, to them, the common values, the universal beliefs, are always defined in ethnocentric terms. They project their values onto others and real differences are swept under the rug.

For example, in Western culture, people value privacy in the bathroom so they believe that all people value privacy in the bathroom. They want several private bathrooms in their home and therefore they believe that everyone wants at least one private bathroom in the home. There is a danger of projecting such a belief onto others, calling it universal. In fact, when planning low-income homes and communities in some countries, Western engineers are surprised to learn that their "clients" do not like their plans. They do not want bathrooms in their homes because they consider them smelly, dirty, and unhealthy, no matter how clean they are. They prefer going to a communal bathroom because it is a valued source of social contact where they can freely interact and groom themselves with others of their gender.

Minimizers also protect their world view by interpreting differences in ways they already understand. They do not try to see another perspective. For example, if someone from another culture brings a gift, a minimizer interprets the gift according to her own cultural norms. She thinks it is a host gift, nothing more than a polite token. Later she finds out that acceptance of the gift meant a commitment to help the giver, and she is angry because she made no such commitment. The giver, on the other hand, assumed that her acceptance of the gift was an agreement to help. When no help is forthcoming, he feels justified in getting angry. Both minimizers projected their own interpretations onto the behavior rather than questioning whether the gift signified something different to different people.

Minimizers often support universal religious, moral, or political principles, like the Earth Charter. They can be important social activists and global civilians. Without minimizers, many important social causes would surely have died out. However, according to Bennett (1991), minimizers cannot always see clearly when they enjoy certain privileges or powers over others. And if they cannot see them, they cannot give them up. That blindness makes their activism suspect to some and hypocritical to others. It might be that Western minimizers are responsible for some of the worst faults of global civil society.

Acceptance

Acceptance is an attitude of understanding and appreciation of differences as viable alternatives in human existence. Accepting people hesitate to project their own expectations onto others of different native cultures. For example, in receiving a gift, an accepter might try to find out what expectations go along with it. In giving a gift, an accepter might try to find a way to articulate what it means. Very culturally aware, they understand that values and judgments of behavior are embedded in social and cultural contexts. However, accepters are generally monocultural and do not feel comfortable about shifting to another perspective. They know that they do not understand other cultures very well. Like minimizers, accepters may be affected by inaction or liberal paralysis when it comes to perceiving their own part in social injustice, according to Bennett (1991).

Adaptation

Adaptation is a comfort zone that combines acceptance with good verbal and behavioral skills for cultural communication. Adapters are often at least partially bicultural. In addition, because of their enhanced cultural awareness, they experience a shift in their own frame of reference. They are comfortable shifting consciously into an alternative world view in order to act appropriately in at least two different cultures. For the adapter, the boundaries between cultures are flexible and permeable. Still, they have to shift consciously to an alternate world view. Adapters perceive behavior in a cultural context. They understand what a gift signifies or might signify in another culture. An adapter who receives a gift knows it may not be a simple host gift. The adapter who gives the gift knows that the other may take it as a host gift instead of as a promise to help. So they consciously adapt their communication to make their intentions clear.

Intercultural communication has come a long way since its early days, but it is still not well understood. At first, people who studied and wrote about cultural communication issues were generally North Americans or Europeans. Therefore, the information gained was one-sided and superficial, full of projection and erroneous interpretation. The standards against which other "exotic" cultures were measured were Western. In the old days it was enough to note that other cultures had different politeness norms (from us) or (to us) different ways of saying no without saying no. Often this information was meant to help transnational businesspeople and foreign service professionals to live and work overseas successfully because relocation costs were high and business deals lucrative. However, increasingly, knowledge about variation in cultural communication is coming from an equal-to-equal dialogue between researchers from a number of cultures. The information is deeper and likely to be more accurate.

In addition, the ever-increasing numbers of multicultural people increase the chances that cultural communication will be more effective.

Integration

According to Bennett (1991), integrated people are tolerant of uncertainty and ambiguity; in fact, they relish them. Because they are capable of complex cultural thinking, they step away from the expectations common to their culture. That is, when they receive a gift from someone else they may act the same way as adapters, by using communication to clarify the giver's expectations. But if they give a gift, it is without any expectations at all because, in our terms, they have adopted a third culture, a cultura franca where local cultural expectations, projections, and attributions do not enter.

Minimizers, accepters, and adapters may be global civilians, but they do not have the most abstract characteristic associated with multicultural identity. Their learning about different cultures and critical reflection have not changed the way they think. Integration is more than a comfort zone. Instead, it

> involves the acquisition of a new mind set, that is, a style of mental and emotional consciousness that allows individuals to negotiate, more readily, new formations of reality. It involves the development of individuals who are more susceptible to change and to the acceptance of the inevitability of the conflict that comes with it.
>
> (Wurzel, 1998)

If Wurzel's ideas are correct, integration is more than an intercultural comfort zone; it is a different cognitive style. *Cognition* is perception, judgment, reasoning, and memory. Kohlberg (1984:219) defines it as observable or imaginative role-taking abilities, the search for logical inferences, relationships and transformations, and the way people find meaning in the world. Thus, a *cognitive style* means that people perceive, judge, reason, and remember in a specific way. They have differing abilities to take roles, see inferences and relationships, and find meaning in the world. A cognitive style does not affect raw intelligence, but it does affect the way people think and view the world.

Bennett (1991) points out that integrated people often feel most comfortable with other people at the margins of cultures because they share a world view. They connect to each other as members of the same community with a common culture that, perhaps, fuses collective and individualist features. We might call this cognitive style the global citizen. It may be possible for connected independent and interdependent people to show global citizenship as well, as I show in Figure 4.1. However, until psychologists clarify the issues, I will use the term *global citizen* more narrowly—for those with multicultural identity and/or a cognitive style that integrates interdependence with independence.

There have been some recent studies of so-called "global leaders" by people in the field of human resource management. Osland and Osland (2005:112) summarized conclusions about expatriates who are closely involved with a local culture different from their own. The more deeply they are immersed in another culture, the more they are confronted with paradoxes and contradictions that change their self-image. A paradox is a situation in which at least two contradictory and mutually exclusive elements are in play simultaneously. Osland and Osland argue that a new cosmopolitan mindset develops when expatriates wrestle successfully with the paradoxes and contradictions of their home culture and their new culture. Resolving paradoxes requires managing uncertainty and balancing global and local tensions. The paradoxes force expatriates to perceive more than one truth; they learn to analyze situations accurately from a variety of perspectives.

My interpretation of some of the paradoxes Osland and Osland studied is that they seem to be on the "fault line" between interdependent and independent selves and agencies, and perhaps the transformation they produce is a shift towards the integration of a multicultural identity. For instance, the expatriates talked about being freed from cultural rules and even some of the norms of the host country, while not being free from all norms. They recalled becoming more world-minded, understanding, and open to new experiences, but also more self-created in their value system. They reported paradoxes of seeing a culture as foreign but also feeling part of a specific community with people they personally knew. They talked about possessing power but downplaying it in order to gain cooperation from others. They gave up some core values like outspokenness and the urge to stand out, while at the same time finding that some core values—like freedom of action, creativity, and agency—became stronger. Finally, they reported paradoxes of feeling at ease everywhere but feeling marginal to their home culture.

It is a paradox that a different identity and cognitive style come from resolving intercultural paradoxes; this multicultural identity rests on both belonging to and marginality to the home culture. It is the *integration* of these various perspectives, insider/outsider and local/global, that makes the global citizen a fusion of independence and interdependence. It remains for cultural psychologists to explore whether people with multicultural identities have fused the qualities of interdependence and independence like empathy, integrity, honesty, and reciprocity.

Metacultural Awareness

Let me approach the same issue from another angle. It is well known among educators that children acquire, or fail to acquire, an awareness of language as an object that can be talked about or studied in the abstract. For instance, people who lack language awareness are unable to separate a word from the thing it refers to. They simply do not get that the word "table" is just a random sound symbol in English that happens to represent a certain type of object in the world. They cannot examine their language because they take it for granted. They have a harder time learning to read and write well if they cannot observe words and sentences, meanings, and intentions, and talk about them. Language awareness is a bootstrap that lets people use language more effectively. To complete the cycle, using language in ever more sophisticated ways leads to greater language awareness.

The point is that people who are aware of language have a cognitive advantage over people who are not. They think in a different way. Their minds have changed because of what they have learned. This cognitive advantage is not intelligence; it is a different cognitive style called *metalinguistic awareness*, derived from "meta" which means "higher" or "beyond." Metalinguistic awareness results in the mental agility that is often found in multilingual people. Their metalinguistic awareness empowers them to use their various languages and knowledge of language itself to perceive, think, and learn differently.

Since language is a subpart of culture, it is reasonable to extend the idea of meta-awareness to culture. That is, I hypothesize that there is a *meta-cultural awareness* that may be analogous to metalinguistic awareness. Just as people can use awareness of language(s) to understand the world, people can use their awareness of culture to resolve cultural paradoxes and contradictions through critical reflection. Just as multilingual people can use metalinguistic awareness to perceive the world in different ways, so multiculturally integrated people can think outside the box in ways that monocultural people cannot. Metacultural awareness does not make people smarter than others. It simply makes them think differently, and perhaps more creatively or more complexly.

If this hypothesis holds true, the intercultural comfort zones and integrated cognitive style show people and groups at various milestones of metacultural awareness and multicultural identity. As people deal with the paradoxes of interdependence and independence, and their relationship to their own culture, to other culture(s), to culture as an abstraction, and to global cultural consciousness and critical loyalty, they gain a cognitive advantage over monocultural people. As they acquire the capacity to integrate various world views, their cognition restructures their sense of identity.

As we saw in an earlier chapter, relativity or deculturalization are terms for world views in which there are no truths; there is no moral anchor. Adler (1976) feared that his multicultural man would lapse into relativity, and that it would leave him morally paralyzed. Kumaravadivelu (2008:168) talks about the same topic when he contrasts Nehru with Gandhi. Both men had traveled and studied extensively outside their local cultures. Both were prominent leaders of their people. But Nehru had an "ambivalent hybrid identity." He found himself "in a cultural limbo— neither here nor there." He was alienated from his culture. "I have become a queer mixture of the east and the west, out of place everywhere, at home nowhere . . . I am a stranger and alien in the West. I cannot be of it. But in my own country also, sometimes, I have an exile's feeling" (Nehru, 1964:16). He was marginal everywhere and not connected.

In contrast, about Gandhi, Kumaravadivelu (2008:168) says, "His encounters with his native and foreign cultures produced in him an enriched and enlightened cultural persona . . . He repeatedly emphasized the importance of embracing the best of one's own cultural heritage, which does not have to be forsaken in order to imbibe what is best in other cultures." Gandhi's cultural awareness was rooted in Hindu nonviolence, but still was open to other cultures. He was comfortable in England as well as India because he was himself in both settings. The fact that Gandhi is now revered across the globe is an indication that his local cultural heritage, nonviolence, resonates globally as well.

The hypotheses in this chapter are tentative. It may be possible for psychologists to tease apart the three hypothesized self-identities related to global citizenship—connected independence, multicultural identity, and connected interdependence—based on the psychological traits they show. It may be possible to find a cognitive style related to metacultural awareness that combines different types of marginality, voice, and agency. The importance of looking at Nehru and Gandhi is to see the necessity for connection or moral grounding. Such moral grounding depends on personal resilience in the face of the perhaps inevitable decoupling of language, culture, affiliations, identity, and values in a globalized world.

Learning is Agency

Adler (1976:375) thought that people with multicultural identity are "shaped and contoured by the stresses and strains which result from cultural interweaving at both the macro and the microcultural levels." To him, multicultural identity evolves in people "capable of negotiating the conflicts and tension inherent in cross cultural contacts." It might be that multicultural identity and metacultural awareness are related to Kumaravadivelu's global cultural consciousness, in that they emerge from complex intercultural contacts as well as critical cultural reflection on trigger experiences, moral dilemmas, paradoxes, and contradictions. Dealing with these complexities produces cognitive conflict in people's minds, and when the conflicts are resolved through reflection, people experience cognitive restructuring. Cognitive restructuring allows for complex thinking, appreciation for uncertainty, and, possibly, metacultural awareness and multicultural identity. Johnston (2003) provides a cogent discussion of many of the complexities and paradoxes facing English language teachers and learners; his book is a good source of moral dilemmas for the English language classroom.

Complex Thinking

The power of complex thinking lies in the capacity to resolve paradoxes and tolerate uncertainty, ambiguity, and ambivalence. When people tolerate *uncertainty*, they are not unsettled by unpredictable or opaque situations where they cannot discern the details or implications. They do not get unsettled when confronting puzzling situations in which there are no clear answers. There are many such situations where people are immersed in another culture or where they only imperfectly understand the language people are speaking. When people tolerate *ambiguity*, they can make the best of situations where there is insufficient information to make a choice between two possibilities. For example, there might be more than one way to interpret what someone says or does; complex thinkers realize the ambiguity and do not let the alternatives confuse them. When people tolerate *ambivalence*, they can live with conflicting emotions or interpretations and they can integrate positive and negative elements. They may both like and dislike someone for different reasons, or they may perceive positive and negative aspects in the same situation. Their thinking is not dichotomous.

In other words, when straddling different cultures, people are confronted with situations involving two or more contradictory and mutually exclusive elements. As they grapple with the contradictory information from their home culture and their new culture, they learn to manage uncertainty and balance more than one truth. They acquire multiple perspectives and become complex thinkers. Complex thinkers do not jump to simple conclusions or accept superficial explanations simply because they do not want to deal with complexity. They can integrate conflicted feelings and emotions in order to move through them and get over them. Few educational systems presently build paradox, uncertainty, ambiguity, and contradiction into their curriculum. It is quite the opposite: the focus is on facts, evidence, and forming firm opinions.

Critical Pedagogy and Resistance

The importance of complex thinking argues strongly for the benefits of study and work abroad for developing global citizens. Critical pedagogy for resistance, which Canagarajah (1999:22) describes as education that leads people to "gain agency, conduct critical thinking, and initiate change," would be a good preparation. Resistance education is elicitive; it makes use of local resources to nudge people along in their understanding of social and cultural dysergy. At first, people are in denial about the paradoxical and contradictory realities that surround them, often in the form of injustice and violence. The challenge for resistance educators is to bring these issues into awareness through a process of *conscientization* or *problem-posing*. Problem-posing requires confrontation with the complex past and present, with other ways of thinking and acting, with uncertainty, ambivalence, and ambiguity. The "givens" of totalitarianism—racism, injustice, and violence—are problematized; therefore they are delegitimized. After this process, people may see other legitimate preferred futures and be willing to make changes in their own attitudes and initiate attempts to make a transition to something better. They use their agency for social and cultural transition and to grapple with conflict.

Problem-posing takes place through dialogue (voice, attention, and acknowledgment) between participants organized around a key concept, object, or experience that forms the basis for Socratic open-ended questions. *Voice* is when participants offer, articulate, legitimate, and become vulnerable. *Attention* is when they listen, accept, understand, and give legitimacy and acknowledgment. *Acknowledgment* is their recognition of what another sees as a truth. The dialogue is aimed at defining issues, discussing the causes and implications, and imagining ways to mitigate them, if possible.

At first, teachers usually generate the issue; it is hypocritical to say that teachers are not in charge of the learning, but they need to minimize their natural authority. Their open-ended questions should leave a lot of room for creative and complex thinking, not shying away from dilemmas, uncertainty, ambiguity, and acknowledging ambivalence. Problem-posing, where the outcome is meant to be agency, is different from problem-solving, where the outcome is some kind of answer. Throughout, teachers need to think about whether to reveal their own opinions. As participants become accustomed to problematizing, they begin to select their own themes and issues.

The Biosphere

The cautionary tales of Kazmi and Nehru point to the need for a glocalized moral grounding for problem-posing. The moral ground can be the principles of the Earth Charter applied locally, or local ideas of responsibility and reciprocity. Spring (2004) separates human rights education from environmental education, identifying them as two goals for educational policy and systems, and in his book *A New Paradigm for Global School Systems: Education for a Long and Happy Life* (2007) he unifies these two goals under a more general goal: happiness and subjective well-being. He points out that there is ever more research into what makes people happy and increases their sense of well-being. To be happy, people need a certain level of material comfort and safety. However, beyond a certain level, economic achievement does not contribute to happiness. It is not true that the billionaire is that much happier than the millionaire. Despite what advertisers tell us, more things do not make people happier.

Naturally, what makes people happy and feel a sense of well-being differs among different cultures and among individuals within those cultures, but as goals, they can be specified and measured. For instance, Spring (2007) discusses research into collectivist and individualist cultures. In collectivist cultures the factors that promote happiness are achievement of collective goals, fulfillment of duty and obligations to one's in-group, and interdependence. In individualist cultures the factors promoting happiness are achievement of personal goals, self-fulfillment, and independence. Multicultural identity may fuse these; if personal goals are allied with social goals, then happiness is connected to achieving and balancing both. There is more about this relationship in the next chapter.

Spring shows how happiness and well-being can be the moral ground for problem-posing. The overarching framework for learning is a human-centered biosphere and how that biosphere promotes (or does not promote) human happiness and longevity. The biosphere is a concept that developed in the Russian scientific tradition. Instead of breaking science down into different fields, categories, and dichotomies (as European and American scientists did), Russian scientists looked at the interdependence of all physical and biological things holistically as participants in a single *biosphere* including air, water, land, plants, minerals, and animals. No single participant is truly free from the other participants in the biosphere.

The methodology is problem-posing, including the use of imagination, to work towards the conditions that increase life-spans and well-being. Spring (2004) includes a number of lessons to illustrate his ideas. In these lessons, the traditional subject matters of school are integrated into holistic units or themes where students learn the physical, biological, political, social, and economic conditions that decrease and increase life-span and subjective well-being. Spring lists content areas of the biosphere, bringing together global human rights and a global environmental ethic in localized study:

- methods of civic activism to protect all humans, other species, and the environment;

- the basic principles of ecology or, in other words, the biosphere;
- a study of the social, economic, and environmental impact and limits of industrialism and technology;
- history of science and its impact on humans and the biosphere;
- sustainable consumption, agriculture, and forestry;
- environmental ethics;
- the effect of poverty on the biosphere;
- human rights as protection of the biosphere;
- peace education as protection of the biosphere;
- the use of traditional (local) knowledge for understanding relationships between humans and interdependence within the biosphere.

Problem-posing helps people understand the contribution that their culture or local knowledge makes to their understanding of and care for the biosphere. If it includes complex thinking, paradox, and contradiction, it may lead to Bennett's integration, multicultural identity, and multicultural awareness. It is crucial for global citizenship because it supports the moral values for sustainable development and social justice. One criticism of critical pedagogy has been that participants are often overwhelmed by the magnitude of the task that confronts them. My students, for example, have despaired as they ask themselves how they can have an impact on racism. They are frustrated with simplistic actions like writing a letter to a newspaper or Congress member.

It is important for teachers to help participants identify a localized, meaningful way for transition and to provide examples of what others have done. One such story is MachsomWatcher, a group of Israeli Jewish women who monitor the behavior of the Israeli military at checkpoints where Palestinians cross, protecting the human rights of the Palestinians, and bearing witness by writing reports of each observation. They cannot change the government and military policy, or the large injustice, but they formed a civil organization to act within their rights to resist on a local level. According to their website, one of the early MachsomWatchers got the idea because she had participated in a similar project in Guatemala, illustrating the glocalized nature of the resistance. It is no coincidence that Spring suggests civic activism as the first area of critical pedagogy.

Part II

The English Language Teacher in Local Civil Society

Chapter 5

Sustainable Peace

[W]e never can have a true view of man unless we have a love for him. Civilization must be judged and prized, not by the amount of power it has developed, but by how much it has evolved and given expression to, by its laws and institutions, the love of humanity. The first question and the last which it has to answer is whether and how far it recognizes man more as a spirit than a machine. Whenever some ancient civilization fell into decay and died, it was owing to causes which produced callousness of heart and led to the cheapening of man's worth; when either the state or some powerful group of men began to look upon the people as a mere instrument of their power; when, by compelling weaker races to slavery and trying to keep them down by every means, man struck at the foundation of his greatness, his own love of freedom and fair-play. Civilization can never sustain itself upon cannibalism of any form. For that by which alone man is true can only be nourished by love and justice.

(Thakur, 1916:113)

Rabindranath Thakur (Tagore) was an ardent early twentieth-century cosmopolitan rooted in the complex cultures of India. In this quote, he argued that a true view of humankind can come only through the relationship of the personal with the social, which he called love of humankind and justice. Cultures can be judged and/or appreciated by examining their laws and institutions to see the extent to which they lead to the well-being of humans. Thakur argued that ancient cultures fell and withered away because the people were callous of heart. They did not value human life and engaged in "cannibalistic" practices like slavery, injustice, and oppression. His use of the term "cannibalism" is striking; it calls to mind primitive societies of people who eat each other. It intentionally contrasts sharply with the civilized concepts of freedom and fair-play. Thakur certainly appropriated his knowledge of English culture and language to resist Britain's imperialist position in India, foreshadowing the fall of the British Empire. Yet he was also looking inside his own culture to the inequities of caste.

In this quote, Thakur displays how critical reflection on "civilization" led him to a fundamental pillar for local and global sustainability and peace: respect for humanity, or species identity as we might call it. Sustainable peace is found in the balanced relationship between self and others, in blending independence and interdependence. When people oppress others, they ultimately become callous and cheapened, and their position is not sustainable. This chapter addresses several ways we can think about and imagine a world of sustainable peace. As seen in Chapter 3, global civic culture is altruistic and goal-directed, with values in opposition to rampant predatory globalization and the culture of consumerism, exploitation, and imperialism. Global civilians share values opposed to the culture of hate, war, genocide, violent conflict, and global terror.

Pennycook (2001:8–9) argues that critical applied linguists need a vision of *preferred futures* that are alternative possibilities grounded in ethics, compassion, and hope. With an anti-prescriptivist perspective, he feels that ethics should not be a normative or moralistic code of practice but a recognition of ethical concerns. He objects to a top-down, outside-in dogmatic moral code, but I think that a bottom-up, inside-out coherent and normative set of guidelines to which individuals, societies, governments, and businesses adhere by consensus, such as the Earth Charter, would offer a better chance of achieving preferred futures for localities and the planet. Failing that, national and international legislation must come into play.

A Just Peace

There is a growing awareness that modern warfare is different from earlier warfare between nation-states. Terrorist warfare and largely unilateral media events like the Gulf War target civilians indiscriminately and do not solve the issues that they are meant to solve. They succeed only in spreading the seeds for future violence and war and make people less secure rather than more secure. Global civil society and its pro-social and pro-human agenda and culture may be, as Kaldor (2003) puts it, the "answer to war." However, just because global civic culture is more coherent and conscious, that does not mean that all global civilians hold identical values. They are pro-peace but this core belief translates into different attitudes and behaviors with respect to war and violence.

Some people oppose certain violent conflicts but not all violence. They believe that only violence in self-defense is appropriate, or they support violence and war if it is "just." The number of people holding this anti-war attitude has grown considerably, as shown by the numbers involved in global anti-war demonstrations over Vietnam, the Gulf War, the Israeli occupation, and the war in Iraq. Protests have grown so influential that governments are increasingly trying to cast wars and armed conflict in the terms of just wars, when they are clearly not just.

Some people will not use or cooperate with any kind of institutionalized social or political violence or war for any reason. Some will not use or cooperate with any violence to any animal life, a perspective that fuses Western and Eastern religious, humanist, and universalist thought. And finally, almost all global civilians refuse to use or cooperate with violence against the earth.

Global civil society has been criticized for its inability to react to wars and conflicts. Instead, it is proactive, emphasizing the building of a just society or a just world to prevent future aggression from murderous governments or terrorist groups. Global civilians have come to the conclusion that violence and war are simply too costly in lives and property, too disruptive, too unfair. They believe that the way to make the world more peaceful is to remove obstacles to peace like exploitative social and economic structures or exclusive and nonparticipatory political systems. They see environmental degradation as a major threat to human security. Like the grassroots movements in Eastern Europe, they exploit the power of the followership. They use organized nonviolent resistance and direct action to bring about change.

There is a new way of thinking: that peace will not come from avoiding war. The world needs a "just peace" based on the Earth Charter consensus of human rights, sustainable development, equitable distribution of resources, and political self-determination, within our biosphere. People are becoming increasingly aware that most national governments and armies do not seem to be achieving peace; and that they may, in fact, have a vested interest in war. So, in a time in which many people feel disaffected from their governments, global civil society, with its affiliated economic, educational, political, and social movements and its pro-human and pro-social values and behavioral norms, is perhaps the best hope for a just and sustainable peace. Global civic culture wants to change the world from the bottom up, without relying on governments, religious leaders, and transnational industry/commerce unless they support the change.

Post-Thinking

In trying to imagine preferred futures, sometimes it is necessary to look into the past. Philosophers and cultural commentators describe our present times as poststructuralist, postpositivist, postcolonial, and postmodern. In other words, the world view today seems to be defined by what it is not rather than what it is. It is defined with respect to the past and not with respect to the future. This is the sign of a world anticipating and building a post-Western, post-Eurocentric, post-American future.

Poststructuralism

Structuralism holds that people understand their world by inventing taxonomies, or hierarchies of categories. The smallest taxonomy is a binary opposition or a dichotomy, two concepts in opposition to each other like good or bad, black or white, East or West. Dichotomies are often ways to draw a line of separation between one thing and another. Structuralism is associated with Western culture, especially with the rise of physical science and technology. Much of the early work in linguistics was based on structuralism: the inventory of phonemes, the invention of the concept of morpheme and its varieties, syntactic categories and phrase structure trees, semantic features. Structuralism takes the existence of structures as a given.

Poststructuralists look at structures and hierarchies critically because they may be false or misleading. Expecting to find structures in the world, we see them, but they may blind us to alternative ways of looking at things. For instance, if we think of parts of speech as rigid either/or categories, then a word must be a noun or a verb, an adjective or an adverb. Recent work in English word meaning, for instance, posits the use of fuzzy categories to describe the way a word can act like a noun or a verb, an adjective or an adverb, at least in English (Birch, 2004). Seeing parts of speech as rigid categories misses important flexibilities of English grammar and makes them more difficult to teach and learn.

Dichotomies like bad and good, white and black, and West and East often carry the implicit assumption that one member is primary and the other secondary. Poststructuralists reject dichotomies as too simplistic. The global is often contrasted with the local, yet we saw that they do not contrast. A clear dichotomy between East and West or collectivist and individualist no longer seems viable. Solutions to the problems we are facing might be found in the latencies between structures or behind hierarchies.

Poststructuralist thinking includes holism, orthogonalism, and constructionism. *Holism* is a world view that "zooms out" to see something as a whole. For instance, quilt makers, after piecing together their quilt patches with pins, hang the "latent" quilt on a wall to squint at it. Squinting brings out another, sometimes unexpected, pattern in the combination of quilt squares, and quilters need to decide if they like the unintended pattern or not. Holism sees not separate compartmentalized units but a functional system of relationships between units leading sometimes serendipitously to a different whole. The concept of the biosphere is holistic.

Orthogonalism refers to seeing cross-cutting relationships between members that might also be in a structural hierarchy. For instance, in linguistics, a lexicalist talks about the relationships among words as captured in their statistical co-occurrences, such as "look" and "alike" or "cross" and "border". These collocational relationships are orthogonal to the phrase and clause structures posited by syntacticians but equally interesting and robust. Human Rights Watch and its connections to associations in Eastern Europe created an orthogonal relationship that cut across national sociopolitical hierarchies. In many parts of the world, local secondary English teachers in the towns look to the capital city and central government for resources and support. Accustomed only to hierarchy, they are reluctant to cooperate with and share resources orthogonally with other teachers in their area even when that might benefit them.

Constructionism refers to the idea that conditions, structures, systems, and hierarchies are socially constructed and therefore can be modified and changed. For instance, under structuralism, people's identities were fixed by national borders, religions, sex, and race. In a poststructuralist world, people construct themselves, within constraints, from their affiliations, and affiliations can change over time. Culture, too, is constructed by individuals, social groupings, and institutions. It is fluid and shape-shifting.

Postpositivism

Positivism is the belief that true knowledge is scientific knowledge, and that it can come through experimentation using the scientific method. It is contrasted with other ways of knowing the truth—say, through intuition, dreams, quests, contemplation, revelation from the divine, logic, and reasoning. According to positivists, scientific knowledge is superior because it is (supposedly) above culture and human foibles; it is objective, explicit and testable, not subjective, abstract, and untestable.

The *postpositive* world view is less enchanted with scientific truth, especially outside of the physical sciences. Postpositivism values both objectivity and subjectivity, both the qualitative and the quantitative. There has been more contact between Eastern and Western philosophers and psychologists, and there is far more respect and equality between them. Eastern wisdom, for instance, emphasizes human abilities to control the mind and body through intense mental and physical training; these abilities involve concentration of a kind not developed through the scientific method. Likewise, inspiration, creativity, and imagination emerge in ways we do not know much about.

Another flaw of positivism is that it was divorced from values and ethics. Knowledge has led to a great deal of hardship, suffering, and "cannibalism" like the atomic bomb, landmines, and other weapons. To achieve a preferred future, science and technology need to be reined in by ethics or moral thinking. For instance, Mohd-Asraf (2005:114) mentions a Muslim word, *Ilm*, a concept of knowledge that combines the senses and intelligence with, "more importantly, the realm of spirit." The pursuit of knowledge for knowledge's sake is less valuable than the pursuit of wisdom for the sake of a better world. Wisdom is a fusion of knowledge and ethics.

Postcolonialism

In its broadest terms, *colonialism* refers to the creation of subjugated states militarily, politically, or economically. When early people first walked out of Africa they found uninhabited regions which they moved into, populating the earth. At some point, millennia ago, people began moving into areas that already had populations. Colonialism has been going on since then, but people generally use the term to refer to the world view, policies, and activities by which European nation-states acquired massive, discontinuous, subordinate regions in Africa, Australasia, America, and Asia. *Neocolonialism* is used to refer to continuing exploitation resulting from turbo-capitalism.

Postcolonialism refers to the past and current legacy of the global land-grab and the chaos it caused in indigenous life and culture. For countries "freed" from their colonial status, the legacy often has to do with political instability, social unrest and injustice, economic debt, and cultural upheaval. Many of the areas with intractable conflict between different groups and ethnicities today trace their divisions to their colonialist legacy. For individuals, the postcolonial legacy involves identity and affiliation issues of race, language, religion, and culture, and the relationship between the colonized and the colonizer. The dichotomy between colonized and colonizer is a false one; the reality is far more complicated. For one thing, colonized people were active agents of resistance, like Thakur. They created new cultures of fusion, and the world is richer for it. The term "postcolonial" also refers to a world where the former colonized nations are economic and political powerhouses or potential powerhouses, and the internal and external cultural changes that come along with that.

Post-postmodernism

Modernism refers to an optimistic world view that predominated in Europe and North America through the closing decades of the twentieth century. It is characterized by a belief that humans could improve life through science, technology, and changes in social and political structures. Humans and human society could progress along a path to a better world. There has long been a humanistic kind of modernism, attempts by humans to improve life and health, human rights, better working conditions and the like, through civil society, science and technology, legislation, and education.

However, modernism has a dark cannibalistic side. There were three flavors of modernistic ideology that were meant to improve people's lives: capitalist, fascist, and socialist/communist. Under these ideological banners, the worst excesses of modernism led to the horrors of atomic bombs, extermination camps, gulags, and cultural revolutions. Capitalistic modernism is also predicated on the idea that people will be happier the wealthier they are and the more possessions they have. Capitalism feeds itself by creating ever more consumers and by exploiting those not in a position to consume. It was disillusionment with these attempts to change society through force, killing, and consumerism that led to postmodernism.

Postmodernists looked back on modernism and towards the future with more pessimism than optimism. They no longer believe that humans can engineer social progress through science and technology and least of all through the efforts of national governments. Progress does not come from political platforms or economic ideologies. Materialism and consumerism do not make people happy and do not lead to just societies. Instead, they lead to superficiality, competition, loss of community, and environmental degradation. Nevertheless, the dichotomy between modernism and postmodernism is also false. We need both optimism and pessimism. Optimism gives people hope that measures taken this year can slow global warming. It gives people the courage to explore ways to resolve the conflicts of today. Pessimism tells us that many of our existing social structures and institutions do not make the grade and that change is hard but possible. Pessimism added to optimism gives people hopeful realism instead of hopeless despair.

In a post-postmodern world we know that a certain degree of material comfort and security lead to happiness, but that beyond a certain level, more possessions do not mean more happiness or more security. Instead, other aspects of life bring fulfillment: achievement of personal/social goals, a sense of community, good relationships, a meaningful job, and the respect of others. Post-postmodernist thinking embraces East, West, North, and South. Progress has not been good for humans or for our earth but it has not been all bad either. Post-postmodernism attempts to peel back turbo-capitalism, environmental degradation and nuclear weapons, but it encourages social relations, human rights, and sustainability through people working together.

Postuniversality

Universality is the name for a debate about whether there are universal moral values or not, whether there is an ethical standard that should govern human affairs. Part of the debate also centered on what the standards were. If the standards were identified and promulgated around the world in a top-down fashion, would that constitute cultural imperialism? That is, are local cultures in danger from cultural imperialism from the outside even if the potential change is for the good? I think we are now in a world of postuniversality because there is now a grassroots consensus of moral values of human rights, peace, and the environment.

If principles like those in the Earth Charter are planetary, the issue of cultural imperialism becomes different also. The Earth Charter does not belong to anyone or to any existing national culture. It is the content of a cultura franca. It is the culture of peace attempting to influence the culture of war, whether that culture is associated with a huge global power or a local conflict between two warlords. It is the culture of global civilians attempting to regulate turbo-capitalism, wherever it originates. It is global civic culture aiming to trickle down to local cultures as ideas of sustainability, at the same time that sustainability concepts from local cultures flow up to global culture.

The opposite of universality is relativity, the belief that there is no ultimate moral truth in the world because values are relative to cultures; and because values are relative, there is no way to judge or select behaviors as worthy or not. Thus, relativity can lead to a paralysis of moral thinking. It is possible to argue that, with the Earth Charter, our world has also become postrelative. In fact, we are in a transition period between latency and actuality; to move forward we must picture preferred sustainable futures, and let go of the past.

Transitional Thinking

Rather than referring to our world today as post-whatever, a few people have adopted a term oriented towards the future: transitionalism. Transitional thinking is a way of articulating and legitimizing the idea that cultures, societies, and people are in transition to more preferred ways of being. Transitionalism depends on people's ability to imagine a different way that the world could be and to figure out how to use their agencies to make this world into that imagined world.

Historical Precedents

For instance, on their Great Transition Network website, the contributors point to historical precedents for other transitional phases in human cultures: the Stone Age, early civilization, and the modern age, as shown in Table 5.1. The transitions are linked to communication technology and economic systems. It took 100,000 years for the Stone Age to make the transition to early civilization, 10,000 years for the transition to the modern era, and 1,000 years to consolidate the nation-state. This suggests that the transition to the planetary phase may take as little as 100 years.

This picture of the past, the present, and the future, although simplistic, is effective as a tool of imagination. For instance, there are still many

Table 5.1 Characteristics of Historical Eras

Milestone	Stone Age	Early Civilization	Modern Era	Planetary Phase
Organization	Tribe	City-State/ Village	Nation-state/ Kingdom	Global Governance
Economy	Hunting/ Gathering	Settled Agriculture	Industrial System	Globalization
Communications	Language	Writing	Printing	Computers/ Internet
Years	100,000	10,000	1,000	100

Source: Raskin, Banuri, Gallopín, Gutman, Hammond, Kates, and Swart, 2002. Reprinted with permission of the Tellus Institute.

hunter-gatherers, herders, and agriculturists; there are still many places where questions of tribe, city, and national statehood have not been settled. Literacy is not universal in the Modern Era. This means that earlier eras continue into the present and will continue in the future. Likewise, industrialism and nationalism will not fade away completely. There is much about the future that would remain the same as now. The question is: what will be different?

Sustainability

Sustainable development is development with a long-term view, the development of land, businesses, and communities in a way that does not damage the world for future generations. Wealth, resources, justice, and education are distributed more equally. Sustainability requires a global transition from old values to new ones. For one thing, cultures with strong individualism and competition need to learn from cultures with a more collective and cooperative spirit. The values placed on consumerism and accumulation will cease to be the path to happiness. There must be responsible reproduction to stabilize population growth. Policies leading to global warming and pollution must be reversed and changed. Although treaties and laws are helping in this regard, they are not enough.

Followership

Sustainability requires a change in followership. If people refuse to be influenced by blind loyalty to governments that encourage war and killing, there will be less of these. If people resist the appeal of advertising to make them want more things to fuel relentless turbo-capitalism, there will be less consumerism and less pollution. If people insist that transnational corporations clean up their toxic waste, the environment will be cleaner. This revolution will be difficult in rich countries because people will need to tighten their belts and reduce consumption, but it will also be difficult in those countries that are starting to adopt a consumer lifestyle. It will require cultural transformation.

People will need to harness their cooperative power and strengthen their orthogonal networks to help each other. But how do we know what is sustainable? What are the criteria for selection? Sustainable development balances individual interest with the collective interest, independence with interdependence. The Earth Charter is its moral code and global civic culture its way of life.

Synergy and Dysergy

Sustainable communities have synergy. The word "synergy" comes from Greek roots for "acting together." In science, synergy means that when two or more things are added together, an unexpected result happens, like more strength or more power. It is a buzzword today, but the anthropologist Ruth Benedict initially described a range of high synergy to low synergy cultures in the world:

> I shall need a term for this gamut, a gamut that runs from one pole, where any act or skill that advantages the individual at the same time advantages the group, to the other pole, where every act that advantages the individual is at the expense of others. I shall call this gamut synergy, the old term used in medicine and theology to mean combined action . . . I shall speak of cultures with low synergy, where the social structure provides for acts that are mutually opposed and counteractive, and of cultures with high synergy, where it provides for acts that are mutually reinforcing.
>
> (Benedict, 1976:415)

In this section I build on Benedict's original concept of synergy and present four distinct possibilities on a "spectrum," as shown in Figure 5.1.

High Synergy

High synergy describes societies where the things that individuals do are both good for them and good for society, like becoming literate and educated, staying healthy and fit, voting, and sharing resources so that everyone has enough. In addition, the things that society does are good for both the society and the members of the society, like providing free education, low-cost healthcare, and safe highways for all. Societies and cultures with high synergy have social and economic structures in which

High Synergy	Low Synergy
What benefits the individual also benefits the group.	What "benefits" some individuals is at the expense of the group welfare.
Affordable preventive healthcare, birth control, cheap mass transport, environmental protection, free access to education, peace.	Driving gas-guzzling, polluting cars, consumerism, price-gouging, gun ownership, gang membership, hoarding.
Synergy	**Dysergy**
What benefits the group is at the expense of (some) individuals (required or voluntary).	What harms individuals also harms the group.
School taxes, building codes, traffic laws and fines, required military service for defense, environmental protection restrictions.	Child abuse and neglect, domestic violence, obesity, smoking, alcoholism, illiteracy, violence on TV, prejudice, oppression, genocide, war.
Voluntary acts of altruism.	

Figure 5.1 Spectrum of synergy

the larger entity benefits only if each individual member benefits. There are institutions that help, support, and guide others if necessary. Resources and privileges are distributed equitably. Conflict is handled proactively. There is little time or energy spent on wrangling and squabbling. The individuals are constructive and fulfilled, and therefore the group is productive and dynamic.

Low Synergy

Low synergy is present in societies where what the members do for their own advantage results in disadvantage for other members or the society as a whole. Examples are hoarding food and supplies when others do not have enough, driving a gas-guzzling and polluting car, or keeping a gun in the home (in my culture, guns tend to be used on domestic partners, relatives, and children rather than on strangers). Some people think those are advantages but they are not, because of their low synergy. Societies and cultures with low synergy have cliques or castes that compete with each other and leaders who play them off against each other. Long-lasting feuds and grudges prevent people from working together. Secrets and behind-the-scenes machinations are used for coercion and manipulation. Since people do not feel safe, they spend a lot of time defending their positions against perceived threats. This takes away from the time they have to be productive and creative.

Synergy

Synergy is present in societies where what is at the expense of the individual member benefits the group. This happens in collectivist cultures where individuals often sacrifice their own good for the good of the group. In individualistic cultures, such sacrifice is common too but it is often cast in terms of "enlightened self-interest." There are two possibilities for synergy within this scenario. One is that the society demands or requires a sacrifice from some of its members, something that does not necessarily benefit them but does advantage the group. Examples of this type of synergy are: paying taxes (a sacrifice for workers) for government services like street repair, healthcare, and schools; conscription or the draft (a sacrifice for draftees) for an army of defense; affirmative action (a sacrifice for those with privilege) to help those who have been excluded from jobs or education; and environmental restrictions (a sacrifice for some workers or corporations) to combat pollution. People accept the sacrifice if the costs and benefits are fairly distributed across society.

Of course, the costs and benefits to the individuals in these cases are relative. For instance, individuals pay the taxes, so the disadvantage is theirs, but they also presumably benefit from them if the taxes are spent in appropriate ways. When people without children pay school taxes, they pay the cost but do not directly benefit. However, because they are members of the society, they indirectly benefit because the society is better educated and more literate. Similarly, draftees and their families benefit from defense from attack, those with privilege eventually benefit from a more just society, and workers and corporate leaders benefit from a cleaner environment. They sacrifice in the interest of reciprocity; they get a return on their investment of time and money. So this is *enlightened self-interest*.

The other possibility for synergy in a society is when its members voluntarily make a sacrifice for the common good without seeking a tangible reward. This is the definition of *altruism*: the crossing guard who goes out early every morning to help neighborhood kids cross the street safely; the doctor who operates on poor people for free; or the person who adopts two orphans with learning disabilities. Naturally, people who make these sacrifices benefit as well. They feel good, they make new relationships, and they become part of a new social network. They have more opportunities to influence change for the better. In fact, altruistic people do not feel that they are making a sacrifice, because they do not think that they are losing anything. The psychic reward is worth any cost in effort, time, or money.

Dysergy

The fourth possibility shown in Figure 5.1 is even worse than low synergy. If low synergy is when people advantage themselves at the expense of the group, in dysergy people do things that do not benefit either themselves or society. Similarly, the group follows policies that do not benefit itself but do harm the people. These situations create a kind of nightmarish culture of fear, revenge, and greed. The society itself encourages the destructive behavior; the culture is "cannibalistic." Obesity is an example of dysergy: people eat themselves sick and healthcare costs for heart disease and diabetes skyrocket for the society. Meanwhile, there are other people within the same society who do not have enough to eat. There are many health-related dysergies because people actively seek to harm their bodies at the same time as society is harmed collectively because it must pay the cost of healthcare. Dysergic cultures are violent: from child abuse and spousal battering, to feuds and showdowns, to oppression and genocide. Low synergy and dysergy lead to a hellish dystopia, the polar opposite of a utopia.

A *dystopia* is the site of the worst of all possible human existences. In modernist literature and videos, dystopias were depicted as totalitarian or anarchistic states. Unfortunately, dystopias are not imaginary. Descriptions of concentration camps, geno-suicide (senseless massive killing within one people), and famine make dystopias real. There are many places where poverty, famine, and instability are on the rise, while 10 percent of the world's population own 85 percent of the wealth. But if dystopias are real, *utopias* can be too, not as boring, perfect places, but as sustainable, local, highly synergistic communities.

The transition is from planetary and local dysergy to planetary and local synergy. People need to use orthogonal, holistic, constructionist thinking to overcome fear and pessimism. People must join agencies to fight inertia and change human tendencies to follow along without thinking, drawing upon peaceful cultural resources from wherever they can be found to foster cooperation and sharing.

Moral Development

There is a relationship between sociocultural synergy and individual morality, because both synergy and morality are all about balancing individual welfare with the welfare of others and the group and avoiding both extremes of egocentricity and sociocentricity. Morality involves both an ethic of justice and an ethic of care for self and others.

An Ethic of Justice

Kohlberg (1981) argues that there are six ways people are oriented towards morality; he calls them universal stages of moral development. These stages are not about particular moral beliefs but about how people reason and explain their beliefs. The method was to ask boys and men how to resolve a moral dilemma. Then researchers prompted them to explain why they answered the way they did. As the boys became adults, they were increasingly able to view the dilemma from the perspective of other people. Their thinking became more complex and abstract.

Heinz Steals the Drug

In Europe, a woman was near death from a special kind of cancer. There was one drug that the doctors thought might save her. It was a form of radium that a druggist in the same town had recently discovered. The drug was expensive to make, but the druggist was charging ten times what the drug cost him to make. He paid $200 for the radium and charged $2,000 for a small dose of the drug. The sick woman's husband, Heinz, went to everyone he knew to borrow the money, but he could only get together about $1,000 which is half of what it cost. He told the druggist that his wife was dying and asked him to sell it cheaper or let him pay later. But the druggist said: "No, I discovered the drug and I'm going to make money from it." So Heinz got desperate and broke into the man's store to steal the drug for his wife. Should the husband have done that?

(Kohlberg, 1981:19)

Kohlberg and other researchers studied males in Mexico, Taiwan, Turkey, Israel, Kenya, the Bahamas, and India using different culturally appropriate dilemmas. Overall, the studies supported Kohlberg's stages and sequence within both individualist and collectivist cultures. Kohlberg found no difference in the way people oriented themselves in these stages among Catholics, Protestants, Jews, Buddhists, Muslims, and atheists. However, people in different settings go through the sequence at different speeds and reach different end stages. Most urban middle-class adults reach Stage 4, with a few people at Stage 5 reasoning. In more isolated villages, however, it is rare to find any adult beyond Stage 3.

At Level I (comprising Stages 1 and 2), called Preconventional Morality (Kohlberg, 1981:17–19), people cannot identify with the values of others. Their moral decisions are egocentric. Reward and punishment are the typical bases of reasoning in this stage.

- Stage 1. Obedience and Punishment. People obey rules to avoid punishment. The value of a human life depends on the social status, possessions, or attributes of the person.

- Stage 2. Individualism and Exchange. People conform to rules to obtain rewards and have favors returned. The value of a human life depends on what that person can do for you. Reciprocity is instrumental: "You scratch my back and I'll scratch yours."

At Level II (comprising Stages 3 and 4), called Conventional Morality, people have a sense of community and reciprocity. They can take the point of view of others into account in making decisions.

- Stage 3. Interpersonal Relationships. People believe that they should meet the behavioral expectations of the family and community. They conform to expectations to avoid disapproval and dislike by others. Human life is valued based on personal relationships.
- Stage 4. Social Maintenance. People meet expectations because they want to avoid feelings of guilt and censure from friends, community members, authorities, and to maintain social order. Human life is valued within a moral or religious context of rights and duties.

At Level III (comprising Stages 5 and 6), called Postconventional Morality, people base their morality on principles thought to be universal. Psychologists found fewer people at this level.

- Stage 5. Social Contract. People believe that there is a "contract" between people and society, a consensus on individual rights and group welfare impartially determined through a recognized procedure. People conform to the social contract to maintain the respect of others within the community. Human life is valued as part of the welfare of the community or as a universal human right.
- Stage 6: Internalized Universal Principles. Universal principles require people to respect the dignity of all people. People follow this guide because they believe in it personally. Human life is valued because there is a universal human right to dignity.

Stage 5 was unusual and Stage 6 was rarely found among people whom Kohlberg and other psychologists studied. Later Kohlberg stopped differentiating between Stages 5 and 6. He admitted that his inspiration for Stage 6 was a small sample of people like Martin Luther King (Kohlberg, 1984:270). He cited King's "Letter from a Birmingham Jail" in his 1981 book as an example of Stage 6 thinking.

[T]here is a type of constructive nonviolent tension which is necessary for growth. Just as Socrates felt it was necessary to create a tension in the mind so that individuals could rise from the bondage of half-truths, so must we see the need for nonviolent gadflies to create the kind of tension in society that will help men rise from the dark depths of prejudice and racism . . .

One may well ask, "How can you advocate breaking some laws and obeying others?" The answer lies in the fact that there are two types of laws: just and unjust. One has not only a legal but a moral responsibility to obey just laws . . . [O]ne has a moral responsibility to disobey unjust laws . . . An unjust law is a human law that is not rooted in eternal law and natural law. Any law that uplifts human personality is just. Any law that degrades human personality is unjust . . . An unjust law is a code that a numerical or power majority group compels a minority group to obey but does not make binding on itself. This is difference made legal . . .

In no sense do I advocate evading or defying the law, as would the rabid segregationist. That would lead to anarchy. One who breaks an unjust law must do so openly, lovingly, and with a willingness to accept the penalty . . . [A]n individual who breaks a law that conscience tells him is unjust, and who willingly accepts the penalty of imprisonment in order to arouse the conscience of the community over its injustice, is in reality expressing the highest respect for the law.

(King, 1964)

Kohlberg's stages of moral development have been controversial. For one thing, women are usually rated as lower in terms of Kohlberg's moral stages than men. Gilligan (1982) felt that the focus on justice was not as relevant to women as it was to men. She thought that women focused more on connections among people and had an ethic of care for people rather than an ethic of justice. In her book *In a Different Voice* she laid out her theory: that growth in moral development for women was related to changes in sense of self in relation to others.

An Ethic of Care

To Gilligan's way of thinking, the first stage of moral development is egocentric and the goal is survival of the self. Next, there is a transition from selfishness to responsibility to others, after which self-sacrifice for the good of others occurs. This is the conventional stage of morality. Then there is a transition from self-sacrifice for the good of others, or sociocentricity, to a balanced view of care for self and care for others. At this stage, women consider their responsibilities in terms of an ethic of care, not merely based on conventional expectations. Staub (2003:246) notes in this regard that "people have to value themselves to value other people, but not value themselves so strongly that others don't matter." For people in individualist cultures at least, a moderate (not high) self-esteem is more closely associated with sensitivity and concern for others.

Psychologists now believe that moral development for both men and women involves internalizing both ethics: justice and care for self and others. It is interesting to note that both justice and care require balancing independence and interdependence, and the personal, the interpersonal, and the universal. Nevertheless, there is a cautionary message in the fact that moral stages do not predict moral behavior; there are too many personality variables and situational and contextual factors, some of which will be discussed in the next chapter.

Learning as Agency

In many parts of the world, children acquire a pro-human and pro-social moral code from their families and faith and social groups. This moral code might be cultural, traditional, and/or religious. However, for social and cultural transformation, English language teachers may get involved to legitimize or reinforce global ethics of justice and care.

Moral Dilemmas

A student of Kohlberg, Blatt, used moral dilemmas as a teaching tool, presenting them and discussing them with sixth-grade students (Blatt and Kohlberg, 1975). His thinking was that if the students heard others explain their moral reasoning, they would hear reasoning just ahead of their own moral level. This was, indeed, what happened. Blatt concluded that cognitive conflict, role-taking, moral awareness, and exposure to moral reasoning just above one's own stage helped develop moral reasoning. Blatt induced cognitive conflict as disequilibrium; his students took one view, became confused by discrepancies and other information, and then resolved the confusion through cognitive restructuring. The method was Socratic dialogue in which the students present their views and the teacher asks open-ended questions to induce them to see paradoxes and complexities so that they formulate better positions. It is consistent with critical pedagogy for resistance. Cognitive restructuring also leads to an increase in empathy for others because the students gain in their ability to take another perspective.

Kohlberg's ideas of moral development were prescriptive, although he was sensitive to the problems inherent in prescription. He advocated creating schools that were "just" communities based on principles of democracy. He wanted schools to initiate children into the moral order of their society. He suggested that "the teacher take the dull routines of classroom discipline and invest them with moral meaning by treating the classroom as a small society with its own rules, obligations, and sense of social cohesion" (Kohlberg, 1981:23). He advised teachers to take the hidden curriculum of the classroom (discipline, social order, hierarchy, management) and make it explicitly empathy-developing, conflict-transforming, and relationship-restoring in culturally and linguistically appropriate ways.

Learning Empathy

Empathy-learning is remedial education for collectivity and reciprocity, and especially for the avoidance of attribution and projection. Learners suppress and manage anger in the service of harmony. Although respecting self-autonomy, there is much less focus on self-esteem and more on other-esteem. When people have empathy for others, they can understand them without having every experience fully explained. Some people are naturally more empathic than others, but people learn or increase their empathy by reflecting on experiences that they have in their lives. Meditation or mind-training also increases empathy; perhaps other forms of spiritual exercise do, too.

To learn empathy, people distinguish accurate perception from creative thinking like projection, attribution, imagination, evaluation, judgment, interpretation, and inference. Accurate perception takes in the details of a person or event without adding interpretations like how good or bad they are or it is, what it means, or what it implies. Perception stays as close as possible to what is in the world. After working at distinguishing perception from creative thinking, learners practice understanding what other people feel, based on their physical cues like facial gestures, body language, and situational cues. Learners try to become aware of what others feel, not what they themselves would feel in the same situation or what they imagine others might be feeling. In order to do so, learners develop the ability to set aside their own feelings in order to attend to what others are feeling, without assuming that the feelings will be similar or shared.

Next, learners develop their own responses to the feelings they perceive in others to increase care for self. The idea is to build up the reciprocal connection between learners and others by situating them in a mental space and establishing a point of contact between self and others. The point of contact is the perception of a feeling and the response to the feeling. It is usually easier to have empathy for people who are perceived as similar, so learners practice empathy with different people.

Empathy involves normative pro-social communication also, especially active listening and paying attention to others. Learners distinguish verbal judgments, projections, inferences, or evaluations from accurate reporting and unbiased labeling. They try to incorporate the latter two into their verbal repertoires and avoid the former. They learn to verify the feelings that they perceive using open-ended questions rather than assuming or projecting. Learners also accurately label their own responses to the perceived feelings and emotions of others, and respond with acceptance and validation before expressing disagreement. If the goal for education is dialogue, then empathy is the foundation for voice, attention, and acknowledgment.

Chapter 6

Local Uncivil Societies

It is because the rulers, if they are bad, are so not necessarily or wholly by reason of birth, but largely because of their environment, that I have hopes of altering their courses. It is perfectly true . . . that the rulers cannot alter the course themselves. If they are dominated by their environment, they do not surely deserve to be killed, but should be changed. But the environment are we—the people who make the rulers what they are. They are thus an exaggerated edition of what we are in the aggregate. If my argument is sound, any violence done to rulers would be violence done to ourselves.

(Gandhi, 1970:179)

Here Gandhi states the reasons why he had fervent hopes for social and political change, and he also puts his finger on the basis for his nonviolent methods. He did not blame leaders as much as he shifted responsibility to the environment, an environment in which the preconditions for bad leadership were present. The environment included, most importantly, the followers who enabled or encouraged the leaders. The leaders reflect the moral culture because they are socialized, acculturated, and educated by families and schools. They respond to difficult life conditions and conflict in ways that advantage themselves or their groups. For social and political change, the environment enabling bad leadership needs to change, starting with the followers. However, Gandhi advocates nonviolent change from the bottom up; sustainable peace does not change leadership through violence. It changes the followership.

Conflict and Violence

The word "uncivil" usually means impolite or discourteous, especially in language. Here I am using it to refer to dysergic societies and cultures in need of "civilizing" because they have a lot of conflict. There are many sources for conflict in uncivil societies. One is difficult life conditions, such as economic, political, and social upheaval, violence and crime, disorganization and rapid changes in social institutions and values (Staub, 1989:35–50). Difficult life conditions, along with diverse ethnic or religious affiliations, are the context for intractable conflicts that become the source for further conflict. But not all conflict results in violence. Conflicts turn violent because of cultural preconditions and moral culture. Some cultures are more aggressive than others, some are more authoritarian and monolithic, and some have systems, ideologies, and institutions that support violence, mistreatment, and scapegoating. Another reason is the interplay of individuals as they contribute to conflict and violence as leaders or followers (Staub, 1989:51–65). In this section, we will look at some of these factors.

Difficult Life Conditions

Natural disasters like drought and famine and unnatural disasters like dislocation, political instability, economic depression, and social injustice make people feel insecure and defensive. Often conflict erupts along ethnic, tribal, or religious lines as people try to gain security and acknowledgment. Identity conflicts embroil whole populations in long-standing uncivil turmoil. For instance, Regehr (1993:8) says:

> Identity conflicts emerge with intensity when a community, in response to unmet basic needs for social and economic security, resolves to strengthen its collective influence and to struggle for political recognition. Almost two-thirds of the current armed conflicts can be defined as identity conflicts, and some estimates count as many as 70 current political conflicts worldwide that involve groups formally organized to promote collective identity issues.

In these divided societies, people's identities form around narrow lines of affiliation: clan, ethnicity, religion, language, or culture. There is little concept of shared identity based on citizen relationships or nationality. For instance, in Kosovo and Serbia, people identify as Orthodox or Muslim, Serb or Albanian. Several groups compete with each other for autonomy and recognition. The groups live near each other or with each other and they share a long history together. At times they have lived in peace but there have also been frequent conflicts and violence. In Macedonia, English language teachers speak English rather than Albanian or Macedonian to avoid linguistic and political bias. In such divided societies, when there is conflict, there may be limited legitimate peaceful means to deal with it, such as just elections, judicial systems, arbitration or mediation, or rule of law.

Reciprocal Causation

Some victims of exploitation, abuse, and violence, when later placed in a position of power over others, may choose themselves to become exploiters, abusers, and perpetrators of violence, simply because that is what they know. Unfortunately, this cycle has often been played out, time and time again, at the individual, local, and global levels throughout human history. As just one example, European Jews, so often the victims of pogroms, expulsions, and finally genocide, have turned into Israelis who oppress and kill Palestinians. And Palestinians kill Israelis. Lerner (2003:xii) characterized it this way:

> As Jews established our state in our ancient homeland, we hurt many Palestinians and evicted many from their homes. When the Palestinian people cried out, we could not hear their pain—because we believed that the genocide we had barely survived proved that our pain was so much greater. Israelis defended themselves against knowing how much violence they had done to the Palestinian people by telling themselves that the Jewish people have never done anything to the Palestinian people even vaguely comparable to the genocide that was done to us in Europe.

Now there are generations of Palestinians who know only violence and displacement. This creates a vicious, intractable cycle of violence and conflict because people cannot put aside their thirst for vengeance, and injustices go unresolved. Lederach (2004:15) calls this dynamic *reciprocal causation*, "where the response mechanism within the cycle of violence and counterviolence becomes the cause for perpetuating the conflict, especially where groups have experienced mutual animosity for decades, if not generations." We might say that this is reciprocity gone horribly wrong.

Many of the conflicts we see today are not so much about political issues as they are about complex and subtle "social-psychological perceptions, emotions, and subjective experiences" that are more difficult to address (Lederach, 2004:15). They make for protracted and intractable conflicts that threaten to drag neighboring regions and possibly international players into world war. Perhaps because of an incident or because of a leader, people come to view others with suspicion. The perceived threat makes people of each group draw more closely together and emphasize their sameness and stereotyping of the other. The conflict lies in the reciprocal relationship of distrust, fear, and paranoia, leading to fundamentalism, ethnocentrism, and violence. School systems become involved in perpetuating divisions. The experience of violence exacerbates. The long history of conflict between two groups makes resolving it very difficult, because there are many social, psychological, and emotional scars at the personal and group level. Such conflicts are too complex to resolve by any conventional means.

Moral Culture

Earlier the idea of synergy was used to evaluate cultures and societies; synergy is inversely related to aggression. Cultures of low synergy are those where individuals' agency is for their own advantage and not for the group. There is less aggression in synergistic societies which emphasize mutual advantage and avoid acts that disadvantage some members. Peaceful cultures have a balance between meeting the needs of the individual and meeting the needs of the group. It is easy to conclude that low synergy and dysergy are associated with aggression and violence because people advantage themselves over others politically, socially, and economically, or they disadvantage themselves and others. Indeed, the cannibalistic nation-state finds that some members of society are expendable.

Kohlberg (1984:264), in his consideration of moral development, also discusses some of the factors leading to the My Lai massacre, in which American soldiers murdered hundreds of Vietnamese civilians. He feels that a large factor in the soldiers' obedience was the moral culture of the group they were in. The *moral culture* is a collective stage of moral development that is legitimate in the group. The collective stage of moral development affects the behavior of individuals in the culture because it sets the values and norms for the group. In particular, the moral atmosphere can be at a lower stage than the individuals' moral orientations. Individuals may value human life out of principle and yet, if the moral culture does not value it, the individuals may behave as if they do not value human life. At My Lai, soldiers who might have disobeyed the orders to kill if they were on their own succumbed to the pressure of a moral culture that did not place a high value on the lives of Vietnamese civilians.

Leaders

Gandhi did not blame leaders but they are a factor in violence and conflict. In divided and fearful societies made up of people of different ethnic or religious identities, it is easy for leaders to create a culture of hate by demonizing or dehumanizing others. Once labels and categories of people are established (Jew, whitey, gook, untouchable, extremist), it is not hard for leaders to manufacture proof that some people's lives are not valuable. They publish textbooks and fraudulent documents, or make films that blame and scapegoat others for current problems.

Some leaders take advantage of difficult life conditions and situations of reciprocal causation to gain positions of power. They exploit divisions and insecurities to build their leadership at any cost. Psychologists have studied some people called *social dominators* in Canada, China, Israel, Mexico, New Zealand, and Taiwan. Social dominators are associated with ethnic prejudice, sexism, militarism, punitiveness, and conservatism. They have a certain cognitive style; they believe that some people are meant to dominate others and they want to be the ones who do it. Not all leaders are social dominators, but social dominators are drawn to politics. Social dominators are raised and educated to be intensely competitive and to disrespect people weaker than they are.

> Winning is the only thing for them. They want power and relish using it, to the point of being relatively ruthless, cold-blooded, and vengeful. They enjoy making other people afraid of them, and worried about what they might do next. They would not mind being considered mean and pitiless. More than most people, they say they will destroy anyone who deliberately blocks their path.
>
> (Altemeyer, 2004:99)

Strategy

Staub (1989) made a study of the Holocaust, the Armenian genocide, the autogenocide (or geno-suicide) of the Khmer in Cambodia, and *los desaparecidos* in Chile. The leaders and perpetrators of each crime against humanity justified it to their followers in a number of ways. They manipulated their followers and covered up what they were doing with a variety of strategies.

One justification was that leaders relied on followers to accept and use *"just world" thinking*: the false perspective that the structures, organizations, and systems of the world are essentially fair. The argument goes like this: "I think the world is a just place. Therefore, if these people are [poor, uneducated, mistreated, denied their rights, enslaved, tortured, killed, etc.], it must be because they deserve it." At the very least, "just world" thinking legitimizes an unjust society; at worst, it leads to genocide. In Hitler's world view, Jews, homosexuals, and others deserved their treatment, and he persuaded and coerced many to agree with him.

Also, perpetrators/leaders engage in careful *escalations* of violence, small increments of crime. They use the small steps to justify further steps. If they are not checked by protest, they ratchet up their rhetoric and demand greater violence. When there was little outrage in the public sphere about Kristallnacht, an early riot against Jewish businesses, Hitler was more free to take the next step in his genocidal plan. And there is an important psychological *pressure* on followers because of escalation. Once followers have accepted or participated in a low level of violence, they are more committed to accepting and taking part in greater violence. They need to find a way to prove to themselves that their earlier action was correct.

In each case of mass violence studied, Staub (1989) found followers who followed along step by step as their leaders committed them to greater atrocities and crimes.

Kelman and Hamilton (1989) were also interested in followership, in particular the My Lai massacre in Vietnam. In this case, there was a military chain of command but there was also a great deal of rhetoric involved in the leaders' attempts to gain the cooperation of the followers. One way the leaders achieve compliance is by claiming *authority* and *legitimacy*. Leaders use their authority to legitimize the crime and to force obedience. They link their power and position to a certain violent course of action. They legitimize the action in the name of country, flag, uniform, or some other abstraction. Anyone who does not follow the course of action, whether they agree with it or not, is therefore disloyal to the leaders or to the abstraction that legitimizes the violence. It is hard to resist the call to commit violence for "love" of country or ideology.

Another way perpetrators/leaders gain compliance is through *routinization*; they make the violent course of action seem routine. They point out that other people are following orders and not questioning the violence. This distributes the potential guilt over a number of people. They also make the process of the violent course of action as job-like as possible, even assembly-line in nature. They use euphemistic language to talk about what they are doing. They *dehumanize* the victims of the violent course of action. If the targets are less than human or even diabolical in nature, then killing them in the name of an authority or an abstraction can be seen as good. The targets are cast as political or religious threats that must be stopped.

The outcome of these strategies is that followers undergo *desensitization* to violence and killing. To be desensitized means that the ordinary emotions that would prevent violence are numbed. What should be shocking and revolting is instead commonplace. Where people might use reason and critical thinking, they instead accept their leaders' rationale. Where they might raise questions or protest, they remain passive. The interior voices of restraint that tell a follower not to follow are shut down. And their acquiescence legitimizes the violence for others.

Bystanders

Within any moral culture, some followers end up as perpetrators, as in My Lai, but some may be bystanders. *Bystanders* witness a crime but are not directly involved in it; that is, they are neither a target nor a perpetrator. Staub (1989) was interested in the effect that bystanders could exercise on violent crime. In the case of the Holocaust, there were ordinary Germans and others outside of Germany who witnessed the genocide and did nothing. Staub found that sometimes bystanders were simply afraid to try to halt the crime; sometimes they thought that someone else should halt the crime. Interestingly, Staub found that the more bystanders there are to a crime, the less likely any one of them is to respond. The fewer the bystanders, the more likely they are to do something.

A large group of people who fail to respond legitimizes the lack of response of each individual in the group. Perhaps the weight of people not responding causes everyone to doubt or misinterpret what they witness. In other words, inactive bystanders rationalize their inertia or indifference with the inertia/indifference of others in their sociocultural network. They say to themselves: "If those people over there aren't doing anything, why should I do something?" So guilt, blame, indifference, and inertia are distributed over a sociocultural network. Rather than cooperating to resist or overcome perpetrators of violence, followers and bystanders do nothing, and their sociocultural network reinforces that decision.

The Banality of Followership

During the Adolf Eichmann trial, Hannah Arendt (2003) made the point that, to the extent that people are involved in genocide, they are not evil but "banal." Eichmann was Hitler's associate in charge of the genocide of the Jews, the so-called Final Solution. Putting herself in the position of a judge for the purposes of her essay, Arendt had this to say to Eichmann:

> You also said that your role in the Final Solution was an accident and that almost anybody could have taken your place, so that potentially almost all Germans are equally guilty. What you meant to say was that where all, or almost all, are guilty, nobody is. This is an indeed quite common conclusion, but one we are not willing to grant you. In other words, guilt and innocence before the law are of an objective nature, and even if eighty million Germans had done as you did, this would not have been an excuse for you.
>
> (Arendt, 2003:374)

Banality

To Arendt, Eichmann was banal because he attempted to justify his behavior by saying that anyone else would have done the same thing. He claimed to be a victim of circumstances and his behavior, to himself, was quite understandable. In other words, Eichmann attempted to shield himself in his sociocultural network, his network of relationships with others within society and culture. If he succeeded in distributing the guilt and blame over many people within his sociocultural network, he could absolve himself. The truth is that he used his military and political position in a sociocultural network to force others to kill. Others either obeyed willingly or did so because they themselves were afraid. He used his agency antisocially, his social capital for dysergy.

Eichmann attempted to defend himself by pointing out the banality of people's reaction. The more widely violence is distributed throughout a network of relationships, the more acceptable or banal it is. The word "banal" came from the Serbo-Croatian word *ban*, meaning ruler or lord, and originally referred to compulsory feudal service owed to rulers. Once in English, the word went through a remarkable semantic drift. It stopped meaning compulsory service owed to a ruler and began to mean "open to everyone." After a while, the word meant commonplace, ordinary, lacking in originality, predictable, tiresome, and drearily "normal."

So, while everyone agrees that Hitler's actions were evil (he was the consummate social dominator), Arendt's point was that Eichmann's actions were banal. They were common, ordinary, unoriginal, normal. He was just doing what he thought everyone else would have done. He was just following orders. Leaders such as Hitler can succeed only if they have such banal people willing to accept the commonplace, remain ordinary, react predictably, and, in short, carry on with business as usual.

Followers

If we cannot prevent the emergence of the Hitlers of the world, we need to affect the Eichmanns of the world. Staub (1989:23) pointed out that there will always be ideological, social, economic, political, and personal reasons for violent leaders to emerge into the public sphere: "there will always be people with extreme views, radical ideologies, and the willingness to use violence who offer themselves as leaders. Cultural pre-conditions, combined with difficult life conditions, make it probable that they will be heard and accepted as leaders." Staub suggests that it is more important to understand followership, what leads individuals to accept such a social dominator as their leader. Thus the way to stop another Hitler is not reactive war but rather to change the dynamic that allows such people to rise to powerful positions where they can do damage. If the followership does not follow, the leader cannot lead.

The Authoritarian Follower

We can learn more about followership by turning again to the field of political psychology. Brown (2004) wrote that in 1938, in Nazi Germany, psychologist E.R. Jaensch published a book that discovered two basic human personality types. One was a despicable "S" type, a creative, unstable, effeminate, liberal personality who made ambiguous judgments. The other was an ideal "J" type, a firm, masculine, nationalistic, social conservative who recognized the importance of blood and tradition. As you might imagine, the J personality was characteristic of people whose ancestors had lived in Germany since time began. The S personality came from a racially mixed background and was especially characteristic of Jews, Parisians, and "Orientals." Naturally, psychology like this served as a justification for fascism and ethnic cleansing.

Later, after the Second World War, American and European psychologists became interested in finding out why the people fell for the Nazi rhetoric, why they engaged in ethnic cleansing of the Jews and others, why they did not question the unspeakable duties that they performed. They wanted to answer the following questions. What kind of people are anti-Semitic? What kind of people get involved with ethnic cleansing? Is there a type of personality that will follow orders without questioning?

Personality

In 1950, *The Authoritarian Personality*, a book by four social psychologists (Adorno, Frenkel-Brunswik, Levinson, and Sanford), answered those questions. "The thousand pages of *The Authoritarian Personality* tell the story of behavior that covaries with attitudes towards Jews. The account moves from anti-Semitic attitudes to ethnocentric ideology to political and economic conservatism to implicit antidemocratic trends" (Brown, 2004:40).

The researchers called this personality type *authoritarian*, not because such people were authoritarian but because they defined the personality by the *submission* to authorities who are thought to be legitimate. Authoritarians adhered to traditional social conventions endorsed by society, and their behavior was easily influenced by outside authorities. It is interesting that attitudes of submission to authority and traditional social conventions are stereotypical of embedded interdependent personalities and collective cultures, yet we see that they were quite common in the independent but conformist US culture studied by Adorno et al. (1950). The authors also found evidence that prejudice and ethnocentrism were associated with antidemocratic opinions. Authoritarian people showed signs of a general aggressiveness which could be directed at others by (legitimate) authorities. The researchers found something like Jaensch's personality types. The J personality was authoritarian, and the S personality was a freedom-lover (Brown, 2004). Some of the research methods the psychologists used to gather the evidence in the book were justifiably criticized, but the results they found have nevertheless stood the test of time.

Since 1950, political psychologists in Western nations have produced a robust body of research using a variety of methods and measures and with a number of people of different nationalities. Time and time again, they have found evidence supporting a personality type which bundles together prejudice against others, resistance to or fear of change, and acceptance of the inequalities of society. People with this personality are more susceptible to propaganda that dehumanizes others and they are willing to carry out orders. They show a marked preference for social hierarchy and inequality.

Cognitive Style

Jost, Glaser, Kruglanski, and Sulloway (2003) re-examined the various studies conducted between 1958 and 2002 on attitudes towards authority. They looked at studies from England, New Zealand, Australia, Poland, Sweden, Germany, Scotland, Israel, Italy, Canada, South Africa, and the United States. Jost and his team found evidence that people with an authoritarian personality have a certain cognitive style. Recall that a cognitive style is different from intelligence or ability. It is a filter or lens that shapes people's interpretation of what they experience. Jost et al. confirmed various cognitive, emotional, and social factors that compose the authoritarian style of thinking in those sample populations.

The *cognitive factors* associated with authoritarian personalities were mental rigidity, closed-mindedness, and dogmatism; intolerance of ambiguity; ethnocentrism; decreased cognitive complexity; decreased openness to experience; uncertainty avoidance; and need for cognitive closure. This means that people with this way of thinking look to authorities to explain and resolve problems. They accept their leaders' simple answers to complex issues because they are dogmatic and hate uncertainty or ambiguity. They are willing to blame and scapegoat others. They want to "close" a complex issue in their minds so that they know what to do. They cling to rigid belief systems because they offer answers to life's complexities. Although lack of critical thinking has been associated stereotypically with hierarchical collectivist cultures, it was quite commonly found in Western studies.

People with an authoritarian cognitive style are not open to new experiences or new people, especially if they are different and might involve learning something new. They dismiss broad-mindedness, distrust imagination, and dislike excitement. Decreased cognitive complexity means that people with this conservative style of thinking are not willing to weigh and balance subtle factors or different perspectives in order to make a decision. They prefer to think that new information that conflicts with their established ideas must be incorrect, a lie, or irrelevant.

Jost et al. found that there are also *emotional factors* associated with this cognitive style. There is often a personal need for order and structure, sometimes combined with pessimism, and disgust and contempt for others. The need for order and structure operates at both the individual level and the social level. People with this social style are neat, orderly, and organized. Socially, in Western cultures at least, they advocate firm parental discipline, comprehensive drug testing, and core educational curricula because society must also be structured. They oppose environmentalism, abortion rights, and services for AIDS patients or the homeless.

People with this cognitive style are fearful. Although the evidence for low self-esteem among authoritarians is meager, Jost et al. suggested the possibility that authoritarians have less stable self-esteem: "they respond differently than others to potentially ego-threatening situations" (2003:361). They feel a generalized fear, anger, and aggression. They fear loss, death, and social and economic deprivation. They feel threatened by social and political instability. Fearfulness makes them punitive, defensive, and militaristic.

It is not surprising that *social factors* also affect people's cognitive style. In a recent study of survivors of the 9/11 terrorist attacks in New York, Bonanno and Jost (2006) found that survivors shifted towards an authoritarian world view after the attacks. This shift was associated with post-traumatic stress disorder and depression, desire for revenge and militarism, and cynicism, combined with increased religiosity and patriotism. It seems clear that leaders exploit social factors to encourage the authoritarian cognitive style.

While more research is needed, especially in collectivist cultures, it is easy to contrast the integrated, globally conscious, tolerant, open-minded, and moral global citizens described earlier with the social dominators and authoritarians described by Altemeyer, Jost et al., and other psychologists. It is also easy to contrast the dominating and authoritarian cognitive styles with the global cultural consciousness of connected independents and interdependents described by Kumaravadivelu (2008). I think this may go partway towards explaining a well-known case of paradoxical cosmopolitanism, one that is well described by Appiah (2006:1–8). Sir Richard Francis Burton was a Victorian whose life was spent traveling, working overseas, and learning many languages; he was seemingly a true cosmopolitan. He appreciated different religions, respected and translated diverse literatures, and enjoyed a variety of customs. He could pass unnoticed in many parts of the world.

Yet he was insufferably prejudiced, like many an upper-class gentleman of his day. He showed contempt for Africans, Arabs, Indians, the Irish, French-Canadians, Jews, Pawnee Indians, and the American army. He did not resist the injustices of the social hierarchies where he went. (He did seem to like Mormons, perhaps because of their order.) So Burton was not really a cosmopolitan; he did not respect other people, and he did not have universal concern. While obviously an intelligent man, perhaps he was both an authoritarian and a social dominator. Social dominating authoritarians had the highest prejudice scores of anyone studied by Altemeyer (2004:105). To Altemeyer, they were "the most worrisome persons" he found in his investigations. From this example we can deduce that mere exposure to cultural variation is not enough to produce a tolerant cognitive style in people. It is not enough to cause integration, which is why Kumaravadivelu (2008) emphasizes the need for critical reflection as a crucial component in complex cultural growth. And it is why Kohlberg (1981, 1984) and Staub (1989, 2003) advocate moral education and empathy.

Building Peace in Local Civil Society

Transition is the responsibility of each individual or group which claims membership in a social and cultural network. To harness the force of synergy, people generate processes and approaches that transform their conflicts into sustainable peace. They understand that most processes and approaches in peacebuilding work in stages, not all at once.

> Peacebuilding is understood as a comprehensive concept that encompasses, generates, and sustains the full array of processes, approaches, and stages needed to transform conflict toward more sustainable, peaceful relationships . . . a comprehensive approach to the transformation of conflict that addresses structural issues, social dynamics of relationship building, and the development of a supportive infrastructure for peace.
>
> (Lederach, 2004:20)

Local uncivil society is where peacebuilding has to happen. Local civil society is the thickening and stretching of sociocultural networks inside a locality but linked to the outside, to global civil society, governments, religions, and the military, such that peaceful or "civilizing" effects of these sociocultural networks are felt at the planetary level itself. It is anything but banal.

> Building peace in today's conflicts calls for long-term commitment to establishing an infrastructure across the levels of a society, an infrastructure that empowers the resources of reconciliation from within that society and maximizes the contribution from outside. In short, constructing the house of peace relies on a foundation of multiple actors and activities aimed at achieving and sustaining reconciliation.
>
> (Lederach, 2004:xvi)

It is safe to say that difficult life conditions will always happen: ethnic or national conflicts, water shortages, viruses, famine and crop failures due to weather . . . the list goes on. It is safe to say that some local leaders will try to take advantage of cultural and social conditions to consolidate their power and provoke violence. Global and local civil society can sometimes react to signs of war and insecurity, intractable local conflicts, terrorism, famines, pandemics, global warming. But local civil society works best when it is proactive about helping people resist demagogues and opening the way for a cycle of peace. Local civil society transforms structures, systems, institutions, and culture to take away the factors that exacerbate dysergy, conflict, and violence. One hope for sustainable peace is to change would-be perpetrators, followers, and bystanders and decouple them from banal sociocultural networks.

Learning as Agency

Leadership training has become an important component in capitalism and democracy; but for sustainability and especially sustainable peace, the focus is on followership training. Informed followership starts with critical thinking, the power to think critically about leaders, peers, and their rhetoric. It is related to the critical pedagogy for resistance and reflection that leads to global cultural awareness and metacultural awareness. Critical thinking is intended to turn embedded individuals, those who cannot oppose or resist their group, into connected individuals who can take a more objective perspective on their group's culture and behavior. It is meant to turn authoritarian, blind chauvinist or isolated individualists into critically loyal citizens, those who can balance universal good with local good.

Critical Thinking

Critical thinking has often been thought of as a prescriptive methodology, but it can also be elicitive if teachers incorporate and model local ways that certain habits of thought, insight, interaction, and judgment can be cultivated. Among the habits of *thought* are impartiality (the ability to suspend immediate judgment, and avoid projection and attribution), humility (the knowledge that no one owns the truth), courage to think and act with agency, and confidence in the ability to engage in complex thinking about paradox and contradictions. Among the habits of *insight* are the ability to see the egocentricity or sociocentricity of self and others, to evaluate the credibility and motives of self and others, and to identify people with authoritarian or social dominator cognitive styles.

Among the habits of *interaction* with the rhetoric of texts and speakers are the following: to identify "just world" thinking, escalations, psychological pressure to be banal, claims of authority, efforts to legitimize certain policies or actions, routinization, and desensitization; to analyze language for generalizations, oversimplifications, euphemistic language, and dehumanization; to listen or to read arguments carefully and pick them apart; to discern what information is relevant and irrelevant to arguments; to question for more information; and to compare and contrast what people say and do or what they say and do at different times. Among the habits of *judgment* are: the ability to see the relationship between emotions, beliefs, and reason to explore and question personal, social, and cultural beliefs, values, standards, arguments, assumptions, and theories; to compare and contrast local, regional, national, and international cultures; to generate solutions, actions, and policies and assess them; and to evaluate evidence and facts.

But like critical pedagogy for resistance, critical thinking by itself can lead to a paralysis of analysis. To avoid this, it should be accompanied by moral grounding and agency. For instance, in many parts of the world bullying starts in the early grades. *Bullying* is a form of antisocial aggression that is among the most stable behaviors during the life of an individual (Eron, 1997). Even preschool children can learn to resist bullying. Critical thinkers who use their agency to resist are *outliers*, people who rise out of banality to make their dissidence known and to intervene to prevent injustice or scapegoating.

Bullying

There are different types of bullying behavior. Independent *bullying* is based on physical intimidation or aggression by one person of a target because of size or age; it is sometimes called "boy" bullying. Most common in the schoolyard or free time outside of class, it is based on control or intimidation. Individual authoritarians, social dominators, or people with troubled backgrounds are more likely to be bullies. Interdependent bullying, *ijime* in Japanese or *relational aggression* in English, is the isolation, ostracism, or shunning of a target by a clique; that is, a disruption of the social fabric among peers to exclude someone perceived as different, uncooperative, unfriendly, unattractive, or the like. Sometimes called "girl" bullying, it depends heavily on an interdependent agency called *peer pressure* to conform (e.g. not reciprocity). Quite well-behaved ordinary people engage in *ijime* because they perceive themselves as maintaining a social order (Mino, 2006). Schools and teachers sometimes even condone or encourage *ijime* because it makes the majority of schoolchildren more manageable. It is also becoming quite common in cyberspace.

Both bullying and *ijime* have important negative effects on individuals and on the group moral culture. Bullying and *ijime* in children become aggression and banality in adults. Staub (2003:237) notes that the behavior of the bystander is an important factor in bullying. There are two aspects of this. First, children who have friends who stick up for them are less likely to be bullied or ostracized from the start. Second, children feel included if others stick up for them when they are the targets of aggression. The critical thinking skills described above should be aimed at helping children resist peer pressure and speak up for those who are victimized.

Intervention

Mino (2006) argues that the *ijime* is a product of the Japanese education system, which emphasizes group conformity. Taki (2001) argues that children engage in *ijime* because they have not learned to manage their stress or how to interact with others because of changes in Japanese families, schools, and culture. Therefore, administrators, schools, and teachers should intervene to stop *ijime*, and not condone or accept it. They should find out what is causing the aggression, then develop a plan for social skill and interaction training followed by traditional Japanese activities like voluntary school or community service so that children increase their sense of effectiveness with others.

Boyle (2005) calls on teachers and school administrators to be aware of bullying, encourage positive role models, and monitor student behavior. They should set limits on unacceptable behavior and impose consequences for breaking the limits. There should be training programs for both prevention and intervention. Boyle suggests that the intervention be done individually since participants in group interventions sometimes simply learn to bully even more effectively. Interestingly, Boyle does not recommend treatment for low self-esteem for independent bullies because, contrary to what many people think, bullies generally have high self-esteem. He also makes the point that conflict resolution does not work between bullies and their targets because of the power disparity, and mediation suggests that the bully and the target share the blame for the conflict, which is unfair.

Staub (2003) suggests that teachers discuss with children any aggressive behaviors or exclusivity and develop with them rules of appropriate interaction. He wants teachers to create a sense of inclusive community in the classroom and the school, and model conflict transformation training. Some children may need help in learning to fulfill their needs in pro-social and pro-human ways or in healing past wounds. Teachers may need to learn positive ways to guide and discipline children, avoiding shame and ridicule. Some children may need more adult supervision. Staub believes that focus groups and community meetings might help schools and classes involve parents in solving problems as well.

Outliers

Mino (2006:3) discusses four participants in *ijime*: the *ijimekko* (perpetrator), the *ijimerarekko* (target), the *kanshu* (audience), and *boukansha* (bystanders). The audience supports the *ijime* and encourages the perpetrator(s). The bystanders do nothing and therefore legitimize the *ijime*. The perpetrator, audience, and bystanders exert a lot of peer pressure on each other to perpetuate the *ijime* because they feel that the target deserves it (just world thinking). They also attempt to use peer pressure to force the target to conform to the majority if possible or continue to face exclusion. To create a post-*ijime* situation, teachers bring another participant into the picture: an *outlier* who sticks up for the target against the bully. Being an outlier does not mean being rude or belligerent, but it may mean being a troublemaker and dissident because outliers reveal their feelings or opinions instead of concealing them. English language teachers can use local resources (stories, myths, proverbs, movies) that encourage people to behave as outliers and to elicit local pro-social communicative norms.

In addition to local pro-social communication, English language teachers may introduce norms from outside. It takes some practice to be an outlier, so some people build up to it in small steps. The first step is mental preparation to overcome nervousness with confidence and to maintain a firm, audible, and pleasant tone of voice. Outliers get the facts, predict potential outcomes, and plan possible responses or questions. The second step is resistance to the bullying through nonviolent communicative strategies. For instance, outliers describe the behavior they see and the effects of the behavior on the target or on others in neutral terms, using the *I-statement*. The statement does not start with "you" because that sounds like blame or accusation, at least in English. Nonconfrontational I-statements take the following three-part form:

> I feel ——
>   when you ——
>   because ——.

The first part contains the feeling; the second part is a neutral and specific expression of the other person's behavior; and the third part explains the connection between the feeling and the behavior, avoiding exaggerated descriptions, blame, and interpretations.

> I feel upset
>   when you say that Karan is stupid
>   because it hurts his feelings and he's my friend.

It is possible to preface an I-statement with agreement to disarm the bully:

> I agree that Karan didn't answer your question.

Another alternative is to ask a lot of open-ended questions to encourage empathy:

How do you think Karan feels when you call him stupid?

Outliers listen to the bully but do not deviate from the message. If they are asked to do something they do not want to do, they might simply say no or they might ask for more time to think about it. They try to brainstorm a win–win compromise using more questions:

Is there some way to change what is happening here?

Teachers might attempt a "contrastive analysis" of these English norms with local norms to show that both are effective at stopping bullying or *ijime*. Teaching critical thinking and encouraging nonviolent communicative competence may change the followership. Early intervention to stop bullying and *ijime* and to encourage outliers may be one way English language teachers can contribute to a local culture of peace and local civil society.

Chapter 7

Pro-social Capitalists

Critical Yeast: Rather than *critical mass*, commonly believed to be the moment of shift when large enough numbers of people get behind an idea or movement, critical yeast does not focus on producing large numbers of people. Critical yeast asks the question in reference to social change: Who within a given setting, if brought together, would have the capacity to make things grow toward the desired end? The focus is not on the number but on the quality of people brought together, who represent unique linkages across a wide variety of sectors and locations within the conflicted setting.

(Lederach, 2005:181)

We saw in the last chapter that sociocultural networks can be banal, spreading blame and guilt so thin that they stick to no one. Leaders use networks to induce followers to commit violent crimes against humanity or, at the very least, keep desensitized bystanders in inertia and indifference. However, sociocultural networks can also provide the cultural infrastructure for peace that Lederach mentions. A cultural infrastructure is a complex, multi-level, multi-actor social network of people in relationships: families and clans, age and gender sets, congregations and clubs, civic organizations and cooperatives, unions and tribes. Local civil society is, or can be, such an infrastructure.

Peaceful local societies rest on the interdependence of the global and the local within the local infrastructure, so that they can take advantage of resources from inside and outside. The infrastructure has many individual and group players operating vertically, horizontally, and orthogonally throughout a social and cultural network of relationships to change the dynamics of the followership. Lederach suggests that people get involved to create a sociocultural network with an infrastructure that supplements national and regional diplomatic efforts to end conflicts. He invites them to commit to social justice and reconciliation. In his 2005 book *The Moral Imagination: The Art and Soul of Building Peace*, he calls such people the critical yeast. English language teachers can be critical yeast.

Lederach coined the term "critical yeast" in response to another common idea, that of the critical mass. The idea of the *critical mass* is that it takes a certain number of people to create social or political change. Once that magic number of people comes together—they form an immovable bottom-up force that causes change at the top: new legislation, a new policy, a new timeline, a new peace treaty, a new way of doing things. We can see this at work in all great social movements against slavery, totalitarian regimes, apartheid, and so on. The idea of *critical yeast* makes the point that a small number of imaginative and innovative people at strategic levels of society who reject banality are the impetus for the formation of the critical mass. In breadmaking, the yeast is the catalyst for the increase in the mass of the bread. Without the yeast, nothing happens, so the yeast is critical. People willing to be critical yeast have moral imagination, which is the

> capacity to imagine something rooted in the challenges of the real world yet capable of giving birth to that which doesn't yet exist. In reference to peacebuilding, this is the capacity to imagine and generate constructive responses and initiatives that, while rooted in the day-to-day challenges of violence, transcend and ultimately break the grips of those destructive patterns and cycles.
>
> (Lederach, 2005:29)

In this chapter I will make the case that English language teachers can be critical yeast, or, to appropriate a dynamic economic term, *pro-social capitalists*, an imagined community of people with moral imagination who invest their agency in synergy. They are my answer to the question: who, within a given setting, if brought together, would have the capacity to make things grow towards the desired end? To imagine pro-social capitalists, we need to look at a few other aspects of sociocultural networks: infrastructures, pro-social capital, and cooperative power.

Infrastructures

There are only a few superstars in peacebuilding; they win the Nobel Peace Prize. However, superstars depend on a lot of other important people elsewhere in the sociocultural network and chain of command. The infrastructure for peacebuilding can be understood as intermeshed vertical, horizontal, and orthogonal sociocultural networks of people in relationship with others. This network of networks operates in, around, and through civil society but also in faith groups, government, the military, and, of course, educational institutions. Lederach (2004) describes a vertical peacebuilding infrastructure.

Verticality

The vertical infrastructure is composed of top-, middle-, and lower-level leaders and followers. The leaders at the top are few in number. They engage in negotiations, settlements, and ceasefires. They are perceived to have power over others, but their ability to influence events may be overrated. Because of their fixed positions, their visibility, and sometimes their isolation from others, their freedom to visualize and create change is limited. They have more information about the conflict, but they themselves (and their families) do not suffer very much from it.

The leaders in the middle of the sociocultural network are more numerous. They are leaders in education, business, health, agriculture, religious organizations, ethnic groups, and civil society. Middle-level leaders work behind the scenes, out of the spotlight, so they have more flexibility and freedom. They are more likely to suffer direct consequences of the conflict. The middle is thick with a horizontal network of relationships among these leaders, described below, but there is also a vertical network reaching up to the top leaders and down to the grassroots leaders and followers. The status and power that middle-level leaders enjoy depend on their position in the social network and their pro-social capital. The network of relationships in the middle level is the space where an infrastructure for peace can develop. If the middle level has a lot of pro-social capitalists, there is already a latent infrastructure of activists for peacebuilding.

At the bottom of this middle section is the grassroots leadership in the local communities, small NGOs, and refugee camps. They create points of contact with the masses of ordinary citizens, the followership. The followers are the ones who know and experience suffering. They are the cannon fodder. Up from the bottom's battle fatigue comes pressure for change.

> From personal experience I can attest to the fact that the process of advancing political negotiation at polished tables in elite hotels, while very difficult and complex in its own right, is both a more formal and a more superficial process than the experience of reconciliation in which former enemies are brought together at the village level.
>
> (Lederach, 2004:55)

Horizontality

At every stratum of society there is a dense mesh of interlocking relationships among families, friendships, sisterhoods and brotherhoods, clubs, tribes and clans, and others. Lederach (2005:10–13) gives two examples of such horizontal relationships among pro-social capitalists and outlines how they contribute to the infrastructure for peacebuilding.

Wajir is in Kenya, near Somalia, and it was caught up in fighting between clans, other fighting groups, and refugees from Somalia in the early 1990s. The women were tired of the violence, rape, and theft to which young girls and women were subjected. They decided to start at the market, trying to make it safe for them to buy and sell. They established monitors to watch what was happening; they reported any kind of abuse. When an issue came up, a committee of women resolved the problem. They made the market a peaceful place and created the Wajir Women's Association for Peace. Over time, they succeeded in bringing together the elders (all men) from the groups to stop the fighting. The elders formed the Council of Elders for Peace to deal with fighting among the clans.

The women's influence reached up the chain of command also. They contacted government officials and received their support. They realized that they needed to organize the young men who were doing most of the fighting, so they identified a few of them and formed the Youth for Peace association. Realizing that employment was a key issue, they engaged the local business community to create jobs for the young men. All of these groups formed the Wajir Peace and Development Committee to coordinate activities designed to stop the violence and lead to a ceasefire.

Carare, Colombia, was the site of another example of horizontal association. It was a very violent place, with a complex combination of guerrilla warfare, private armies, and government troops. People were prohibited from talking about anyone who was killed. One particularly violent government captain called together 2,000 country people and gave them an ultimatum in the form of "forgiving" them for supporting the guerrillas if they would arm themselves and support the military. He ended by giving them four choices: "You can arm yourselves and join us, you can join the guerrillas, you can leave your homes, or you can die." At least one of the *campesinos* did not fall for this rhetoric. He responded for all when he said to the captain:

> You speak of forgiveness, but what do you have to forgive us? You are the ones who have violated. We have killed no one. You want to give us millions in weapons paid for by the state, yet you will not facilitate even the minimum credit for our farming needs. There are millions for war but nothing for peace. How many men in arms are there in Colombia? . . . We have arrived at the conclusion that weapons have not solved a thing and there is not one reason to arm ourselves . . . Captain, with all due respect, we do not plan to join your side, their side, or any side. And we are not leaving this place. We are going to find our own solution.
>
> (Lederach, 2005:14–15)

That outlier was not alone. He and others formed an association to pursue civilian resistance, the Association of Peasant Workers of Carare. Their first act was to speak openly about those who had been killed. Their motto was "We shall die before we kill." Their principles were solidarity instead of isolation, speaking out instead of secrecy, transparency instead of hiding, dialogue and understanding instead of fear. The association identified and recruited key people to be liaisons to all of the areas and groups. They sent delegations to all of the armed groups and succeeded in reducing violence by connecting with people.

In the cases of the Wajir women and the Colombian *campesinos*, ordinary people exercised their pro-social capital to be outliers together. They saw in their violent and unjust reality a potential for change. They found ways to use solidarity in relationships with others to see violence and coercion rather than other people as the enemy. They did not minimize the complexity of their situation or look for quick fixes. They found a path that wove through the complicated structure of the injustice. They found creative ways to cut through complexity to the heart of the matter, even at great risk to themselves. Like the Eastern Europeans who brought down totalitarianism, they founded civil associations to harness the power of cooperation against oppression and war.

Orthogonality

The orthogonal infrastructure can be seen by taking a holistic perspective of a complex situation. There are always cross-cutting sociocultural networks among members of different strata and groups which transcend the borders of affiliation and identity. The orthogonal infrastructure is constructionist in the sense that culture and society, power relationships, and authority structures are taken as givens, but they can be modified or worked around. Lederach (2005:7–10) gives the following two examples.

In a conflict between two groups in Ghana that stretched back to the days of slavery, mediators finally brought together a paramount chief from the dominant Muslim group with all his entourage, and a spokesman, a young man, from the Christian Konkombas, who had little organization or power. In a tense and frustrating meeting, the paramount chief blasted the Konkombas for not having a chief and for sending a "boy born yesterday" to negotiate. When he responded with surprising power and dignity, the young man transformed the meeting, the process, the relationship, and the direction of the conflict.

> You are perfectly right, Father, we do not have a chief. We have not had one for years. You will not even recognize the man we have chosen to be our chief. And this has been our problem. The reason we react, the reason our people go on rampages and fights resulting in all these killings and destruction arises from this fact. We do not have what you have. It really is not about the town, or the land, or

that market guinea fowl [the original cause of the dispute]. I beg you, listen to my words, Father. I am calling you Father because we do not wish to disrespect you. You are a great chief. But what is left to us? Do we have no other means but this violence to receive in return the one thing we seek, to be respected and to establish our own chief who could indeed speak with you, rather than having a young boy do it on our behalf?

(Lederach, 2005:7)

After the chief thought for a moment, obviously affected by the young man's words, he answered.

I had come to put your people in your place. But now I feel only shame. Though I insulted your people, you still called me Father. It is you who speaks with wisdom, and me who has not seen the truth. What you have said is true. We who are chiefly have always looked down on you because you have no chief, but we have not understood the denigration you have suffered. I beg you, my son, to forgive me.

(Lederach, 2005:8)

The moment was charged with emotion. The young man knelt before the chief and gave him a sign of great respect. Although that was not the end of the problems between the two groups of people, this equalizing moment had a positive impact on everything that followed.

Another example of orthogonality occurred during the civil war in Tajikistan, when a philosophy professor was asked by the government to visit one of the renegade warlords and ask him to enter into negotiations. During the visit, the professor discovered that the warlord shared his interest in philosophy and Sufism. They talked for two and a half hours. After numerous visits and conversations about poetry and philosophy, the professor asked the warlord about ending the war. The warlord said, "If I put down my weapons and go to Dushanbe with you, can you guarantee my safety and life?" The philosopher could not do that, so he answered, "I cannot guarantee your safety . . . But I can guarantee this. I will go with you, side by side. And if you die, I will die." The warlord agreed to meet the government, and several weeks later they came down out of the mountains together. The warlord told the government mediators, "I have not come because of your government. I have come for honor and respect of this professor." The philosophy professor had the courage to step outside of his boundaries to change the course of events.

Bystanders and Dissidents

Studying these examples of verticality, horizontality, and orthogonality reveals that there are two special outlier roles for pro-social capitalists besides forming associations to create an infrastructure for peace. First, they can act as *heroic bystanders*, paying attention and responding to acts of leadership that do not fit with the Earth Charter. Second, they can be *principled dissidents*, critically thinking people who resist and replace antisocial and anti-human values and behaviors with pro-social and pro-human ones. These functions are risky; to transform a status quo always involves risk.

The Heroic Bystander

When Staub (1989) studied followers and bystanders, in each case he found a few heroic bystanders. Staub discussed the inhabitants of Le Chambon, France, who, following their pastor, saved several thousand Jews by sheltering them. Other well-known heroic bystanders who saved Jews were Oskar Schindler and Raoul Wallenberg. Some characteristics made these heroic bystanders very different from their neighbors who did not help. They did not use "just world" thinking; they noticed but did not participate as the violence escalated. They used moral imagination to see that there was a different way to look at things. They felt responsibility and empathy towards others, and rejected polarized thinking (we versus they). They responded with courage and self-confidence and took risks to change the course of events. In terms used here, they were not banal authoritarians or social dominators. They were motivated to fulfill moral and humanitarian values. They applied the same standards of right and wrong to all people. Often, they themselves were marginal in their groups.

Alternatively, Staub found that some heroic bystanders were not people of moral imagination. Instead, some were influenced by the moral culture, the norms and values of the group they belonged to. Although they themselves were not particularly altruistic, they went along with the pro-social capitalists in their network of relationships. They conformed to their groups by adjusting their behavior to fit others' expectations. This means that pro-social and pro-human networks and highly moral cultures can influence individuals' altruistic behavior and ultimately have an effect on oppression and violence. For instance, although Bulgaria did have some anti-Semitism and was an ally of Germany in the Second World War, when the government was asked to deport Jews, the protests of Orthodox bishops and professional organizations of doctors, lawyers, and writers (civil society) persuaded the King to intervene. In the end, 82 percent of the Jews in Bulgaria survived the war because of these heroic bystanders. Similarly, in Italy, thousands of Jews were saved when their neighbors hid them and refused to turn them in for rewards.

The Principled Dissident

Principled dissidents actively resist demagogues or oppressors who use authorization, routinization, dehumanization, desensitization, and coercion. Principled dissidents refuse to collaborate with those who advocate actions that are against their principles. Schell (2003), in his book *The Unconquerable World: Power, Nonviolence and the Will of the People*, discusses Václav Havel, a Czech writer and activist who spent years in prison for his opposition to the state and who advocated nonviolent resistance to communism. Havel saw such resistance as a form of integrity, as a way of life. He made a distinction between what he called "living in the lie" or "living in truth."

When people live in the lie, they bow obediently to the demands of an oppressor. Havel says that, by conforming unquestioningly to an oppressive system, "individuals confirm the system, fulfill the system, make the system, are the system." To comply with violence or injustice is to live out a lie because it, like banality, legitimizes the violence or injustice. Further, by living the lie, people alienate themselves from what Havel called their "essential existence" (Schell, 2003:196). In contrast, when people live in truth, they go about their daily lives within their sociocultural networks with honesty and integrity, following their own moral code instead of leaders. To Havel, ordinary people face, in every small decision they make, a choice between compliance and resistance. When asked to do something that runs counter to their principles, they are dissidents, but, paradoxically, that is not their intention.

Havel points out that people who live in truth are, in effect, protesting something with their noncompliance. They are of necessity the opposition because they choose to do what they think is right and say what they think is true without regard for the demands of their government. But the opposition, the protest, is the byproduct, and not the intention, of the truthful behavior. The intention of living in truth is for it to be a powerful affirmation of truth and not a fearful negation of the lie. The person living in truth is the principled dissident. This is what Kohlberg meant with his Stage 6 morality, as exemplified by Martin Luther King.

Pro-social Capitalists

The term *social capital* is generally used in two ways. First, it refers to the support and resources that individuals have because of their participation in the relationships in a sociocultural network. Participation in a network of relationships is not the same as a position in a vertical work hierarchy, a social class, or even a family. Instead, it is a psychic participation that does not derive from a position as superior or subordinate, co-worker, mother, daughter, or cousin, although obviously those affect people's agency. In a relationship, people both get and distribute support and resources to each other. The support is not always tangible; it may be emotional or moral. The resources are not always concrete like money, budgets, or expense accounts; they are assistance, kindness, friendship, encouragement, generosity, caring, wisdom, and so on. Second, people use the term "social capital" in another way, to refer directly to the independent or interdependent agencies that people have to "invest" because of their position in a social network. To summarize, social capital is something people have, and if they have it, they can use it in altruistic pursuits.

Pro-social capital comes from pro-human and pro-social resources, support, and participation. Pro-social capital has its origin in the attributes that an individual has—like credibility, empathy, and trustworthiness— which give people legitimacy, and legitimacy is agency. For instance, psychologists have found that members of a group who care about others' needs, values, and opinions are much more influential than members who try to control others and discount the needs and ideas of others. These are, in fact, often the least influential members of a group (McMillan and Chavis, 1986).

Connected individuals have more pro-social capital than isolated or embedded individuals. Teachers may have more pro-social capital than their school administrator because they do things for others and others do things for them. Because their ability to influence comes from caring about others and trust (not coercion, manipulation, or neediness), their pro-social capital benefits the individual and the group, and it is synergistic. It strengthens the network of relationships and the group moral culture. Pro-social capital sustains relationships and effects change in the group. If enough pro-social capitalists invest their agency altruistically to influence the culture, they get a return of synergy in their community. The cumulative agency of many pro-social capitalists in a community both sustains the community and generates cooperative power through consent.

In sustainable communities, pro-social capitalists influence others altruistically towards synergy, using both their *independent* and *interdependent* agencies to sustain relationships with others in the network. These agencies are interrelated and depend on notions of self and other.

- Individual accountability: taking responsibility to meet others' expectations within a moral code, which inspires trust.
- Influence: getting the willing consent of others.
- Transition: changing oneself or the situation.
- Reciprocity: responding to others positively and expecting others to respond positively in return.

Individual Accountability

Individual accountability is independent agency because it comes from people's self-identified recognition that they are subject to an obligation. They acknowledge that the obligation creates an expectation that something will take place or they will behave in a certain way. Because they recognize and acknowledge the obligation and the expectation, they complete what is necessary to meet the obligation and to fulfill the expectation. They feel responsible for something, and they accept the responsibility.

Individual accountability means that people feel that they are answerable to other people; thus it exists within the context of relationships with others. The relationship creates complex roles for people to play. The roles are both socioculturally created by tradition and constructed or negotiated by the individuals in the relationship. The obligations and expectations depend on what the roles and relationships are. There are different accountabilities for managers and workers, friends, mothers, fathers, daughters, sons, citizens, teachers, and students. Individual accountability means that people recognize and meet the obligations of their role within the relationship. The most general type of individual accountability is *moral accountability*, where people feel accountable to others at the Stage 3 level or higher of the ethic of justice and care. Species identity is moral accountability to all humans.

Influence

People's pro-social capital in a sociocultural network comes from their ability to elicit or generate willing consent from others. Eliciting willing consent from others is independent agency because it comes from individual and moral accountability. Thus, people earn the consent of others because they care about others and others trust them. People do not give their willing consent to those who are not accountable, or who attempt to control or are not trusted. Thus, pro-social capital is a way for those trustworthy, caring people to influence others even in a potentially unequal power structure, because they can get the willing consent of others. The more pro-social capital people have, the more active they can be and the more impact they can have.

Jonathan Schell (2003:230) posed the question: if coercion and control rely on fear and intimidation, on what does cooperative power rely? His answer was stunning. Cooperative power is based on the power to generate or receive willing consent from others. The most powerful people (that is, the people with the most pro-social capital) are those with "the capacity to create or do something that inspire[s] the respect, admiration, loyalty, faith—all of which, again, is to say the love—of others." Cooperative power comes from "the capacity to create or discover something . . . that other people cannot help but love."

Transition

This interdependent agency comes from the recognition that it is impossible for anyone to change others without their willing consent; people can change only themselves or something about the situation. The ability to change oneself or the situation is interdependent agency because the self perceives a need to change something in response to another in a relationship. I could write an entire book about this topic, but here I am limited to a few observations. Changes can be major, minor, or anywhere in between. Minor alterations occur within the confines of self-identity or roles and relationships. Major alterations are life-changing.

The first step is to perceive that something needs to change. In collective cultures, the perception of a need to change comes from empathy for others and highly developed concepts of others. Kitayama and Uchida (2004:139) discuss this kind of interdependent agency, where "action often takes the form of adjustment—namely, changing one's own behaviors in accordance with the expectations and needs attributed to others in a relationship." In other words, people in collectivist cultures adjust their own behavior in an attempt to fit into the expectations of others. Besides empathy, other types of accurate perception (lack of projection and attribution) will also help people see the need for change. Another important quality is the humility to be willing to initiate a change.

People can change either themselves or something about the situation, condition, structure, or system. Changing themselves might involve changing attitudes or behaviors. For instance, teachers in the habit of getting defensive take questions about exams or grades as challenges to their authority or competence. Their defensiveness makes any conversation difficult and awkward so students hesitate to ask questions and become disgruntled. In this case, teachers can change themselves by changing their attitude. They might begin to see that students have the right to ask questions about exams and grades, and that questions are not attacks. Therefore, they stop becoming defensive and begin to feel comfortable about discussing the exams and grades. This change alters the teacher/student relationship and increases pro-social capital.

Changing the situation or condition might involve the timing, the space, the setting, or any other detail so as to alter the dynamics. In the example above, teachers might request that if students have questions about their grades, they ask them after class, during lunch or study hour, or after school, when there are fewer people around. Or, if they have an office, they might ask students to come in during office hours. In a different setting, they might sit down face to face and discuss any issues with more tranquility. Changing the structures or system might also involve finding ways to "civilize" by improving living or health standards, abolishing social injustice, or cleaning up the environment.

Transition sometimes evokes a pro-social response from others, a kind of serendipitous influence. If teachers are less defensive about explaining grades, students will not be disgruntled. If students get calm explanations, they may feel more respect for teachers. Although people cannot change others, if they change themselves or the situation, sometimes others' behavior changes reciprocally.

Reciprocity

In collectivist cultures, the concept of reciprocity is crucial. Naturally, the idea of reciprocity also operates in individualist cultures. However, to people in collectivist cultures, reciprocity seems to be a stronger kind of glue that binds relationships together. People within collectivist sociocultural networks conform to norms of the group to avoid conflict. They place the good of others above their own good. They have highly developed representations of other people and they tend to look at themselves as others see them. They adjust their behaviors to meet the expectations of the group and they expect this to be reciprocal. That is, they expect that others will have elaborate representations of them and that others will try to meet their expectations.

Such strong reciprocity seems to be crucial to the idea of interdependent agency. For instance, Markus and Kitayama (1991:238) discuss the Japanese emotion of *oime*, an unpleasant emotion of unmet obligations that pressures people to reciprocate and therefore return the relationship to balance. My experience with Western culture tells me that this is seldom an emotion that independent people feel strongly. However, it is interesting that in individualistic cultures, doing something truly altruistic means that there is no reciprocal expectation; the person acts pro-socially and pro-humanly without any expectation of return. I would guess that completely disinterested altruism is alive and well in collectivist cultures too.

Pro-social capitalists are people who have a strategic position in an infrastructure, pro-social capital to invest, and moral imagination. People need to be positioned in strategic intersecting points on vertical, horizontal, and orthogonal networks in the infrastructure. They are in positions to use their social capital for synergy. They use their independent and interdependent agencies like individual accountability, transition, influence, and reciprocity. The result is cooperative power.

Cooperative Power

To generate cooperative power, sociocultural networks must have cooperative cultures with reciprocal relationships. Within a cooperative culture, everyone participates to the extent that they can with the resources, pro-social capital, and agencies they have available. People lead when necessary and follow when necessary because it takes both independent and interdependent agencies. One person or group legitimizes an idea, but others must consent to help or to subordinate their own wishes, time, resources, or goals to the group because of altruism or reciprocity. Egocentricity, selfishness, and self-assertion are inhibitory.

In the Japanese concept of *sunao*, "working with others is an appropriate way of expressing and enhancing the self. Engagement and harmony with others is, then, a positively valued goal and the bridge—to openhearted cooperation, as in sunao—is through sensitivity" (White and LeVine, 1986:58). Cooperative power emerges when people want a group goal so much that their own happiness and well-being are identified with the group happiness and well-being. They are willing to relinquish egocentricity because contributing to cooperation to achieve goals enhances their self-esteem as much as or more than achieving private individual goals. It seems to me that in Western classrooms, cooperative learning usually fails in this respect.

But cooperative power needs direction, a goal, so the third prerequisite for the pro-social capitalist is moral imagination, the "capacity to imagine something rooted in the challenges of the real world yet capable of giving birth to that which does not yet exist" (Lederach, 2005:ix). Moral imagination is the ability to see latent peace even within the harsh realities of violence, economic exploitation, and environmental degradation. When selfless pro-social capitalists select a common pro-social and pro-human goal to invest in, there is no limit to what they can accomplish. Thus, within the sociocultural networks, independent and interdependent agencies create sustainable local communities through cooperation. An infrastructure of such communities, local civil society, supported from the outside, might be an answer to violence.

Learning is Agency

English language teachers, in my experience, have a lot of pro-social capital and moral imagination. They have the courage to reject the commonplace, become extraordinary, respond unpredictably, and refuse to cooperate with business as usual. They create infrastructures with neutral spaces where people from different sides can come together. They invest their pro-social capital to bring peace from latency to actuality.

Pessimism and Optimism

Moral imagination is a balance of pessimism, facing the challenges of the real world, and optimism, seeing something latent and better, preferred local and global futures. *Pessimism* is people's tendency to perceive and interpret the present in light of their experienced past, leading them to recognize potential difficulties and challenges down the road, and to doubt their agency. Teachers may be surprised to think that pessimism is a powerful gift because it puts a brake on our expectations. Lederach (2005:54) notes that pessimism tells us that change does not come easily or quickly, and that we should be suspicious of people who offer quick-fix solutions. We should judge any change by its real effect on people, because promises of change are easy to make but difficult to keep. Pessimism tells us that it may take a long time to transition to another way. To survive, people need to find spaces for joy and fulfillment, for laughter and kindness. Pessimism makes us question our ability to create change, but it is not cynicism, a negative postmodern attitude of scorn and distrust that leads to passivity.

Optimism is also a gift. It is people's tendency to perceive the difficulties and challenges of the present in light of an as yet unexperienced but imagined future, leading them to hope and work for change. Lederach (2005:5) believes that

> Transcending violence is forged by the capacity to generate, mobilize, and build the moral imagination . . . Stated simply, the moral imagination requires the capacity to imagine ourselves in a web of relationships that includes our enemies; the ability to sustain a paradoxical curiosity that embraces complexity without reliance on dualistic polarity; the fundamental belief in and pursuit of the creative act; and the acceptance of the inherent risk of stepping into the mystery of the unknown that lies beyond the far too familiar landscape of violence.

Values-Based Perspective Development

Wenden (2004a) talks about educating for a culture of peace, carefully linking sustainable peace with both peace education and sustainability education. Her approach, called *values-based perspective development*, is a methodology that intends to change students' attitudes, their perspectives, by learning about new values and imagining different preferred futures. The values are nonviolence, social justice, ecological sustainability, intergenerational equity (each generation is the steward for the next), and civic participation. This approach combines optimism with pessimism.

Wenden starts by raising some issues limiting our imagination and agency as we attempt our transition to synergy. One difficulty in converting a latency, sustainable peace, into an actuality is that we have no picture of sustainable peace. Wenden laments a lack of (moral) imagination that paralyzes us when we try to think about the future. We do not understand the bad effects of what we are presently doing (the dysergy), nor can we visualize the means we could employ to bring about positive alternatives.

Another constraint to autonomy of thought and action is the inability to think in alternative and creative ways about the future. In the case of those social and ecological realities that inhibit the achievement of a culture of peace, while it is agreed that violence is abhorred, our imaginations often appear to be prisoners of the present, apparently incapable either of visualizing the consequences of continued violence, be it physical, structural, or ecological, in the long term future or of creating positive alternatives. Reasons put forth to explain this paralysis include the belief that things cannot change or fear, and therefore the unwillingness to face what present realities portend. It is also true that the educational system does not usually try to change such beliefs and attitudes or help students acquire skills related to thinking in terms of the distant future.

(Wenden, 2004a:161)

Wenden attributes this lack of imagination to paralyzing fear, pessimism, or denial. In other words, because of our fear and pessimism we are prisoners of the past and present. We cannot think autonomously. We are in denial about the present, so we cannot see any paths through the complexities of the past and present and into a different future. Because of our paralysis, we are unable to respond creatively to challenges with optimism. Because of our fear, we do not have the courage to take risks for change. We cannot harness the power of cooperation if we do not know what to do or how to do it.

Wenden does not talk about the imagined communities of global civilians, global citizens, pro-social capitalists, heroic bystanders, and principled dissidents. She does not take into account an existing global civil society with a latent global civic culture based on the Earth Charter. But still, she has a point. Many people seem unable to imagine a different reality. It could be argued that one important place for such imagination to take place is school, but Wenden argues that our education systems do nothing to foster such imagination. Students and teachers are trained to understand the past, in some way, and deal with immediate issues. As Wenden says, our imaginations appear to be prisoners of the past and the present. As teachers, we cannot see that what we are doing contributes to inertia and paralysis. The method Wenden suggests includes three areas: critical reflection, analytical skills, and imaging alternative futures. All of these involve both individual and collective activities.

Through critical reflection, classroom participants question assumptions and values in local culture. They examine alternative values, and test and assess new values, as in global cultural consciousness. Through analysis, participants classify problems, identify systemic causes and consequences, link them with their impacts on human societies and earth systems, and determine the scope of the problem, as in problem-posing. To image alternative futures, participants attempt to overcome the constraints that prevent them from thinking creatively about the future. Following up on one problem they have analyzed, they write a social goal statement for the change they wish to see in three decades' time without being concerned about practicality or realism.

Then the participants engage in some culturally appropriate activities designed to stimulate their imaginations. For example, first they describe a memorable incident from the past to partners. Second, they are led through an exploratory "trip" that will enable them to imagine moving from present to future. Third, they use their goal statement to go into the future and see what the world is like. They describe what they see to their partners. Finally, they go back into the future to observe and record what they see in greater detail, creating a mental model of what they see. Upon sharing their models with classmates, group members synthesize what is similar about their individual models. Then, to complete the task, groups evaluate the models based on the values that they have studied in the critical reflection part.

Wenden describes some of the difficulties of her "complex and difficult" approach. It is difficult for people to change values once they have been acquired. Students may not have enough background knowledge. They may view social and ecological problems as irrelevant to them. They may not feel empathy, may not value cultural diversity, or may not appreciate global interdependence. For all these reasons, they may not find the activities compelling and may not appreciate the utility of values-based perspective development. However, if successful, Wenden (2004a:163) concludes:

> [L]earners will be provided with an integrated way of thinking about and assessing obstacles to its achievement [a culture of social and ecological peace]. This should lead to an understanding of the dynamic relationship between injustice, war, ecological degradation, and an apathetic citizenry. It should, further, provide citizens with a shared vision of a social and ecological order, towards which they should strive, that is, one that is ecologically sustainable, nonviolent, and just and in which citizens take responsibility for the well-being of all life in the present and future.

Chapter 8

Education for Global Citizenship

> ESD [Education for Sustainable Development] is fundamentally about values, with respect at the centre: respect for others, including those of present and future generations, for difference and diversity, for the environment, for the resources of the planet we inhabit. Education enables us to understand ourselves and others and our links with the wider natural and social environment, and this understanding serves as a durable basis for building respect. Along with a sense of justice, responsibility, exploration and dialogue, ESD aims to move us to adopting behaviours and practices which enable all to live a full life without being deprived of basics.
>
> (United Nations Decade for Education for Sustainable Development, 2008)

If we take the Earth Charter seriously, we are charged to "[i]ntegrate into formal education and life-long learning the knowledge, values, and skills needed for a sustainable way of life." The United Nations General Assembly has approved a Decade for Education for Sustainable Development (DESD) for 2005 to 2014. The goals for the decade are to promote a vision of and transition to sustainable development through education and to highlight the importance of education and learning in sustainable development.

All education has an agenda. ESD is intended to integrate many perspectives from pro-social and pro-human areas like human rights, peace and human security, gender equality, cultural diversity and intercultural understanding, health, HIV/AIDS education, governance, use of natural resources, ecological protection, rural development, sustainable urbanization, disaster prevention and mitigation, poverty reduction, and corporate responsibility and accountability. The pedagogies of sustainable development are intended to be interdisciplinary and holistic, values-driven, multi-method, participatory, and locally relevant. Methods are experiential and exploratory, with dialogue, problem-solving, and critical thinking.

Yet, as the quote above makes clear, education for sustainable development and peace is about the moral values consistent with respect and responsibility for self and others—that is, species identity. It is radically different from current goals for education; it aims at social justice and human welfare through dialogue. Martusewicz, in her book *Seeking Passage: Post-structuralism, Pedagogy, Ethics*, puts it this way:

> I am committed to the notion that as educators we must be engaged with others in questions about the kinds of communities we want to live in, the kinds of knowledge and experiences that are most worthwhile, and the kinds of people we want our students to become, even while we may never completely agree upon the answers to those questions. I am committed in particular to asking students to look carefully at suffering in whatever form it may present itself, as the ground zero of all our ethical decision-making.
>
> (Martusewicz, 2001:6)

Using the Buddhist term *dukkha* for suffering, Martusewicz refers to the destructive choices or dysergic conditions that are parts of life as we know it. This is highly relevant for English language teachers. In Kosovo, English language teachers like Molly Staeheli and Adria Winfield taught English and inter-ethnic understanding to mixed Serbian and Albanian or Bosnian, Turk, and Albanian teenagers through communicative activities. In the Balkans, English language teachers like Leonora Molnar and Izabella Pricop participated in summer camps for teaching tolerance with middle-school students and teachers from Hungary, Romania, Serbia, and Slovakia, including Roma children. Lydia Stack and Mary Lou McCloskey gave seminars to the teachers who then applied what they learned with their students (Dicker, 2006). Many other examples of reducing *dukkha* occur around the world in English classrooms within and outside national systems of schooling.

Education for the Nation-State

In many parts of the world, there are both public and private schools. Public schools have a prescribed curriculum to follow, grade standards that need to be met, and tests that serve as gatekeepers for further education or employment. National governments support education to the best of their ability. The amount of money that goes to schools varies in each country. Some countries have a national school system with national teacher training in the subject matters deemed important. Teachers receive credentials after following a course of study at university. Other countries have localized school districts organized under states or provinces. Private schools do not necessarily follow the same standards or curriculum; their teachers may not need teaching credentials. Globally, there is vast diversity in the quality of both public and private schools.

Patriotic Education

Spring (2004:5–10) provides an excellent summary of the educational paradigm that has spread to most parts of the globe, along with other aspects of colonialist culture. He suggests that mass compulsory public schooling plays an important role in creating and maintaining a national identity in a number of ways. Children are separated from all adults except for those who have been trained and hold an official capacity. Children and their behaviors are standardized through following official curricula and methods and patriotic rituals like flag salutes. They are taught to accept the legitimacy of the state, a common culture, and a common history. They learn about their government and their geography, their literature, art, and culture, although lip service is sometimes paid to superficial diversity. In some places, schooling overtly associates the nation-state with a divinity, implying that the divine has a special interest in that nation and its people. Any criticism of the nation-state and government is minimal; history is sanitized. Critical thinking about their country and region or their school system inside the classroom is minimized.

Children learn their own role to play in the social, economic, and political organization of the state. They derive much of their identity from their interactions with teachers and peers in school.

> The teaching of national boundaries and literature convince the student that the territorial boundaries of the state are the real territorial boundaries of the people. The student is taught that they are separate and different from those living outside the borders of their nation-state. Students are taught to think of those living within the territorial boundaries of their state as their people while all those outside the state's boundaries are the others or foreigners. Thinking and feeling that one belongs to a nation's people interferes with thinking that one belongs to humanity. By dividing the world into separate peoples, rather than one humanity, schools contribute to war, racism, and other forms of inhuman and unjust actions.
>
> (Spring, 2004:10)

What Spring discusses happens in many national school systems, but in some places children learn in school that there are first-class citizens of their country and others who are of a lesser or a different class. Thus, these school systems fail at two tasks. They fail to legitimize us as one humanity and they fail to legitimize that all people who live in that nation share a citizenship relation, and deserve the respect of fellow citizens.

A transition in values is unlikely to come from patriotic educational systems. Changes come from above through national or federal mandates in some countries, or through programs where schools are threatened by loss of federal aid if they do not comply with changes. National governments do not tend to be progressive; they are reactive to trends they see as threats. Sometimes change comes from teacher training, universities and credentialing agencies, but they too tend to be conservative and reactionary. Local civil society and school administrators, parents, and teachers themselves are perhaps the best chances for change, but the potential differs from region to region.

Paranoid Education

Some nation-states, especially those that deny freedom and participation to their people, seem bent on using schools to make their children submissive and orderly rule-followers with the authoritarian cognitive style. In such nations, the ideal citizen is prejudiced against others and sees enemies everywhere. Ideal citizens fear to change the status quo; they are taught to accept the inequalities of society. If there are social inequities, ideal citizens are taught that the world is a just and fair place, so obviously if people are poor, it is because they did not work very hard, they drank all their money away, or they are stupid and lazy. If they are illiterate, it is because they could not or did not want to learn to read.

These nations want citizens to serve the state, so they abhor critical and tolerant thinkers. Studying abroad is discouraged or prohibited. Schools are to teach the basics of education so that ideal citizens accept their leaders' explanations without question and resistance is suppressed. Neatness and cleanliness are highly prized. These nation-states sometimes create and promote biased curricula that demean and dehumanize others, either inside or outside of their territorial boundaries. It is very difficult to change these educational systems from within as there may be spies in the school, or even in the classroom.

Religious Schools

Within nation-states there are also religious schools which are supported by religious institutions, endowments, donations, and fees. The purpose of the religious schools is for the religious organization to maintain its hegemony over the minds of the people and/or to recruit religious workers from among the students. In many cases, teachers are not credentialed by any government agency and they may not have university degrees. They have a religious vocation or calling. The schools naturally reflect the religious traditions and beliefs of their associated religion, be they liberal, conservative, or fundamentalist.

Sometimes religions limit the amount of schooling children have because advanced knowledge and reasoning abilities are considered unnecessary. Since they are enrolled by parents, the students in religious schools, especially fundamentalist schools, are usually homogeneous. The school administration also selects students and can disenroll those who do not fit in or are disciplinary problems. Religious schools are also sometimes sex-segregated. Thus, students who attend religious schools may not have much exposure to people of the other sex or different belief systems, or to cultural or ethnic diversity. Students may not be allowed to think critically; they simply memorize texts without questioning their faith. Of course, there may be resistance among some students.

Some religious schools have the same curriculum as the national schools with an added compulsory religious component. Others have a curriculum that differs from the state-certified one, and reflects their creed and heritage. They advocate a particular social order, history, and science as depicted in sacred texts and ideologies. Their curricula and textbooks are slanted to favor their community, religious history, or beliefs. Some also teach intolerance of other religions and hatred for people who hold different beliefs; they have some similarities to paranoid school systems.

Education for the Global Economy

National and religious schools in some parts of the world are pressured by global influences. The World Bank, for instance, has criticized religious schools in the Middle East, saying that they do not prepare their students for the global economy. The World Bank lends a lot of money to poorer countries for education, and, as happens at the national level, top-down funding can change educational systems, curricula, and training for teachers. Spring (2004) suggests that the World Bank has a globalized focus on creating workers and consumers in developing countries. The World Bank claims its assistance is

> aimed at helping developing countries equip themselves with the highly skilled and flexible human capital needed to compete effectively in today's dynamic global markets. Such assistance recognizes first and foremost that the ability to produce and use knowledge has become a major factor in development and is critical to a nation's comparative advantage. It also recognizes that surging demand for secondary education in many parts of the world creates an invaluable opportunity to develop a workforce that is well-trained and capable of generating knowledge-driven economic growth.
>
> (World Bank, 2008)

The World Bank attempts to accomplish this in two complementary ways. One is the formation of "human capital" as a resource, and the second is the creation of educational systems that teach higher-level "skills" to more and more of the human capital. These promote life-long learning because workers in today's turbo-capitalism may need to retool in reaction to changing market demands. Their efforts include high school instruction for an agile workforce, university education to create capacity to produce and utilize (but not criticize) knowledge, science and technology, and cross-cutting or orthogonal efforts to support education (besides the state). They also support school-based management, an attempt to reduce dependence on decision-making at the national level.

In other words, the World Bank's global agenda for education, which it enforces through capital investment in education, does not involve global citizenship or global cultural consciousness at all. It involves human capital within a nation. The better the human capital a country has, the better able it is to compete with other countries for turbo-capitalistic opportunities. Knowledge is a commodity that, if specific aspects of it are spread around in a country, increases that country's competitive edge over other countries to attract multinational companies. Education is designed to develop a flexible and agile workforce that can react to changing demands in a global market economy, such as when corporations relocate in search of lower wages and less unionized workers. The workforce in a nation may need to retrain, change jobs, or move to another location to keep in work. (An example was the Mongolian government's partially successful attempt to switch unemployed Russian teachers to teaching English, giving them a year of retraining to learn English. This happened in the 1990s as Russia lost its hegemony over Mongolia and people lost interest in studying Russian.)

At the same time, the World Bank also encourages developing countries to rethink the role of government in national education. This reflects the neoliberal bias of the World Bank, which favors privatization of those functions that have traditionally been reserved for the state. When an education system is privatized, it generally needs to charge user fees to the families of the children served. This excludes the people who are unable to pay unless scholarships are given. Therefore, the World Bank is also interested in alternative funding sources for schools, possibly from corporations.

The ties that the World Bank makes between economics and education make many educators nervous. To lift people out of poverty and to improve health through access to education is a high-minded goal. But education is not merely a means to some worthy ends. Education shapes people. Seemingly, World Bank education does not aim to contribute to individuals emotionally or mentally except insofar as they can find better jobs or make more money. Its attempts at values development or sustainability within education seem more geared to promoting capitalism than to modifying it.

There is a washback effect. The World Bank gives money to schools in poorer countries to make students more technologically savvy so that their countries become more competitive in the global marketplace. Schools then revise the curriculum towards creating global workers and consumers. The consumer earns more money so that the country consumes more. This is what is ultimately unsustainable. Turbo-capitalism is based on the premise that people can keep consuming at the same or a higher level and that the spread of capitalism will make everyone able to consume equally.

As we saw with the national and religious education systems, schools are places where values are taught and management goals are inculcated. For national schools, the progress of the nation-state is primary. For religious schools, maintenance of the religion is primary. For schools funded by the World Bank, the global economy is primary. None of these three types of education system takes us through the transition to education for sustainable development, which includes all of the principles of the Earth Charter.

Nevertheless, many others have written extensively about curriculum and pedagogy for global issues, so in the rest of this chapter I would like to focus on Principle 16 of the Earth Charter, which sets a new goal for education: to promote a culture of tolerance, nonviolence, and peace. This goal comprises three objectives. First, education should aim to encourage and support mutual understanding, solidarity, and cooperation among all peoples and within and among nations. Second, education should aim to prevent violent conflict through collaboration and conflict transformation, to switch offensive military security systems to defensive or peaceful purposes, to eliminate weapons, and to ensure that "outer space" remains a place of environmental protection and peace. Third, education should aim to legitimize peace as "the wholeness created by right relationships with oneself, other persons, other cultures, other life, Earth, and the larger whole." I believe that this goal is where English language teachers can exert influence and create transitions. This is where their pedagogy has the power to change relationships.

The English Language Teacher as Pro-social Capitalist

Many English language teachers feel isolated in their classrooms. English, along with other languages, may be on the second tier of required classes. Their professional relationships are with other teachers in their own school, school district, or the central government. Teachers are often so overworked and underpaid that time for daily networking is limited. Their methods and curricula are dictated from above and they have little say in their choice. Despite that, teachers often have some autonomy in the classroom, if only because no one is looking over their shoulders.

Nevertheless, many English language teachers have the prerequisites to be pro-social capitalists: a strategic position in an infrastructure, pro-social capital to invest, and moral imagination. In our schools and classrooms, we have positions in strategic intersecting points on vertical, horizontal, and orthogonal networks in the infrastructure. We are in relationships with administrators, school boards, and higher authorities as well as subordinate employees. We interact with the parents and families of our students, and others in the community. We are connected to people every which way.

English language teachers are often strategically placed to make decisions that affect curriculum and pedagogy. We sometimes give our input into the goals and objectives, the methods, and the norms of classroom management, and we can turn these to global citizenship. Teaching English is also strategic because so many people from all strata of society want to learn it, both leaders and followers. Our students are the future presidents, prime ministers, and diplomats; they are the cultural leaders, the artists and businessmen, the grassroots organizers and activists, the commanders and police chiefs. Our students are also the followers: the store clerks, secretaries, laborers, builders, soldiers, policemen, husbands and wives, and mothers and fathers. Our students are future peacebuilders: global civilians, global citizens, and pro-social capitalists. We can have a strategic effect on the present and the future by incorporating norms of pro-social communicative competence into our curriculum and classroom management.

English language teachers are strategically placed on the intersecting point of the global and the local, between global civil society and local civil society, and between global civic culture and local civic culture. English language teachers percolate local ideas upwards to global civil society and global civic culture. They get external resources and knowledge and gather internal resources and knowledge. Externally, there are specialty associations like Teachers of English to Speakers of Other Languages (TESOL), the International Association of Teachers of English as a Foreign Language (IATEFL), the International Technology Education Association (ITEA), and the International Reading Association (IRA). TESOL has a caucus called TESOLers for Social Responsibility, a community of TESOL members interested in integrating language teaching with social responsibility, world citizenship, and global issues like peace, human rights, and the environment.

English language teachers are an important conduit for information flowing up and down and crossways, so as to inform global and local cultures and contribute to the worldliness of English. International associations are dominated at present by teachers from core nations, and mostly members from wealthy nations can attend international conferences. Costly membership fees make these associations problematic. However, some of these civil organizations have local affiliates or websites with news and resources. Local conferences for English teachers are less expensive because they are supported by the United States Embassy, the

Regional English Language Officer, the British Council, and large multi-national publishers. In Japan, Kip Cates and his colleagues organize the Global Issues in Language Education special interest group (GILE SIG) within the Japan Association of Language Teachers (JALT). Still, many teachers do not attend local conferences because of time, distance, and money constraints, or because they are simply not interested in improving their skills as they do not earn enough money to make it worth while.

Teachers are also connected orthogonally through memberships in civil organizations like clubs and labor unions. Education International claims 394 member organizations representing 30 million teachers around the globe. They are concerned with the rights of teachers and students, and credential evaluations. Another type of civil organization for teachers is Education Action, which assists educators in war-torn communities in Africa and the Middle East, with links to the UK. There are, in fact, many parts of the world in which school systems barely function or have completely broken down because of local conflict. Schools and teachers must be resilient in order to withstand conflict, or seek alternative ways to continue educating despite the chaos. Children, instead of being in school, are fighting battles, being injured, and dying.

> Education is vital to restoring hope to war-torn communities and bringing long term peace and development to the next generation. Education Action helps communities keep schools going and provide a sense of normality for children during conflict. We also work with local communities and teaching unions to rebuild shattered education systems and train teachers in countries recovering from the effects of war. Furthermore, education is the most important way for communities to change the situations affecting them. We provide training for people marginalised by conflict or displacement to help improve their lives and the lives of others and work with schools in the UK to widen understanding of the issues affecting [refugees and asylum-seekers].
>
> (Education Action, 2008)

The second prerequisite for the pro-social capitalist is investing pro-social capital. English language teachers are in positions to use individual accountability, transition, influence, and reciprocity in cooperative and critical pedagogies. They are strategically placed to use their pedagogical power for global citizenship by helping students imagine a global community of civilians with a global civic culture based on the Earth Charter. They can teach pro-social communicative competence, global cultural consciousness, critical consciousness, critical loyalty, complex thinking with paradox and contradiction, constructive patriotism, moral development, values development, and critical thinking to reduce the number of people with authoritarian or social dominating cognitive style.

The third prerequisite for the pro-social capitalist is moral imagination. To have moral imagination is to have a power based on a sense of relationship with the other, an ability to see paths through complexity, a capacity to respond creatively, and courage to take risks for change. My long association with English language teachers around the world tells me that there is no lack of moral imagination among my colleagues.

Education for Global Citizenship

Education is shaped by the values and skills of global citizenship: moral imagination, tolerance, acceptance, peace, species identity, and reconciliation. These values are both internal and external to local cultures. The goal for education is to transition to preferred futures by civilizing uncivil societies, drawing on the Earth Charter for content and civil society as the form. Learners are encouraged to explore social and cultural complexities and creative paths through them, so that they might be willing to take risks for preferred futures. Education aims to create global civilians, global citizens, pro-social capitalists, heroic bystanders, and principled dissidents. Global citizenship is legitimized as a relationship of species identity with planetary duties, privileges, rights, and responsibilities. In particular, education aims to restore relationships and reciprocity among people where they are lacking or broken. Teachers use classroom management and discipline to teach moral values like justice, caring, and interdependence.

Education for global citizenship goes towards understanding the origins of violence and interfering with them. The destination is species identity and synergy, passing through the transition zones and resources of conflict, paradox, and moral dilemma. In working through conflicts, paradoxes and dilemmas, people learn and change. Thus, conflict, paradox, and dilemma arising from culture, prejudice, identity, and history are examined from insider/connected and outsider/marginal perspectives. Curriculum design starts by answering certain basic questions about language, learning, roles, methods, and goals. I turn to that task now.

What is Language?

Language is one form through which dialogue takes place. Dialogue means human connection through voice, attention, and, ideally, acknowledgment. Through dialogue, relationships between self and other can be repaired in order to transition to sustainable peace, which emerges from latency into actuality when people work through conflict, prejudice, and pain to reach reconciliation. Voice is offering, articulating, and becoming vulnerable. It legitimizes itself and asks for attention and acknowledgment. Attention is listening, accepting, understanding, and giving legitimacy and acknowledgment to voice and to what is voiced. Acknowledgment is recognition of what another sees as a truth. Reconciliation can take place only if there is some degree of acknowledgment. Dialogue is facilitated when people adhere to pro-social norms of communication.

Let me give an example. I was teaching in Pakistan in 1988 when my country shot down a passenger flight from Iran. There was little about why this happened in the news. I could not ignore it; I needed to pay attention to it because I knew that my students would identify with Iran. My relationship with them was at risk, so I wanted to be attentive to my students. When I went into class, I apologized to the students on behalf of my government, expressing my genuine horror and outrage. In doing so, I showed my students that I legitimized their feelings. I listened to them as they voiced their response to the event and worked through their feelings of attack and anger. I acknowledged the truth of their perceptions. For my Pakistani students it was enough, that day, to express their shock and outrage to me and to accept my acknowledgment.

What is Learning?

Learning is self-transition through dialogue that legitimizes synergistic visions of preferred futures and imagined communities.

What is the Role of the Teacher?

Teachers are pro-social capitalists who use their strategic positions, pro-social capital, and moral imagination to create experiences in which participants use dialogue (voice, attention, and acknowledgment) for learning.

What is the Role of the Learner?

The learner uses independent and interdependent agencies to participate in dialogue so as to transition self, others, and society to preferred futures.

Goals for Instruction

- Content goals: the content goals for Principle 16 can be found in the definition of peace as the wholeness created by right relationships within the biosphere. In particular, I deal with the relationship among humans within the biosphere by addressing conflict transformation, tolerance, remembrance, reconciliation, and forgiveness.
- Language goals: pro-social communicative competence in global and local nonviolent norms of dialogue (voice, attention, and acknowledgment).
- Cognitive goals: cognitive styles and identity for global citizenship (connected interdependence and independence, multicultural identity),

metacultural awareness, global cultural consciousness, critical loyalty, critical consciousness, constructive patriotism, critical thinking, complex thinking including tolerance of ambivalence, uncertainty, and ambiguity.

- Cooperative goals: individual accountability, influence, transition, reciprocity, *sunao*.
- Emotional goals: empathy, responsibility, species identity.
- Social goals: moral development to Stage 4 or above
- Agency goals: global civilian, outlier, heroic bystander, principled dissident, pro-social capitalist.

What is Pedagogy?

Pedagogy is intended to be personally and socially transitional; it is participatory, glocalized, normative, and formative. The learners and teachers participate actively in dialogue working in, out, and through conflicts, paradoxes, contradictions, and moral dilemmas. If the experience is successful, participants voice, attend to, and acknowledge their own and others' truths with humility. Through reconciliation, participants repair relationships and restore reciprocity. Participants imagine preferred futures and commit their independent and interdependent agencies and cooperative power to achieving a different future. Participants have a sense that they can bring something out of latency and into actuality.

Glocalized pedagogy is pedagogy that balances insider/connected and outsider/marginal perspectives. It honors the knowledge and experience of local teachers who are the experts in the cultural and social resources for learning and the participants' openness to learning. The pedagogy is designed to emancipate participants, leaving intact their roots in their home culture but branching into global cultural consciousness or multicultural identity. It attempts to start in the chaotic and creative tension in the meeting place of the local and the global. It respects indigenous knowledge and traditions at the same time as it looks at them critically. It takes note of how they contribute to global civic culture or where they might be modified.

The pedagogy is normative and formative. Participants learn certain norms of behavior that belong to global civic culture, including language. However, glocalized pedagogy ensures that the behavior and linguistic norms are appropriate to the local culture or modified as needed. Thus, the global is expected to form and inform the local culture. Pedagogy is also a way to legitimize local norms of nonviolent behavior and language and to (in)form global civic culture and global norms of pro-social communicative competence. Pedagogy contributes to the worldliness of English through the adoption of terms like *ilm* and *sunao*.

The pedagogy is post-method in the sense that it is not primarily a language learning methodology. Instead, English is conceived of as a neutral ground for learning global citizenship, for transition through work and study overseas and for critical pedagogy and reflection. The resources are moral dilemmas, trigger events, contradictions and paradoxes, and classroom management choices. The pedagogy encourages participants to use local cultural and linguistic resources, borrowing and code-switching as needed so as to contribute to the worldliness of English. If there is a preferred approach, it is classically Socratic: teachers ask open-ended questions and guide learners to certain insights through summarizing, highlighting, and debriefing. However, the pedagogy is post-method also because insiders, not outsiders, make the important pedagogical decisions.

Part III

The English Language Teacher and Pedagogies of Transition

Chapter 9

Pedagogies of Conflict Transformation

[I]n a world characterized by deep inequities and power differences, the principle of universal responsibility would not have much practical meaning if not coupled with a principle of differential responsibility. "Universal responsibility," here, refers to the moral dimension of a global ethic that can be shared by all humans. "Differentiated responsibility" refers to the "capacity to respond," depending on our actual capacity to do so. Thus, although we may all be equally obliged to respond ethically to meet the challenges we face, our actual capacity to respond depends on the powers and resources one has at hand.

(Brenes-Castro, 2004:82)

Like Appiah's two strands of cosmopolitanism, universal concern and respect for diversity, Brenes-Castro's approach to peace education also combines the universal with the diverse. He tells us that the principle of universal responsibility—that we are all responsible for our contribution to synergy, morality, and sustainability—is meaningless without differential responsibility, that people are able to contribute in diverse ways. For one thing, universal responsibility can easily become the responsibility of someone else because the more it is spread out, the less responsible each particular person feels. Brenes-Castro challenges us to respond to deep inequities and power differences with whatever outsider or insider capacities, resources, and pro-social capital we have available. The infrastructure for peacebuilding depends on connecting and reconnecting in both independent and interdependent ways.

Universal responsibility is global, personal, and collective responsibility; it is both inside and outside. In Eastern Europe, principled dissidents gained strength from their post-totalitarian methods. Taking the totalitarian culture as a given, they still found spaces for resistance. They found powers and resources within their culture to live in truth. This gave them the capacity to transform their moral culture and bring down a regime. The same notions apply to conflict; taking conflict as a given, English language teachers find spaces for post-conflict dialogue.

Conflict

There has been an evolution in thinking about conflict over the years, at least within individualist cultures. *Conflict avoidance* is a strategy which people use when they have a conflict but they deny it because they associate conflict with fear, anger, and confrontation. They believe that conflict is abnormal and bad, and that negative emotions are inevitable. Conflict, to them, is a threat to the relationship. Sometimes people avoid conflicts because they do not care enough about the relationship to confront a dispute. Conflict avoidance comes from personality, isolation, embeddedness, and experience, but also from power imbalances in relationships. The more vulnerable member is more likely to avoid conflict than the more powerful member.

Some conflict avoiders simply give in to the other and fail to achieve their own goals or needs, proceeding with their life philosophically. More proactive conflict avoiders sometimes seek outside help to resolve the conflict or ask for a go-between to communicate their needs. Instead of confronting someone directly, face to face, they write a note or an email. Some conflict avoiders seek more indirect ways of achieving what they want, becoming manipulative, controlling, and resorting to emotional blackmail. They seek to punish those whom they see as creating conflict or winning the conflict. They guilt or shame the other into complying with their wishes.

Conflict resolution takes it as a given that conflict is bad and abnormal, that it should end as soon as possible, and that it can end with both disputants satisfied. Often it is superficial; it avoids the underlying social, economic, cultural, and psychological issues in the relationship between individuals or peoples. It stays away from morality and avoids dealing with injustices and power imbalances. Above all, because it deals only with present issues and not with the past or the relationship, conflict resolution does not lead to sustainable peace. Much of the time the disputants are left unsatisfied, or one of them is.

Conflict management holds that a process or method can contain a conflict even if it can never be resolved. A mediator "manages" the process from the top down, leading the disputants step by step down a predictable path from the beginning to the end. When a conflict is managed, it may never go away; thus, the process is not sustainable in the long run. Because no one gets satisfaction on the underlying issues, it is always prone to break out or worsen. Also, a lot of agency must go into constant negotiation and renegotiation to "tame" the conflict.

Conflict transformation starts with the recognition that conflict is a given in any society, so it is a *post-conflict* bottom-up process of restoring a relationship between the *conflict partners*, the people involved in the conflict, through ongoing dialogue. It acknowledges that conflict can be good because significant learning takes place as a result of confronting the conflict and finding ways through it and beyond it within a relationship. Working through conflict is a way for people to learn about morality and critical consciousness in action. Taking interpersonal and intergroup conflict as givens, pro-social capitalists find spaces to draw on whatever resources there are to create a social and psychological space for voice, attention, and acknowledgment. They try to bring peace from latency into actuality by cooperating with others to transform social and political structures and systems that contribute to conflict and dysergy in a locality. They take risks to repair broken relationships with others, and build relationships that did not exist before. They associate together in communities that create and nurture an infrastructure (vertical, horizontal, and orthogonal) to address conflicts before they get out of control.

Conflict Transformation

People transform conflict into learning and agency through a cooperative dialogue among members of a society. People in a sociocultural network use their agencies to build and restore relationships and to address inequities. They try to stop the cycle of reciprocal causation by increasing pro-social and pro-human reciprocity. They use influence to resolve conflicts over resources, needs and wants, and to establish legitimate systems for the rule of law. The process of conflict transformation is a dialogic way of life for a culture; it is not a technique or an outcome. Ultimately, it aims to restore relationships with justice, forgiveness, and reconciliation.

Universality

Conflict is inevitable because people will always want, need, or value different things and have different resources available to them that others may want, need, or value. Conflict is everywhere, but sometimes difficult life conditions or sociopolitical structures in localities increase the number and intractability of conflicts. In many countries, the relationships among various ethnic or religious groups are made more difficult because of past injustice and current economic and social injustice.

The issue is not the presence or absence of conflict but rather how people respond to it. It is not the denotation of the word "conflict" (differences of needs, wants, values, or resources) that is the problem; it is the connotations (avoidance, disruption of relationship, disharmony, anger, fear, threat, suspicion, violence, ethnic cleansing) that are problematic. To put it another way, the concept of conflict has baggage. People should not fear conflict but rather its sociocultural associations. Just as the word "conflict" is different in different languages, the concept of conflict has different baggage in different cultures as well.

Particularity

Conflict transformation is glocalized. It requires acknowledging that different people react to or respond to conflict in different ways, even within the same culture. Behavior is not completely predetermined by sociocultural context. Conflict transformation requires the understanding that the sociocultural context is dynamic, and therefore it can change. The way that people customarily understand conflict in terms of its connotation and baggage can change. Conflict transformation requires the conscious awareness of the expectations, experiences, and knowledge people bring to a conflict, as well as their particular feelings in reaction or response to a conflict. It requires looking at the sociocultural context for indigenous ways to respond positively to conflict, for ways to lose the baggage of fear, threat, suspicion, anger, and potential violence.

Pro-social capitalists discover or create indigenous methods to settle intercultural disputes before they escalate into violence. In some cultures, conflict in relationships is dissolved in a good way; people use their interdependent agency to find a solution before the conflict erupts. In some cultures, people do not respond to conflict with anger and aggression but with cooperation to resolve the conflict equitably. But in some cultures, conflict is an excuse to intimidate others into surrendering. In some cultures, conflict arouses people's fears and frustrations so that they try to control and coerce others, turning the conflict into chaos. In some cultures, people realize that there must be an ongoing dialogue over needs, wants, resources, and values within an interdependent relationship. Thus, people of different cultures have different ways of reacting and responding to conflict and different norms of communication in talking about it in relationships. There are different ways of repairing a relationship in which conflict has occurred. Conflict and resolution of conflict are both embedded in sociocultural expectations, experiences, and knowledge.

If conflict is inevitable and everywhere, then it follows that conflict transformation must be inevitable and everywhere at all times. It must be proactive so that it occurs before and instead of avoidance, frustration, and violence. That is why conflict transformation is an ongoing dialogue among many members of a society and culture. It takes many people and groups in cooperation to increase justice, reduce violence, and restore broken relationships. Conflict transformation is a universal and a differentiated responsibility to be part of a transition in the moral culture in a locality.

Conflict Dialogue

Conflict dialogue is an interpersonal interaction where any power imbalances are neutralized. If there is a power imbalance, then true dialogue will not occur unless power is reclaimed. When people dialogue as equals, conflict transformation can occur at both the personal and the social levels. People themselves change in relationship with others, and they see ways to make changes to their situation or system. But there are some pitfalls in conflict dialogue.

> The training began in Guatemala. The four-day event seemed to go well overall, but one incident stands out very clearly in my mind. We had reached the mediation aspect of the training. In preparation for this component I had put together some fifteen role plays, all of them developed from real-life situations in Central America. As I had always done, and as I had always seen other mediation trainers do, I started the introduction to mediation by providing an overview of the process and then giving a direct demonstration through a role play. The situation was a family conflict and I invited two participants from the group to take the roles of a father and an adult daughter, and I took the part of the mediator. I had developed the role play directly from a situation that had been described to me by a Guatemalan. The demonstration took about an hour, and in the end we reached some understanding between the two. I then opened the floor for observations, comments, and questions. The first person to speak did not address himself to me, but rather to his two compatriots, and said in a single sentence, "You two looked like gringos!"
>
> (Lederach, 1995:37)

Lederach asked himself, if the language was Spanish and the participants were Guatemalan, what turned the two Guatemalans into gringos. There were two issues. One was that there were underlying assumptions and expectations about conflict and the best ways to transform it, assumptions and expectations appropriate in their original cultural setting but not in another. The other problem was the hidden cultural imperialism, that outsider ways were the best means to resolve conflicts and that the Guatemalans should learn to work through conflict using these methods. One of the main criticisms of conflict resolution methods is that too often they are transmitted from the outsider-trainer to trainee in a prescriptive, culturally insensitive manner. The applied linguist knows that pragmatics do not transfer from one language to another; individualist norms of conflict resolution process and language sound peculiar in a collectivist culture. Voice, attention, and acknowledgment are culturally embedded.

Indeed, such stilted norms of conflict dialogue are native to very few at this point in time. The process of conflict resolution evolved as a procedure to reach agreement in disputes between labor and management within a business context in the US. It became a cultura franca, codified in such classic texts as *Getting to Yes: Negotiating Agreement without Giving in* (Fisher, Ury, and Patton, 1991) and *Getting Together: Building*

Relationships as We Negotiate (Fisher and Brown, 1988). Conflict resolution spread to psychologists and counselors, and it acquired set procedures like active listening, I-statements, and various ways to mediate. (For a less business-oriented example, see Rosenberg, 2005.) More and more people learned these new norms of communicating, and although they first seemed alien because they are not "natural" ways of speaking, they became familiar over time. Conflict resolution and management became a profession, and mediators became consultants in conflicts outside the US. However, attempts to export norms revealed how much more alien and alienating they can be in other cultures and languages.

Conflict Dialogue, Individualist Style

Individualist-style conflict dialogue is a normative way of communicating between individuals or people in a relationship who wish to remain in that relationship. If the conflict dialogue allows them to transform the conflict, the situation of the people in the relationship improves and so does the relationship. Conflict dialogue aims to change so-called normal (but sometimes dysfunctional) communication patterns, creating new norms of communication that allow individuals and people to learn from conflict. The pedagogy of conflict dialogue is a transition between the common experience of conflict as threatening disorder to the experience of conflict as a learning opportunity. It is a transition from old norms of communication to new pro-social and pro-human norms of communication.

Ordinarily, conflict partners prepare ahead of time by practicing empathy-enhancing and anger-management activities. They learn how to listen actively to the other without projecting or attributing. Then they ask themselves whether a conflict with another can be resolved through dialogue. If it cannot be resolved, there are potentially three available options. People can change themselves, change the situation, or leave. For example, if one person, Juan, wants to have coffee with another person, Marie, but she does not want to go, talking about the situation is not likely to help because it will not change. They are not conflict partners. The only way to resolve this conflict is for Juan to realize that he is out of luck (changing himself) and look elsewhere (leave).

If the conflict is amenable to working through, an appropriate atmosphere must be established between the two partners. The attitudes of the two partners should be as favorable and open as possible; they should participate voluntarily. The timing is important. Sometimes the best atmosphere for resolving a conflict is during an argument or fight, where maximal learning and transformation can take place. Sometimes it is best to delay the process, so that the partners are more rational. The delayed timing must be convenient for both partners and enough time must be allotted to work through the conflict without rushing. The physical environment should be neutral and allow for each partner to sit side by side on an equal level.

Working through the conflict is based on the idea that the people are separate from the conflict. That is, the conflict is about interests or behaviors and not how good or bad the partners are. The basis for working through a conflict is for the partners to focus not on the positions that they may have taken, but on the interests, goals, needs, or resources that they have. Conflict transformation involves learning norms of dealing with emotions (empathy, nonjudgmental attitudes, and anger management) and communication.

These are the basic norms for conflict dialogue:

1. Active listening:

    a. Decide if you really want to hear what the other has to say.
    b. If so, clear your mental agenda.
    c. Show understanding and acceptance by authentic verbal and nonverbal behavior such as nodding or saying "yes" or "I understand."
    d. Try to empathize with the other.
    e. At appropriate times, restate what the other person said with a paraphrase. "In other words, you want to use the computer for your homework."
    f. At appropriate times, ask an open-ended question—that is, a question with a "wh-" word: "What have you already tried to resolve this problem?"
    g. When listening, do not judge, evaluate, interpret, advise, predict, or analyze.
    h. Careful active listening will often reveal hidden offers, apologies, common ground, or positive intentions to explore as resources for working through conflict.

2. Clear speaking: know what you think and state it clearly by using I-statements. Do not start sentences with "you."
3. A second statement may be added following the I-statement, not as an ultimatum, but rather as the beginning step in a negotiation. The second statement should be clear and specific about your wishes for the other person or for a change in the status quo.

    a. "I would like to try ——."
    b. "Could we talk about a way to change this situation?"
    c. "Could we work together to set up a new way of doing this?"
        The conflict partners take turns talking about what they need and want, and brainstorm ways to transform the conflict and repair the relationship.

Conflict Dialogue, Collectivist Style

Some people have the idea that the collectivist prescription for resolving conflict within a relationship is to circle around confrontation and give in. Bond (1986:262) looks at China, where communicative strategies designed to prevent conflict from getting out of control are common. Conflict partners first present the problems they have in common and identify all of the constraints each partner faces. Only then do they state their own views. When they use this discourse strategy, it "results in their appearing diffident and vague to most Westerners, but effectively prevents a polarization of positions."

We have already seen that some people are more interdependent, they have more empathy for others, and they are better at controlling negative emotions. They are not prone to attribution; they do not interpret others' behavior in light of an internal characteristic which may be wrong. They are less prone to project their own feelings on others. Interdependent people use their agency (adapting their own behavior or potentially the situation) in order to reduce potential conflict with others. They are less likely to use independent agency (influence) to change another's behavior; instead, they rely on the idea of reciprocity. They expect that the other will be equally empathic and change their behavior to reduce conflict as well, perhaps by giving in also. They feel a strong moral obligation to help others, at least those within their group. Conflict is handled through nondissension.

Aikido is a Japanese nonviolent martial art used for self-defense, not attack. In aikido, practitioners learn to anticipate and block attacks, turning the force of the attack away without defensively attacking the opponent back. Aikido adepts do not attack their opponents because that makes them less able to defend themselves. Therefore, their lack of offensive attack, their *nondissension*, becomes their invulnerability. Making an analogy with aikido, Tohei describes nondissension as follows:

> The non-dissension we are speaking of arises when we do not harbor feelings about our opponent, but with the magnanimity of the sea that accepts all tributary streams, maintain a waveless calm in our own hearts . . . Once a person has penetrated to the real meaning of the principle, strength and body size cease to matter.
>
> As an example, strength and body size are important if, when an opponent attacks you, you receive the strength of the blow *in a collision-like situation*. If, however, *you brush the blow aside*, the opponent must himself manage the force he has generated . . . After all, in a case like this, you are actually making him go where he wants to go and turn in the direction he wants to turn . . . The way of non-dissension enables you to overcome any reversals without spiritual

pain, to laugh off any slander, and to lead astray any attack, without yourself receiving the blow.

(Tohei, 1972:155–9; emphasis added)

I think that the collectivist prescription is far from conflict avoidance; it is *conflict proactivity*. In other words, because people have empathy and concern for others, because they can control their emotions, because they are willing to change themselves or the situation, they use their agencies to reduce conflict before it arises. If there are fewer conflicts, it is not because conflicts are suppressed or avoided; they are simply not there because people have learned how to decide things and make choices without overt conflict and confrontation. In Mongolia, some people talked about how 300 years of Buddhism converted the Mongols from a warlike culture to a culture where equanimity is valued.

Individualist Conflict Dialogue Revisited

A critical examination of individualist conflict dialogue shows that it mimics the collectivist style. The conflict arises because two people assert their independent agency to influence the other, but it creates an impasse, a conflict. To resolve the conflict and repair the relationship, the conflict partners learn empathy enhancement to reduce projection and attribution and anger management to control their negative feelings. They learn that they can change only themselves or the situation since they really cannot change others. That is, they learn that the only option is interdependent agency to transform a conflict. If they value the relationship, they attempt a negotiation without influence or pressure. If they do not value the relationship, they leave (if that is possible).

The norms of individualist conflict dialogue are meant to be formative as well. When people learn to have empathy, when they learn to manage their negative emotions, they transfer that ability to other situations. When people learn to use the I-statement, it becomes a nonconfrontational way to assert their needs proactively. People who learn conflict dialogue norms are often surprised to see how effective interdependent agency can be. It can be more effective than influence or pressure. Once one person in the conflict changes behavior, it often causes the other to change as well. That's reciprocity. The expression more commonly used in English for nondissension is that people become "slower and less likely to take offense." This makes people proactive about dealing with conflicts before they escalate, so they are reduced in number and intensity.

Cross-Cultural Conflict

I taught a class on conflict resolution at a TESOL Summer Institute at St. Michael's College in 1995. The students in the class came from a variety of backgrounds, among them Japan and Egypt. I taught them individualist conflict dialogue, but I openly discussed how uncomfortable it felt because it seemed like cultural imperialism. I asked them how they resolved their conflicts in their home countries. The Japanese students talked about how they "avoid" conflict. The Egyptian students said, half jokingly, "We just yell at each other until someone gives in." The students wondered aloud what would happen if a Japanese person had a conflict with an Egyptian person.

It was then that a common ground of conflict dialogue made more sense. It tones down aggressive pressure and increases interdependent agency, but it also makes less assertive conflict partners more able to express, through I-statements, what they need or want, increasing independent agency. This is a good example of using both inside and outside resources for reconciliation. On the one hand, if people know the individualist style, it becomes part of a cultura franca for global civilians. On the other hand, the cultura franca must grow to accommodate many pro-social and pro-human ways of resolving conflict from all cultures.

For instance, Lederach (2004:28) describes how, in Nicaragua, the local people involved in reconciliation started their village meetings with Psalm 85 from the Bible. The final line is "Truth and mercy have met together; peace and justice have kissed." Later, at a training session with local peace commissions, he elicited their cultural understandings of truth, mercy, peace, and justice and how they related to reconciliation. What he learned from the commissions informed his notion of reconciliation henceforth. In a perfect example of glocalization, the outsider learned from his Nicaraguan participants and published it for us all.

Elicitation

Lederach got into trouble when he prescribed individualist conflict dialogue, and from his experience he realized that a conflict resolution "product" cannot simply transfer from one culture to another. He was inspired by problem-posing and ethnography to do the social and cultural research necessary to develop glocalized conflict dialogue. He calls the process the *elicitive approach* (Lederach, 1995) in contrast to prescriptive or traditional approaches. Lederach describes the elicitive method as ethnographic, but it is not ethnographic in the strictest sense, where outside observers make notes on a population different from theirs and attempt to find the common themes behind artifacts, values, and behaviors. Instead, the facilitator, who may be an insider or an outsider, uses particular methods to help participants access the themes and resources available to them. I am adapting the elicitive approach to the English language classroom.

English language teachers and their learners may share culture and language or they may not. The common element is English, so it serves as a framework to explore the local norms of conflict transformation and dialogue. Learners are the experts on indigenous methods of responding to conflicts and using conflict dialogue. The resources and processes for transformation are embedded in local cultures, languages (English and local languages), and ideologies, and learners' knowledge of these is the primary resource for transforming conflict. Teachers facilitate a process of uncovering and verbalizing the knowledge. Learners uncover, name, evaluate, adapt, and apply indigenous conflict transformation processes with their own ways to dialogue.

In the elicitive approach, English language teachers, in a sequence of steps, help learners bring into consciousness and articulate what they know, using English and concepts, words, and phrases borrowed from local languages as needed. The "products" articulated in this fashion are normative and formative processes that are then resources for people in the culture to transform conflicts, but they also become resources globally as English language teachers spread them upwards and outwards. Learners appropriate English as a resource for conflict transformation locally, but they also make English more worldly. For instance, in Kosovo, indigenous processes of conflict transformation draw from Serbian language and culture and Albanian language and culture. Global civic culture and English can gain from this knowledge.

The first task is *needs assessment*; teachers help the conflict partners identify what they are hoping for or what the conflict is. Do they have a decision to make? Do they want a third party to help them repair a relationship? Do they have a past hurt that needs to be addressed? Is there an injustice that needs to be acknowledged? Is there a cycle of reciprocal causation that needs to stop? The conflict partners' needs are the goals of the process and inform its design. Needs assessment, goals, and design are discussed in sequence, but actually they come up throughout the process.

The next part of the process is called *discovery* because the purpose is to discover or uncover some of the facts, feelings, and events involved in the conflict. Discovery takes place through open-ended discussion and role plays, word cards and storyboarding, and narrative analysis. Learners, in small homogeneous or heterogeneous groups, discuss their real-life experiences. Teachers invite learners to think about a time when they had a conflict and answer the question: if things got difficult and you felt you needed help, who would you go to for help? After some individual time to think, they share with their group the answers to the following questions. Why did you choose this person? What characteristics does he/she have? What do you expect from this person? They describe their experiences as case histories and/or present them as role plays to the whole group.

Learners also use word cards and storyboarding to discover cultural resources for conflict transformation. Teachers divide learners into small groups to answer the question: what is conflict? Each group shares indigenous words and images with the whole class. The teacher puts the images, metaphors, and words on a blackboard or piece of paper within their social and cultural context. Then, the teacher makes a set of words and images for each small group, and assigns them the task of arranging them by some commonality of meaning. The groups try to categorize the images and words by criteria that they themselves define like sequence, relationship, similarity, or difference. The groups report by placing their cards on a storyboard and explaining their commonalities, steps, or other arrangements. Teachers and learners articulate the cultural resources using common terms from English and local languages. For instance, instead of using the term "third-party mediator," they might say shaman, guide, or elder, or they might transfer their own first-language words (e.g. *viejo*, *sabio*, *guia*) to English.

Narratives include analogies, fables, metaphors, stories, and even jokes that contain traditional wisdom and experience. They are holistic and symbolic, dense associations of emotions, events, and relationships. Sometimes there are contrasting narratives that show contradictory or paradoxical feelings about conflict. Learners can translate the narratives into English or study them in their original language, but use English to talk about them. Other resources for understanding conflict and its transformation are proverbs and sayings, such as these from Chinese culture:

- It is better to be a dog in times of peace than a man in times of war.
- Balance is the great schema of the cosmos; harmony is the universal path of life as a whole.
- In a family of a thousand, only one is the master.
- A word once altered cannot be drawn back, even by a team of four horses.
- Haughtiness invites ruin; humility receives benefits.
- You cannot clap with a single hand.

Next, with the teacher's help, participants extract, name, and categorize the constructive social and cultural tools such as activities, approaches, and roles that would be appropriate to conflicts in that setting. Learners evaluate what helps resolve conflicts and what does not, and they adapt old ways into a new context. They articulate the processes, perhaps resurrecting some that have died out because of social turmoil. Learners then attempt to test the processes by practicing them in real life. They report back to the group about the success or failure of the methods, and further refinement or evaluation can take place. Finally, they discuss what more needs to be done in the future, the obstacles and new ideas. It is important to emphasize that these steps are described in sequence but they can occur out of order or in different orders.

A Preferred Future

Using outside prescriptive and inside elicited resources for transforming conflict through voice, attention, and acknowledgment is a way for people to assume universal responsibility as well as differential responsibility for peace. When people no longer fear conflict but embrace it as a means for learning and transition, a post-conflict social space for peace becomes possible. In that space, people continue the dialogue about prejudice, remembrance, reconciliation, and forgiveness.

Chapter 10

Tolerance

> I have come to see white privilege as an invisible package of unearned assets that I can count on cashing in each day, but about which I was "meant" to remain oblivious. White privilege is like an invisible weightless knapsack of special provisions, maps, passports, code-books, visas, clothes, tools, and blank checks . . . My schooling gave me no training in seeing myself as an oppressor, as an unfairly advantaged person, or as a participant in a damaged culture . . . My schooling followed the pattern . . . [that] whites are taught to think of their lives as morally neutral, normative, and average, and also ideal, so that when we work to benefit others, this is seen as work that will allow "them" to be more like "us."
>
> (McIntosh, 1992:33–4)

Many conflicts are complicated by issues of prejudice, privilege, and injustice. McIntosh's quote describes many people's upbringing and schooling in the United States years ago; a schooling that ignored inequality and racism. In a segregated world, it was quite possible for whites to remain oblivious to our damaged culture. We were white, we spoke standard English, we were middle class. We looked like everyone else in the community, including the police officers. Because we looked the same, we trusted each other. We did not realize the social, economic, and political privileges that we enjoyed. Some people remember that time as idyllic, but all the while it was a dysergic façade. Our schools did nothing to prepare us for the reality that ours was and still is a deeply divided society.

Post-racist Society

In his 1959 "Sermon on Gandhi," King spoke of his goal for nonviolent resistance, his concept of the "beloved community," when a relationship of reciprocity between races would emerge from latency. More recently, the feminist and anti-racist thinker bell hooks, in her 1995 book *Killing Rage: Ending Racism*, has argued that King's vision was simplistic. She claims that a post-racist community can come about only when all human differences are embraced and valued. The beloved community will come about when people cherish their own diverse affiliations but are willing to give up the baggage that comes with most of them. When people critically evaluate their socialization and enculturation to see their expectations and opinions of themselves and others clearly, they use their agencies to transform society.

Pro-social capitalists question their feelings of being above others, of being privileged. In this unlearning process, people accept, for example, their whiteness, their maleness, their heterosexuality, but they give up the baggage: their feelings of privilege, normality, or supremacy over others who are not white, male, or heterosexual. They stop feeling that they are entitled to special treatment because of their position at the "center" of the social structure. They stop seeing themselves as the center and accept that there is no center. Likewise, disadvantaged people need to unlearn their feelings of being under others or in the periphery. King's beloved community will come about when people do not see differences through the lens of their personal, cultural, or social stereotypes, and simply perceive them and embrace them as differences.

hooks (1995) makes the very interesting point that in the early days of the civil rights movement in the United States, many blacks felt empowered because they believed that their resistance would end injustice and racism. Decades later, faced with a more subtle form of racism and white supremacy, some blacks have an attitude of victimization and entitlement because they take white supremacy as a given; it can never change because people will always be racist.

> Collective failure to address adequately the psychic wound inflicted by racist aggression is the breeding ground for a psychology of victimhood wherein learned helplessness, uncontrollable rage, and/or feelings of powerlessness and despair abound in the psyches of black folks yet are not attended to in ways that empower and promote wholistic states of being. Until African Americans, and everyone else in the United States, are able to acknowledge the psychic trauma inflicted upon black folks by racist aggression and assault, there will be no collective cultural understanding of the reality that these wrongs cannot be redressed simply by programs for economic reparation, equal opportunity in the workforce, or attempts to create social equality between the races.
>
> (hooks, 1995:137–8)

When people simultaneously and collectively unlearn their socioculturally induced feelings of supremacy over others and the socioculturally induced feelings of victimization or entitlement in which they position themselves under others, the beloved community will come about. hooks' point is that superficial economic programs do not get to this alteration in world view and positioning when social transformation is absent. The psychic trauma must be worked through by both those with feelings of supremacy and those with feelings of victimization. The concept of species identity offers a way for people to interact self to self with (not over or under) others and a way of seeing others as similar while cherishing those things that make people different from each other. People accept their own and others' affiliations while critically examining the baggage that comes along with them.

For instance, I cannot help but be seen as a white person, because I am white; however, I can seek out and reject my internalized feelings of supremacy or fear of others based on their appearance. I cannot help being seen as a woman by others, because I am a woman; but feminist intro-spection can help me explore and discard any feelings of victimization and entitlement that I may have learned. When I have shed not my affiliations but my baggage, I can relate with others from my self. Nevertheless, I cannot free myself completely from my baggage unless others free them-selves from their baggage also. I cannot truly escape my whiteness unless others see in my color not a potential racist but a human. I cannot escape the social and cultural baggage of womanhood unless others see me as an equal human and as a woman. People must be in this process of stripping away baggage together. As individuals, one by one, lose the stereotypes and expectations they have of one another based on personal and cultural affiliations, a truly equal society will come about. In a post-racist world, species identity will be widespread because, first and foremost, we will all be human.

Inequality and Bias

In divided societies, hatred and prejudice are rooted in the baggage associated with group affiliations. People's group affiliations are culturally determined but usually certain characteristics define the group. It may be physical characteristics like skin color, eye shape, hair, or gender, or it may be cultural characteristics that are more intangible like nationality, heritage, ability, intelligence, caste, religion, nomadism, social class, language, or accent. The baggage starts with a historical component, rooted in different forms of domination. When two peoples have a history of mistreatment, they sometimes use history to justify hating each other. It is a rationale for the status quo and for just world thinking. Because they have suffered at the hands of the other, they view themselves as victims and the others as oppressors. Or they want to continue oppressing for the privileges and conveniences that it gives them.

Prejudice

Prejudice refers to negative attitudes and behaviors that derive from historical trauma. Prejudicial attitudes include feelings of superiority over others because of a sense of greater worth, productivity, morality, or intelligence. Prejudice may also include feelings of victimization or oppression. It also refers to negative behaviors that stem from these feelings. Prejudicial behavior runs the gamut from genocide, hate murder, and rape to subtle rudeness and disrespect.

Prejudice is a group and an individual phenomenon at the same time. Any group or individual may be prejudiced. The crucial problem lies in the institutionalization of prejudice, the power of one group of people to maintain a culture of pervasive prejudice that excludes or diminishes others through the structures and institutions they create and sustain. Thus, this prejudice is *structural prejudice*—that is, part of the structure of society. In some areas of the world, structural prejudice seems to have declined over the past half century, as people achieve human rights. However, it is still rampant, and under certain conditions has reached the point of genocide.

Avoidance

In those areas where structural prejudice has declined, it has not disappeared altogether. Even though overtly prejudiced speech and behavior are unacceptable now, people are still biased. They simply do not talk about it because they know it is bad. Prejudice or bias sometimes manifests itself as *avoidance*, where people avoid socializing or working with the other. Avoidance may be due to anxiety rather than hostility. People simply feel more comfortable and less stressed when they are with people whom they know and trust, and those tend to be people they perceive to be like themselves. In western Mongolia, the Kazakh people and the Mongolian people live separate lives with little interaction between them. Although there is little violence, the "peace" comes from self-segregation.

Privilege

A more subtle form of prejudice is privilege. In the United States, because Christian heterosexual people of European descent have been more numerous for a long time, because they, especially men, hold most positions of power in the government and society, because they are the most instrumental in establishing the predominant culture of that society, and because they have prejudices towards other groups, those groups that are not Christian, not heterosexual, not white, and not male find themselves living in a society that is not fair to them. Some people enjoy certain privileges just because of who they are or what they look like.

Another subtle privilege is that of being an expert English speaker, as any trip to a non-English-speaking country will show. Captions in museums and signs are in the local language and English, and people in the tourist industry usually speak English. For English-as-a-first-language speakers, it is a privilege not to have to learn English as one more subject in school. Simple equity is one more reason for native English speakers to become bilingual and bicultural.

Paternalism

In *paternalistic prejudice*, the privileged group look down favorably on the disadvantaged group (Glick and Fiske, 2001). For instance, whites might look favorably on the blacks who live in their town. Men might value the traditional feminine characteristics of the "little women" in their social group. The disadvantaged group are treated as children who are tolerated and indulged despite their "flaws" and "incompetence." Sometimes the disadvantaged group are "protected," and some of its members actually like and maintain the protection.

When members of the less privileged group undergo conscientization, they try to move out of their inferior position and show themselves to be competent. When this happens, a few of them are tolerated as "tokens" as long as they act like members of the privileged group. Women are tolerated in business, for instance, as long as they act like men. People of color are accepted in certain realms to the extent that they act white. Gay people experience greater acceptance the more straight they act. Nevertheless, if the numbers of these people grow, the feelings of threat in the privileged group increase.

In paternalistic prejudice, fear, scorn, derision, or violence is reserved for members of the less privileged group who attempt to change their status or the social norms while not conforming to the image of the superior group. Women who act like women in business face negative evaluation, charges of incompetence, and putdowns. People of color who insist on maintaining their culture and ways of speaking are viewed with suspicion or as inferior. Obviously gay men or lesbians who do not or cannot hide their orientation face discrimination.

Bigotry

Irrational hatred of different others is bigotry. Such hatred and fear are not rational because most of the time their targets have never done anything against the bigots. Bigots hate others simply because they exist and they are different. They often stereotype a group with negative characteristics and do not see any of its members as individuals because they avoid contact with them. Sometimes, if they do know a few members of the other group, they consider them the exceptions that prove the rule. Bigots eagerly seek confirmation for their opinions. They accept on faith any shred of misguided research, crackpot theory, or forged historical documents. They are easily duped into joining hate and supremacy groups. If bigots hate foreigners, they are called *xenophobic*.

Hate Crimes

Bigotry and prejudice are often accompanied by defensive and aggressive rhetoric about the mental or moral inferiority of the other group. If others are seen as less than human, it is easier to beat them up or kill them. If others are portrayed as agents of the devil, then violence against them is justified. Demonization and dehumanization are often the precursors to violence. On a smaller scale, the violence of prejudice may result in a hate crime such as a threat, a beating, or a lynching. On a larger scale, the violence of prejudice is *genocide*, when one group attempts to kill many if not all of the members of another group. *Gynocide* is the term for rape as a tool of violent prejudice.

Ethnic cleansing is the name for a violent process that includes genocide, gynocide, and the forced relocation of people away from their homes. It is prejudice with a political agenda and power, with weapons and a military force. Unfortunately, much ethnic cleansing is done in the name of religion. It is not a new process; in any history book or religious text there are frequent instances of it. However, the extremes of ethnic cleansing in the twentieth century were the impetus for the United Nations Declaration of Human Rights in 1948. Now, ethnic cleansing is illegal, by international law, but it has not stopped because bigotry and prejudice have not stopped.

Instead, in recent examples, ethnic cleansing was cast as a civil war. Since the United Nations and other international organizations are forbidden to interfere in the internal matters of a nation, they are reluctant to get involved. The European Union can, by agreement, enter into its member states. In recent years, partly because of pressure from global civil society, international tribunals have brought some genocidal leaders to justice, but they have not addressed the trauma of the targets, the followers, and the bystanders.

Attitudes towards Prejudice

It is possible to be unaware of prejudice, just as one can deny cultural difference. People of privilege can think that their society offers a level playing field and that anyone who works hard enough can make a good living. Society is just, so if people do not enjoy a decent life in the society it must be because they are not hard-working, intelligent, moral, or honest.

To them, poverty will always exist because there are lazy people who cannot rise above it. To them, this has nothing to do with any prejudice or privilege. Once people admit that their society has prejudice, there are several stances people take towards it. Some are more characteristic of people of privilege (minimizing and blaming) and some are more common to people without privilege (quitting, resisting, and struggling).

Minimizing

Minimizers believe they have nothing to do with prejudice or privilege, even though they do. They intentionally minimize inequalities and take no responsibility for social injustice, at the same time as they benefit from the system because they are the ones on top. They do not understand that they exercise power over others. They do not see that they play a part in structural prejudice or privilege in their society just by being part of it without opposing it. To minimizers, hatred and fear are problems for others, namely bigots, women-haters, homophobes, and the like. They themselves condemn violence and those who make prejudiced remarks. They do not consider themselves a problem because they say things like "I am not responsible for the past, so I am not responsible now." But they are part of the problem in a divided society because they do not see the need to take part in a dialogue that addresses historical trauma.

Quitting

Quitters do not deny their part in prejudice because they are on the receiving end of it; they have simply resigned themselves to it. They quit instead of resisting. They live with bias, but act as if they do not. They may believe that their chances of assimilating or getting ahead are better if they play along. They live in the lie. Quitters often live lives of *double consciousness*; they exist as individuals who judge themselves through the eyes of the dominant group. Some feel alienated from their own group. They themselves look down on their culture or language because they have internalized the viewpoint of the people of privilege. They go to great lengths to avoid conflict, saying, "I have forgotten the past," which justifies the status quo for minimizers. Minimizers and quitters can, under some difficult life conditions, turn ugly because the unhealed historical trauma lurks beneath the surface, ready to explode. But they get along with each other because they avoid situations that might spark a conflict and deny conflicts when they exist. Conscientization causes minimizers and quitters to become conscious of structural oppression and their part in it. Problem-posing and critical reflection often lead people to the next two attitudes towards prejudice: blaming and struggling.

Blaming

Blamers are aware that they or their people have a history of prejudice and oppression against others. They and/or their ancestors engaged in slavery, genocide, ethnic cleansing, discrimination, racism, or privilege. They were and are the cause of historical trauma. And whether they like it or not, they enjoy the benefits of privilege in the present. They sometimes teeter between wanting to maintain their privileges and accepting the changes that must happen for an equitable society. During this time, many frightening feelings make blamers unstable. They feel pain, sorrow, grief, and anger about the past, and their (or their ancestors') participation in it. Because they are defensive, they are hypersensitive to criticism at times. Their feelings of guilt make them blame themselves excessively or, worse, blame others irrationally. Their anger causes violence to erupt; angry blamers justify their violence by saying that the other group deserved it.

In the later part of the twentieth century, males have been confronted with the issue of gender privilege. Males who do not want to give up their privileged position over women blame "feminazis," mythical men-haters who cause trouble by making demands. They maintain their paternalism over docile women. Other males want to extend equality to women without giving up the benefits of the old system. It is okay if women want to work outside the home, but their wives still have to do the housework. The conflicts contribute to domestic violence against women. Some men are willing to give up the privileges because they see greater benefits in sharing responsibilities and because they welcome change.

Struggling

Strugglers feel difficult emotions as they stop resisting and denying knowledge of the effects of historical trauma on their group. Opening themselves up to trauma stirs up old wounds and anger, which increases conflicts and violence. Strugglers feel rage against the perpetrators of prejudice and violence in the past, as well as the minimizers and blamers of the present. They have not yet experienced psychic conversion, so they are still caught in a self-defeating cycle of victimization and power-lessness. Guilt and grief also come up for some strugglers when they realize that they have internalized the oppression from the society. They know that they themselves have played a part in unjust structures. They do not want to see that, when they tacitly accepted their fate of being slaves, targets of genocide, battered wives, or in the closet, they played into the hands of those who wanted to exploit them, kill them, hurt them, or ignore them.

This may seem like blaming the target but that is not the intent. The point is that the conscientization of people's own complicity in injustice is the key to overcoming violence and oppression, as Václav Havel pointed out. Gandhi recognized the part his people played in their own oppression; his power was in becoming the principled dissident to the oppression. He was the critical yeast that changed the followership. His American disciple, Martin Luther King, often told his people that to accept an unjust system passively is to cooperate with that system and that therefore the oppressed people become as evil as the oppressor. That is a very difficult concept to swallow for many people; it is part of the struggle. King called upon people to be "maladjusted" to violence and injustice (King, 1986:14).

As Walcott (2000) points out in his discussion of slavery and creolization, we play out our roles as slave, slaver, and slave-owner; abuser and abused; predators and prey; robbers and robbed; winners and losers. Each region of the earth has different versions of the same story. Walcott cites Glissant's term "poetics of relation" for this view of human history as a turbulent creativity "born of impacts and breaking" in which we are all connected.

> We have not yet begun to calculate their consequences: the passive adaptations, irrevocable rejections, naïve beliefs, parallel lives, and the many forms of confrontation or consent, the many syntheses, surpassings, or returns, the many stubborn outbursts of invention, born of impacts and breaking . . . which compose the fluid, turbulent, stubborn, and possibly organized matter of our common destiny.
> (Glissant, 1997:138)

Blamers and strugglers have stormy emotions as they begin to see their role in the turbulent poetics of relations. They do not see a common destiny. When they are together in a divided society, their interactions are difficult. Sometimes they play into the hands of unscrupulous and violent leaders with their own political purposes. When people are in blame and struggle, their rage, guilt, grief, and victimization can be exploited and perpetuated by unscrupulous and violent leaders who want power. Blamers and strugglers are not resistant to propaganda, rhetoric, and demagoguery that inflame their passions and demonize the other. On the contrary, they thrive on them. Violence occurs because defensiveness meets rage, blame counters blame, and guilt confronts anger.

Pedagogies of Tolerance

We know that people learn to be prejudiced; they are not born with biases. They absorb prejudice and privilege from their families, cultures, and schooling. That means people can unlearn prejudice. One main way that prejudice is reduced is through direct, uncoerced contact between people who are different in the classroom, in the schoolyard, on sports teams. This expands people's comfort zones with others so they feel less hostility and anxiety. Cooperative learning provides an environment for diverse people to come into contact with each other in the classroom. But to reduce prejudice, the contact must have certain characteristics. It must be supported by the school administration, social institutions, and society. It must lead to meaningful relationships among the students. In cooperative activities, learners must enjoy equal status. However, mere contact is not enough when there is historical trauma. With great insight into human nature, Bruno Bettelheim, a survivor of the Holocaust, said, "What cannot be talked about can also not be put to rest; and if it is not, the wounds continue to fester from generation to generation" (Bettelheim, 1984:166).

Voice

The universal "facts" of prejudice and the attitudes people assume in relation to prejudice must be voiced. It is a transitional pedagogy in two ways. First, tolerance is a pedagogy that can take us from the present to a preferred post-discriminatory future, perhaps Martin Luther King's "beloved community." Second, tolerance is a transition from the present to a future place where we can remember our historical trauma. The pedagogy of tolerance is a universal learning experience, as we all play our parts in the poetics of relation. Such dialogue can take place only in a safe place.

One way for English language teachers to create a safe place is to separate the universal from the particular. The universal creates a context for the particular; the global informs the local. Conscientization traditionally requires a key or a series of keys to begin and extend the process. A key is usually a symbolic object or activity that represents the oppression and opens up people's feelings about it. Sometimes a more neutral or universal key makes this discussion safer for participants. It is safer to discuss prejudice or oppression in another part of the world.

Keys

In a university ESL class I taught many years ago, there were students from various backgrounds, including several women from Korea and Japan. It was near Martin Luther King Day and I played a recording of his "I have a dream" speech for a listening activity (King, 1986:217–20). That began a conversation about race relations in the US. I did not feel qualified to "remember" racism and slavery for African Americans, so I brought in a video the next day that demonstrated racism better than I could do. There was further discussion of the video during the next class period.

The following class period I intended to return to the syllabus but a Japanese student put a note on my desk which I found and opened before class. The note said that she did not want to talk about racism any more because of what her country had done to the Koreans in the past. The

Korean students were her friends in the class and it embarrassed her to talk about racism in their presence. Talking about prejudice in the United States sparked her feelings of self-blame and guilt. Without revealing the student's name, and having acquired her permission, I communicated the contents of the note to the class. The note became a key to discuss the fact that there were Spaniards, Filipinos, Puerto Ricans, Japanese, and Korean students in the class. We recognized the past and present power relations, including oppression and violence, between our respective nation-states. I asked the students if they could do anything about the past. They said no and it felt as if the recognition was leading to despair and paralysis. I asked if they could do anything about the structural prejudice or privileges of the present. After they answered in the affirmative, they discussed a variety of things that people can do to change the present and imagine a different future.

The students were still not finished with the topic of prejudice and privilege. After some discussion, they agreed to organize an informal debate. Several topics were put on the blackboard. The one chosen was "Resolved: homosexuals should be barred from occupations in which they work with children." As the groups prepared their pros and cons, the debate question was the key to exploring the topic. At the conclusion of the debate, those who had chosen to support the resolution had opened their minds to alternatives to homophobia.

In this elicitive pedagogy of tolerance, we started with a topic that was largely neutral to the learners, racism in the United States. I was able to model responsibility, regret, and neutrality while talking about my own country. Then the learners themselves related what they learned to their own ethnic and national experiences with responsibility and regret, so they experienced both the particular and the universal. The Koreans and the Japanese, because of their relationship, were able to overcome their feelings of blame and struggle. They became committed to change in the present and future. Reciprocity was restored. Then we applied the learning to a different kind of prejudice and privilege.

Pro-social Communication

Making a safe space for a pedagogy of tolerance sometimes means that teachers need to establish normative guidelines for the discussion. These guidelines are created by the learners for the learners, perhaps with some prompting and input from teachers. They are not top-down norms from the school administration but bottom-up norms from the students. They are culturally appropriate and are best generated through cooperation and by consensus, although voting may take place to ratify them at the end. They are not about what ideas, attitudes, or opinions are right or wrong, but rather about how they are expressed and not suppressed in the group.

They are both general and specific. I would expect culturally appropriate versions along these or similar lines:

- Communication will be respectful. For example, no yelling, no bullying, no teasing.
- Everyone is entitled to have an opinion and express it. For example, no saying, "Shut up," no bad looks, no judging.
- People do not need to express an opinion if they do not want to. For example, they can say, "I pass."
- People will speak generally and neutrally about prejudice and attitudes towards prejudice. For example, do not refer to people in the class.
- People will listen to each other. For example, no interrupting, no shouting down.
- People will control (but not deny) any negative feelings. For example, count to ten. If necessary, leave the room for a few minutes.
- If people get angry, others will not take it personally. For example, do not get angry in return.
- If people forget the guidelines, the teacher will stop the discussion, remind them by saying, "Time out," and explain why the discussion was stopped in neutral terms.
- We will stop and renegotiate the guidelines at any time if someone asks to do so.

The process of coming up with the norms of communication may take a while but it is important because the norms are meant to be formative as well. Although keeping to cultural appropriateness, the norms established by the students are to form the basis for their pro-social communicative competence for global citizenship. The norms of communication are the forms used in the cultura franca, in global civic culture.

Attention

To get beyond bigotry, prejudice, paternalism, avoidance, and privilege, people need to understand what it is like to walk in another's shoes. To understand the issues, people need to listen without being defensive. We need to listen even though it hurts. Here is what Martin Luther King said very eloquently years ago:

> I guess it is easy for those who have never felt the stinging darts of segregation to say, "Wait." But when you have seen vicious mobs lynch your mothers and fathers at will and drown your sisters and brothers at whim; when you have seen hate-filled policemen curse, kick, brutalize and even kill your black brothers and sisters with impunity; when you see the vast majority of your twenty million

Negro brothers smothering in an airtight cage of poverty in the midst of an affluent society; when you suddenly find your tongue twisted and your speech stammering as you seek to explain to your six-year-old daughter why she can't go to the public amusement park that has just been advertised on television, and see tears welling up in her little eyes when she is told that Funtown is closed to colored children, and see the depressing clouds of inferiority begin to form in her little mental sky . . .

(King, 1986:292)

The civil rights activist W.E.B. Du Bois talks about the *double-consciousness* of his fellow African-Americans: "this sense of always looking at one's self through the eyes of others, of measuring one's soul by the tape of a world that looks on in amused contempt and pity" (cited in West, 1994:138). Cornel West, discussing Malcolm X in his book *Race Matters*, uses the term *psychic conversion* in which African-Americans "would affirm themselves as human beings, no longer viewing their bodies, minds, and souls through white lenses, and believing themselves capable of taking control of their destinies" (West, 1994:138). After psychic conversion, feelings of double-consciousness, victimization, and entitlement disappear.

No country in the world is inhabited by just one gender, one sexual orientation, one ability, one race, one religion, one social class, or one language group. Modern national borders do not match the fluid boundaries of the ancient world, so many countries include different nationalities or ethnic groups. Wars cause refugees to settle outside their areas. Even nations that were at one time fairly homogeneous have become more diverse because of increased immigrant and refugee populations from elsewhere. Many societies are facing the tensions brought about by prejudice, bigotry, avoidance, and privilege. The experience of double-consciousness and the need for psychic conversion are not limited to African-Americans. The challenge for pro-social capitalists is to eliminate prejudice and double-consciousness from within themselves and transition through psychic conversion.

Acknowledgment

Throughout the dialogue, teachers keep the discussions on topic and neutral. They monitor to make sure that pro-social communication norms are being followed, and highlight and reinforce insights and ideas as they are expressed by learners. They summarize, generalize, and draw conclusions. The outcome of the dialogue should be students' expanded acknowledgment of these and similar points:

- A history of injustice and prejudice is given in every culture and society.

- Past injustice, prejudice, and violence cannot be undone because the past cannot be changed.
- Injustice, violence, and prejudice can only be acknowledged in the present to make a post-prejudiced society.
- In a post-prejudiced society, the enemy is not the other but the conditions that perpetuate inequality, injustice, and violence, in the present and the future.
- In a post-prejudiced world, people are responsible for dismantling the structures that support inequality, injustice, and violence.

It may not be time to address the particular, the local feelings of inequality, injustice, or the historical trauma that must be healed. Dealing with historical trauma brings up complex emotions like blame and struggle. It is easy for the process to go wrong and reinforce stereotypes and prejudice or revictimize the targets. Revictimization means that a survivor of trauma becomes a victim again or feels like a victim again by having to revisit the trauma. The educator is now trying to create a safe place in which to discuss the historical trauma and potential reconciliation when participants are ready. The pedagogies of conflict transformation and tolerance lay the groundwork for dealing with historical trauma through pedagogies of remembrance.

Chapter 11

Remembrance

Although Hamdo [a witness] provided few new revelations about [the war crime], Judge McDonald was riveted by his testimony. The reason why she would never forget what he had to say, however, had nothing to do with [the crime] at all. It was due to the fact that Hamdo had been the principal of Bosnia's largest elementary school—its largest multiethnic school. The school had been integrated. It had graduated class after class of students, who had added their sums, played catch, elbowed their way through the lunch line. Its teachers, like Hamdo, had preached the lesson of brotherhood and unity. And still ethnic strife had erupted in [the town]?

[She asked,] "How could you explain some of the atrocities that we have heard that have been committed . . . Given your background, your experience, knowing that [everyone] lived together, went to school together, intermarried, how did that happen?"

Hamdo paused. "It's difficult to answer, this question," he replied. "I am also at a loss. I had the key to my next door neighbor's house who was a Serb and he had my key. That is how we looked after each other . . . Who bothered to destroy the health clinic, the school? . . . Most of this was done by my students, the students I was teaching about World War II, Tito's version of it. And that can mean only one thing: I was teaching all those generations about history the wrong way."

(McDonald, cited in Neuffer, 2001:184–5)

This quote comes from the Yugoslav War Crimes Tribunal. The American judge Gabriel Kirk McDonald, like many Americans, believed that violence between people in Bosnia went back centuries and she was surprised to learn that they had lived together peacefully for a long time. As an African-American, she had a special interest in understanding the issues. While she was interviewing Hamdo, she wondered whether all of her work for civil rights in the United States had been for nothing. She asked herself if sustainable harmonious multiethnicity was possible or impossible.

Under Tito, Yugoslavia enjoyed relative harmony among Slovenians, Croatians, Serbs, Macedonians, and Albanians. In schools, children were integrated under the banner of brotherhood and unity. The historical injustices and crimes that deeply divided Croats, Serbs, and Muslims were never dealt with. At the death of Tito, some politicians consolidated their power and territory by playing groups off against each other and demonizing Muslims. The result was the largest example of ethnic cleansing in a European country since the Second World War, as Muslims were exterminated and relocated. The world stood by while thousands were killed. In the aftermath, Judge McDonald wondered if divided societies would always face the threat of internal war.

Hamdo's realization that he had been teaching history the wrong way is crucial to any understanding of what happened. His life's work had been teaching the sanitized version of history that was demanded by the Yugoslav national school system, which preached brotherhood and unity despite the strong tensions and hatreds that existed. Yugoslavia was a deeply divided nation, but conflicts were swept under the rug; they were not acknowledged.

Bar-On (1989) interviewed almost fifty German children of Nazis and found that they were in an immense struggle to understand what had happened, to maintain a relationship with their Nazi fathers, and to build an identity with the past hanging over them. There was a lot of denial and distancing from the past. In the aftermath of the war, German schools ignored their history and allowed silence to drown out healing. Similarly, when I was teaching English in Spain during the time of Franco, my students told me that their history books stopped at 1939, with the victory over the communists. Many young Spaniards had no idea that Hitler had supported Franco and a fistfight broke out among the students when a Basque student brought it up. Forgetting can be an important political and social strategy to maintain a false façade of peace and to avoid dealing with prejudice and injustice.

In the last chapter, we saw that there is a universal aspect of prejudice and trauma in a poetics of relation, a turbulent creativity and tension "born of impacts and breaking" in which all humans seem connected. Yet this universality does not diminish the particular, the local. That is why teachers dealing with their own difficult historical memories need to look for ways to work through the traumas of the past. Teachers need to find local resources to help in the process of remembrance in the classroom. Much of my discussion here comes from the poetics of relation as it plays out in North America, as people attempt to deal with genocide of native peoples, slavery and ongoing racism, violence against women, and anti-Semitism and the Holocaust. In this chapter, I focus on remembrance of historical loss or trauma as a pedagogy of working through difficult conflictive emotions and memories so as to learn acceptance.

The Passage of Time

A primary concern for remembrance pedagogy is its timing in relation to the loss or trauma. The remembrance can be long after, shortly after, or very shortly after. In the first case, an event is remembered—that is, brought from the past into the present, across decades and possibly centuries, through sagas, histories, and myths. A trauma or loss thus becomes part of the cultural history of a people and it takes on a life of its own. Since the original event/loss has vanished, it is unknowable by present-day people and therefore its meaning and function are constructed by the culture of the day.

Each generation reinterprets a past event; that is the job of historians, folklorists, holy people, elders, and other cultural workers. In my lifetime the holiday Columbus Day has been re-remembered as Indigenous People's Day. It used to celebrate a prideful event for European-American culture, but now it commemorates the loss to native peoples of their land, culture, and languages. The strategic value of the name change is an important recognition and acknowledgment of different perspectives about the past.

Short-distance remembrance is a few generations removed from the trauma or loss. Survivors of trauma sometimes feel guilty about surviving when other people did not. They may have been psychologically damaged or emotionally numbed by their experiences and the effects of the trauma are passed down to their descendants. Children, grandchildren, or great-grandchildren may be affected by secondary emotions related to their parents' or grandparents' experience of turmoil, upheaval, fear, and prejudice. They too may feel guilty if they do not live up to their parents' expectations, if they assimilate to another culture, or if they do not carry on with vengeance. Remembrance for the descendants of survivors may be healing. Recently the President of Israel joined the President of Poland in commemorating the armed uprising against the Nazis of some of the inhabitants of the Warsaw ghetto in 1943. It was one of the few times that Jews actively resisted their deportation to death camps; so, although they lost, the event is a source of pride for relatives of those killed in the Holocaust.

Finally, a traumatic event like genocide or gynocide can be so recent as to be incomprehensible by the sufferers of the trauma. In shock and denial, they may be angry and vengeful. They know what happened but cannot understand it. Their loved ones are gone, often without a trace. Remembering, for them, is a way of trying to make sense of a trauma directly experienced and therefore it is a therapeutic process of working through traumatic events so as to comprehend them and go on living. This remembering is different because oftentimes the targets still live with the perpetrators and possibly still feel the immediate threat of terror.

Strategy

Remembrance is a conscious process of bringing a past event into the present. It can serve a variety of social, political, cultural, and personal functions. According to Simon, Rosenberg, and Eppert (2000:1–8), it is sometimes used for its political and social power to legitimize ethnocentric values in the population. The remembrance is a strategy to bring past glories, events, or heroes that possess noble qualities or achievements into the present, to enhance collective pride or esteem. Sometimes it is a way to honor lost ones or to heal survivors with a special monument or a holiday. Sometimes the remembrance is a way of reinforcing barriers between groups instead of removing them. Remembering is a value-laden political and sociocultural strategy.

A political system can recall and reinterpret stories of past traumas and indignities, sometimes centuries old, to strengthen nationalism, to reinforce stereotypes and prejudice, or to incite anxiety in people so that they support the regime. Mythological one-sided stories lend credence to a traditional enemy, a convenient notion for any government. There are splendid heroes and evil villains in the folklore. This is indoctrination, and education of and for fear.

Simon et al. (2000:1–8) also discuss another strategic use of remembrance based on the idea that "those who don't remember the past are doomed to repeat it." What is created in historical remembrance is an interpretation and depiction of the event, a history of facts and truths. There may be false comparisons, as when Milosevic is compared to Hitler or the Armenian genocide is compared to the Holocaust. Traumatic instances cannot be compared with each other because they are not similar. Traumatic events cannot be measured off against each other. The purpose of the strategy is to turn people away from prejudice and genocide, but the strategy does not work if it is superficial or perceived as indoctrination. It neither heals the psychic wounds that people still hold nor inspires empathy for those who went through the trauma.

Strategic ways of remembering sometimes fail to address the *voyeur effect*; that some people find depictions of death and cruelty fascinating and seductive. Rather than feeling shock, some people cannot look away. Ethnocentrism cultivates the voyeur effect, but historical remembrance usually ignores it. Strategic remembering also overlooks the potential for *revictimization*. Traumatized people or those who are descended from them may be retraumatized by the depictions in the remembrance. Furthermore, these methods sometimes do nothing to relieve the unhealed wounds that persist after the historical trauma.

Healing

Psychologists talk about "melancholia," in which individuals or groups experience loss or trauma, and instead of mourning and working through it, they *incorporate* the loss or wound into themselves. The trauma becomes part of their self-identity; they cannot relinquish it. This also happens at the national level. For instance, the Serbian defeat in the Battle of Kosovo in 1389 seems to have been incorporated as part of the Serbian psyche. Remembrance as healing is an attempt to get at that incorporated wound through dialogue, to work through it and let it go, whether it is at the individual or the national level.

Memorialization attempts to deal with pain and loss by creating a tangible memorial in the form of a monument, shrine, or museum, a space like a cemetery or a battlefield, or an event like a ceremonial reenactment, an apology, or a conference. The memorial is supposed to symbolize the meaning that the event or the loss has taken on in the culture and becomes a place or a time to mourn. Nevertheless, the symbolic nature of the memorial can be controversial and can take on different meanings (Rosenberg, 2000). There is also a danger that the completion of the memorial implies that the trauma is healed; that understanding of the event is complete and no further dialogue is necessary. A physical monument also becomes an important part of the history and mythology of the people and it too can be used strategically as well as therapeutically.

Memorialization can also be strategic in the sense that it may demonstrate a current government's or society's break with the past. For instance, the House of Terror in Budapest, Hungary, shows how the fascist and communist police oppressed the civilian population. The museum represents a repudiation of that history, a strategic "let's not let this happen again" message; also, through controversy, it provokes dialogue and, perhaps, healing. The museum contains names of targets and perpetrators; descendants of those targets and perpetrators are active in community life today. The challenge is to move through the trauma and loss to a different future.

The psychologist Staub, who spent his adult life researching the psychology of good and evil, describes how he was reluctant to go to a conference of people who survived the Holocaust as children by hiding or being hidden (Staub, 2003:470). He was such a child. He was hidden by a Christian family from the Nazis and the Hungarian Arrow Cross, and then his family was saved by Raoul Wallenberg, the Swedish diplomat in Budapest who saved thousands of Jews. Staub's interest in the heroic bystander comes from his experience. He suggested that his reluctance may have been because he did not want to revisit what he called the "dark times" of his wartime experience. At the conference, there were both speakers and small group dialogues which allowed the survivors to understand and share their experiences. In the end, Staub felt moved and uplifted by the conference and was glad that he went.

Counseling

It is quite easy to see the bystander effect in Rwanda. Despite all the rhetoric surrounding the United Nations Universal Declaration of Human Rights, the world stood by knowingly when another genocide began. Once it gained momentum, it could not be stopped. Ranck (2000) discusses the aftermath of the genocide and gynocide in Rwanda, during which humanitarian aid arrived in the form of counseling for post-traumatic stress disorder (PTSD), a syndrome identified by Western medicine and consisting of various symptoms which occur after something traumatic has happened, such as an accident, natural disaster, or attack. The most common symptoms are a re-experiencing of the event again and again in memory, avoidance of trigger situations, and emotional numbness.

There is a set of procedures that counselors use with PTSD, and the humanitarian aid from UNICEF trained local personnel to counsel survivors of the genocide/gynocide. This aid was well intentioned, but it was unclear if the procedures were culturally appropriate for Rwanda (Ranck, 2000). It seemed that local methods of healing were displaced. For one thing, PTSD is diagnosed and treated as a mental disorder, making it a medical problem instead of a social, political, or spiritual process that empowers people as they work through it. In the Western world, PTSD is considered a neurosis, something to be cured as quickly as possible with medication, discounting its potential for initiating a cultural transformation. In addition, some people find that counseling actually makes things worse, because it emphasizes the trauma or accentuates the negative emotions.

Staub and Pearlman (2003) went to Rwanda to train local facilitators to help victims of trauma after the genocide. They worked with a local Rwandan psychologist to come up with a program that integrated some outsider ideas with some local traditional ideas of healing. They trained a number of Tutsi and Hutu facilitators in the program and then had them work with survivors of the genocide. They also set up a program in which other facilitators used local traditional methods of healing with other survivors. Then they tested the survivors on various measures of reconciliation, taking care to make their trainings and tests culturally appropriate. They found that the facilitators who had the integrated training were more effective at reducing trauma and encouraging reconciliation among the survivors.

Their integrated training included, presumably as the Western components, content-based lectures on the origins of genocide and mass killing from difficult life experiences and the frustration of basic human needs, the psychological effects of genocide on survivors and perpetrators, and the stages of grief. They encouraged participants to engage in discussions with empathy. Unfortunately, Staub and Pearlman do not discuss the traditional Rwandan means of healing that were integrated into the program, although they did make sure that all of the content-based lectures and discussions were made relevant to Rwanda and its culture. During the training, the participants told powerful stories that they had not told before. They found that the participants were profoundly moved and healed by understanding why genocide happens and that it is a universal problem. The actions of the perpetrators seemed more comprehensible, although still horrible.

Truth Commissions

Truth commissions and war crimes tribunals are more recent attempts to remember the past in codified governmental processes that end in a product: a report or a trial record that memorializes the genocide or war. Both the processes and the products of truth commissions and war crimes tribunals have been criticized. Each can be part of a system of retributive justice. Zehr (1990) provides a good summary of the differences between retributive and restorative justice.

In *retributive justice*, the purpose of the process is to fix blame on guilty individuals who have broken the laws of a society. Justice is codified as a set of laws, and when laws are broken, the state assumes the role of accuser, and the target and the target's suffering are left aside. There is rarely any restitution to the target or the target's family. While the state attempts to prove that offenders are guilty of crimes, the offenders attempt to prove that they are innocent of those crimes or that there was justification for the crimes, so the process is very adversarial. The resolution is either freedom or a sentence in which the offender is punished by a fine or imprisonment. If a guilty offender is freed, there is no sense of justice. Remorse, repentance, and forgiveness are ignored. An offender who is found guilty is banished from society as a criminal.

In *restorative justice*, the focus is on problem-solving so that the future is different. An offense has been perpetrated on a member of a community; justice lies in restoring the relationship between the offender and the target. Targets get a chance to voice their truth and offenders attend, so the suffering is lamented and acknowledged. Offenders are given a chance to make things right with targets through some kind of restitution so that they can show remorse and get over feelings of guilt. The state is not really involved, except for facilitating the process of restoration. Repentance, forgiveness, and reciprocity are encouraged.

Retributive truth commissions or war crimes tribunals are not really meant to reach down to the bottom levels of society; they are designed to find those who are guilty and punish them. They are not designed for reconciliation among people; therefore, they are often not healing processes at all. Witnesses may be revictimized and there may be a voyeur effect. Retributive processes do not lead to a working through of trauma for healing. Discussing the Truth and Reconciliation Commission (TRC) in South Africa, Desmond Tutu put it like this:

> Those who brought to birth the TRC process also ought to be commended for their wisdom, which has recently been demonstrated no more clearly than by the trial of Dr. Wouter Basson. Without making any judgment on the correctness of the judge's decision, the case has shown clearly how inadequate the criminal justice system can be in exposing the full truth of, and establishing clear accountability for, what happened in our country. More seriously, we have seen how unsuccessful prosecutions lead to bitterness and frustration in the community. Amnesty applicants often confessed to more gruesome crimes than were the subject of the Basson trial, yet their assumption of responsibility, and the sense that at least people were getting some measure of truth from the process, resulted in much less anger. For the sake of our stability, it is fortunate that the kind of details exposed by the Commission did not come out in a series of criminal trials, which—because of the difficulty of proving cases beyond reasonable doubt in the absence of witnesses other than co-conspirators—most likely would have ended in acquittals.
>
> (Tutu, 2003:1–2)

In a restorative truth and reconciliation process, perpetrators take responsibility for their actions and truths are acknowledged, resulting in less anger. The outcomes of truth and reconciliation commissions are different from the outcomes of criminal trials. In the next chapter, we will see that restorative justice is related to reconciliation as well.

Pedagogies of Remembrance

Indigenous practices such as spirit work, exorcisms, sweat-lodges, and ancestor worship are means of remembering and healing that are in danger of cultural subtraction. To think of remembrance as pedagogy is to respect local ways of remembering, and bring them, as appropriate, into the classroom. In addition, English language teachers can turn to the study of history for transformative and transitional dialogue to lay ghosts of the past to rest and to envision a different future, one of relationship. Remembrance is a transitional pedagogy because it provides the transition from prejudice awareness as a "universal" through the particular historical trauma to the latency of reconciliation.

> Remembrance as a hopeful practice of critical learning extends to reworking notions of community, identity, embodiment, and

relationship. In effect, this reworking requires us to contemplate a revised notion of the political beyond conventional questions of power—questions, for example, of who gets to decide for whom what privileges, opportunities, and resources will be made available and withheld within any given community. While never disregarding this dimension of the political, what we are attempting to bring to the fore is the recognition that remembrance as learning fundamentally reconfigures a "politics of relationality." In saying this, by no means do we diminish the importance of contesting ongoing systemic structures of violence such as racism, sexism, and anti-Semitism. Rather, we emphasize that a politics of relationality is additionally needed, implicating us in an examination of how it is each of us listens, learns, and responds to those whose identities, bodies, and memories have been fundamentally impacted by such violences—impacts that cannot ever be reduced to versions of our own troubles and traumas.

(Simon et al., 2000:6)

Simon et al. say that remembrance is a critical pedagogy, a critical learning process that transforms our ideas of community, identity, and the self in relationship with others for a different future. This process situates agency not in the conventional political structure but in the orthogonal "politics of relationality." Remembrance as critical pedagogy emphasizes voicing and attending to, learning from, and acknowledging those who are suffering psychic wounds, without comparing them to those we may have suffered.

Mourning

Remembrance as a transitional pedagogy makes a place for mourning in the classroom. *Mourning* is a dialogue of working through the pain and loss to find meaning, relationship, and comprehension. Salverson (2000) recalls her experience writing a play about landmines for Canadian high school students to see. She distinguishes between mourning (or grieving) and melancholy. In mourning, people pass through stages like denial, anger, yearning, and vengeance to acceptance. In melancholy, the pain is incorporated or internalized as part of the self and acceptance is delayed or prevented. Acceptance of loss allows for contact between the mourner and those who are listening. Naming and experiencing pain and resistance in dialogue, not ignoring and incorporating them, in culturally appropriate ways may open the way to "surrender to the fact of loss" and contact with others. The isolation of the survivor is broken; reconciliation with others is imaginable.

> Working through . . . requires naming and experiencing (but not repetitively recycling) the shock of the encounter: anxiety, pain,

resistance. Working through is by no means a simple task, and, it may be argued, the task itself is never completed, nor is mourning completely distinguishable from melancholy. Attention to and consciousness of the task of working through, however, may make possible, or at least imaginable, an eventual surrender to the fact of loss; and, paradoxically, make equally possible movement toward a regaining of contact between the story (or story teller) and the listener, a contact that was previously made impossible by the preoccupation with the constitutional element that began the encounter—that of loss itself.

(Salverson, 2000:63)

Reinterpretation

Rinaldo Walcott, in his work with young blacks in the United States, attempts to have his students name and experience the social, cultural, and political power of "creolization" as the painful birth of a new people instead of the shame and defeat of slavery. This is a concept that would transform the thinking of white students as well. They cannot change the past, but they can reinterpret its meaning and make the transition to a different future.

This way of thinking about New World blackness means that slavery is not merely signaled as a moment of defeat for Africans. Instead, slavery also becomes a site for signaling the various possibilities for living human life differently and for demonstrating the dynamism of human cultures in their violent and pleasurable encounters. In this regard, creolization challenges us to consider how to think beyond the framework that renders the narrative of slavery as one of defeat, rage, and shame. But creolization also allows us to consider what it might mean to resignify rage, shame and defeat into mobilizing moments for the production of a new humanity. In this sense, history becomes a process of learning fraught with the risks of arriving at an elsewhere that cannot be known in advance.

(Walcott, 2000:146–7)

The pedagogy of remembrance is a difficult and risky road to choose. There is no clear method, no rules to follow, no certain outcome, but there are certain to be strong emotions of minimization, defense, resistance, blame, and anger. There is a danger of revictimization. For instance, when Walcott discusses the problems inherent in teaching young African-Americans about slavery, he notes that, if not done carefully, the cruel and humiliating details of the slave trade can cause modern young blacks to feel defeat and shame, not transformation. They feel immobilized, not energized. In a defensive reaction, they deny the cruel "facts" of their past, and look nostalgically for an alternative past in Africa, skipping over the trauma of diaspora.

Universality to Particularity

Some students are farther removed and their need to mourn may be less than their need to understand the past and gain a private perspective on it. The pedagogy of remembrance attempts to help students find their relationship with the past so that they can be engaged in the present in a different way. Baum worked with children of Holocaust survivors. Her concern was with literal as well as figurative "second generations," those who were children of survivors but also those who were not so directly involved but became involved through remembrance pedagogy. Both of these populations may feel resistance, shame, and guilt and need to work through their relationship to the past and to the present. She writes, "It seems to me that my students who speak of picturing themselves in the death camps are trying through the imagination to place themselves in relation to the Holocaust" (Baum, 2000:98).

For instance, in my own journey through remembrance, I learned about the bloody and misguided history of the United States, including slavery, genocide, relocation of peoples, and unjust wars fought overseas. This process brought up ambivalence, resistance, and guilt. My first inclination was to deny that it had anything to do with me. Then, although my own ancestors were not directly involved, I needed to recognize that I am the beneficiary of stolen land, slave labor used in building the prosperity of my country, and exploitation/murder of people in other countries. Resistance and guilt became responsibility and regret. There are some positives to this poetics of relation. My country is now enriched by having a multitude of people and cultures, including hybrid ones that do not exist elsewhere. I cannot do anything about the past, but I can do something about the present and the future.

In the example of my students grappling with prejudice and trauma discussed in the last chapter, we started out with an example of remembrance of trauma in a neutral place to them. Then students remembered their own peoples' historical experiences of trauma. The Japanese and the Korean students, because they valued their relationship as classmates, were able to move beyond the guilt or pain to another psychic space that allowed them to take responsibility for a different future.

Voice and Attention

Remembrance as a transitional pedagogy does not have a prescribed method, sequence, or procedure to follow. However, like many critical pedagogies, it usually starts with some kind of object, activity, person, or piece of writing as a key that opens the way through desensitivity, numbness, and denial. Objects might be a photo or a monument, a relic owned by a survivor, a visit to a museum, or a novel. Liss (2000) discusses seeing in a museum a railroad boxcar that had been used to transport Jews to the concentration and extermination camps and the emotional response it evoked. An activity might be writing and performing a role play or dance in which characters are structural devices to show common attitudes. It might be a ritual cleansing or exorcism. It might be a visit to a museum like the Museum of Communism in Prague or a carefully preserved but weirdly clean and empty concentration camp in Germany. Sometimes survivors are willing to share their memories with others.

Novels, dramas, and poems by survivors or their descendants remembering their historical trauma and working through it can challenge traditional histories or rumors that students may have heard. Writings from traditional or sacred texts, koans, moral dilemmas, and the like can also be used. Several contradictory texts from different perspectives might present paradoxes for participants. I believe that teachers should admit their own relationship to the key, especially areas of resistance or lack of shared memory. In my case, I could claim Martin Luther King as a fellow American, but I could not remember for the students the experience of racism or slavery. It would not be authentic, so I tried to find a more authentic representation of that point of view. I could admit my experience of privilege and my pain of living in a racist culture and society, but I could not remember and relate the experience of victimization. The video about racism (see p. 161) opened the way to remembrance of being oppressed and being an oppressor.

Recall also the use of narratives and storytelling as means of getting at cultural resources for conflict transformation. Likewise, autobiographical journaling or storytelling is useful for people to understand trauma and loss, if culturally appropriate. Students may write or speak in response to such questions as: What happened? How do I feel about what happened? What does the event mean to me? What wisdom can I gain from this experience? Writing is more confidential and thus less threatening, perhaps, than speaking out loud. Teachers need to decide how much information they will read, if any, and how much might be shared with classmates. They need permission before disseminating anything a student has written.

Norms of communication must be established by the students with the assistance of the teacher. The guidelines are similar to those laid down in the pedagogy of tolerance and conflict transformation and are also formative. People need to find ways to talk to others about their own and others' historical trauma without fear. In discussion, students are never forced to contribute. They most certainly need to be allowed to pass their turn.

Not Reconciliation

The pedagogy is meant to open a path through feelings of minimization, denial, and resistance so that participants work through struggle, blame, and anger. However, participants have the choice of whether or not to work through their feelings. They have a choice about how fast and far they want to go if they decide to do so. A space must be created for those who refuse. This is what makes remembrance different from reconciliation. In a process of reconciliation, only those who self-select for potential reconciliation should be involved. There is more about this in the next chapter.

Another difference between remembrance pedagogy and reconciliation is that remembrance may take place within one ethnic group or one type of survivor. It might be a group of women who have experienced gynocide or it might be a group of former East Germans coming to terms with their history. Because people remember and name their traumas best in a safe place, teachers need to place limits on who is included. It is not necessary for remembrance to take in a variety of conflict partners, as it is for reconciliation. Remembrance is a more inward-looking process, whereas reconciliation is outward-looking, towards the other in a relationship. Within the pedagogy of remembrance, struggle, blame, double-consciousness and other attitudes are named and brought into awareness without judgment. They must be accepted as part of the history of trauma. For many people, but not for all, it is only through struggle and blame that they begin to see the potential for a different attitude, freed from such cultural baggage as oppressor and oppressed. It is only then that reconciliation can come out of latency.

Not Indoctrination

Teachers need to be prepared to learn from students; they are not presenting the "truth." They do not indoctrinate students with their version of events. It is a process of learning that teachers initiate and facilitate, but cannot dictate where it will go. They are limited to highlighting certain insights over others, remarking on paradoxes and contradiction, accepting ambivalence and uncertainty, summarizing important conflicts and breakthroughs, and reflecting on their own relationship with the discussion, the students, the key, writing, and the process. Throughout the pedagogy, teachers assist and take part in the mourning. They direct students away from melancholia and incorporation by explaining what it is. They help students liberate themselves from the past.

Acknowledgment

At a certain point, some of the students may feel free to explore their own ancestry and history with some objectivity. They feel neither power over nor power under others. Without prejudice or feelings of victimization, they are willing to channel their pain, loss, and anger into agency for dismantling social injustice and constructing a tolerant society. Not all students get to this point. That is to be expected if the process is truly free. When students can own their past truthfully, they realize that they can do nothing about it. They understand that they can only do something about the present and the future. They mourn their loss but they can go on. They liberate themselves from melancholia; they let go of the incorporated trauma.

At first tentatively and then more automatically, they take responsibility for carrying out the personal, professional, and institutional changes that eliminate positioning over or positioning under. As active bystanders, they speak up against injustice. Whenever they see bias or prejudice, they identify it without fear and resistance, even in themselves. They take personal and group responsibility for stopping the behavior even at personal cost. As principled dissidents, they refuse to listen to those who would incite them to violence. They do not avoid people of other groups; they function as multicultural people within the dominant society. They are pro-social capitalists because they imagine a different reality in the future.

When students see society, not people, as flawed, they realize that their enemy is not the other; the enemy is injustice and violence. They are willing to work together in inclusive coalitions to prevent, through a just peace, the potential for genocide, ethnic cleansing, and gynocide in the future. They are open to a latency, potential affiliation, species identity, and reconciliation with the other. To help them, communities can develop a culturally appropriate infrastructure for healthy grieving and remembrance.

Hamdo, the history teacher and witness in the War Crimes Tribunal in Yugoslavia, realized that he had been teaching history the wrong way. Grieving prejudice and historical trauma were thwarted and proscribed by the official curriculum of brotherhood and unity. Transitional pedagogies of remembrance offer other ways of teaching history, ways that have a chance of healing the wounds that otherwise fester, and a hope of reconciliation.

Chapter 12

Reconciliation

We have been privileged to help to heal a wounded people, though we ourselves have been, in Henri Nouwen's profound and felicitous phrase, "wounded healers." When we look around us at some of the conflict areas of the world, it becomes increasingly clear that there is not much of a future for them without forgiveness, without reconciliation. God has blessed us richly so that we might be a blessing to others. Quite improbably, we as South Africans have become a beacon of hope to others locked in deadly conflict that peace, that a just resolution, is possible. If it could happen in South Africa, then it can certainly happen anywhere else. Such is the exquisite divine sense of humor.

(Tutu, 2003:2)

Tutu sees the need for reconciliation and forgiveness if we are to have a future without war, oppression, and genocide. He acknowledges the paradox that South Africa, so long a cruel example of repression and apartheid, is now a "beacon of hope" to the rest of the world. The hope is that injustice and oppression can be overturned peacefully. With justice restored, people long at odds are free to reconcile. This happened because both Nelson Mandela and F.W. de Klerk were able to see reason and want a different future for their country. They shared the Nobel Peace Prize. Perhaps because they themselves were wounded healers, they were able to lead their country to a preferred future. It did not happen overnight. There were political changes, criminal justice trials, and a long truth and reconciliation process which addressed emotional and cultural needs for acknowledgment and responsibility.

Reconciliation, in essence, represents a dialogic place where people meet in species identity to address their concerns about the past, the present, and the future. People acknowledge the past and let it go. They tell their stories, talk about the facts of the conflict, the systemic nature of it, and how it impacts their lives in the present. They try to envision a different future and brainstorm how they can work for that. People balance pessimism and optimism, tradition and innovation, independence and interdependence.

Lederach (2004) describes what he learned about reconciliation in Nicaragua; it is the meeting place of truth, mercy, justice, and peace. There must be truth: honesty, revelation, clarity, open accountability, and vulnerability. There must be mercy: compassion, forgiveness, acceptance, healing, and a new start for a healthy relationship. There must be justice: making things right, creating equal opportunity, rectifying the wrong, and possibly restitution. There must be peace: harmony, unity, well-being, respect, and security. Reconciliation addresses emotions to meet needs. "The immediacy of hatred and prejudice, of racism and xenophobia, as primary factors and motivators of the conflict means that transformation must be rooted in social-psychological and spiritual dimensions that traditionally have been seen as either irrelevant or outside the competency of international diplomacy" (Lederach, 2004:29).

Reconciliation is a place of paradoxes. People confront the past to free themselves for a new future. They become vulnerable in order to be stronger. They expose wounds so that they can disappear. They work through wrongs in order to put them aside. They take responsibility in order to be free of guilt. They accept responsibility for going along with violence in order to have personal peace. They acknowledge that they were passive bystanders in order to become active agents of change. They admit their own complicity in oppression in order to resist it. They legitimize a relationship with another in order to build and repair it.

Reconciliation is not remembrance. Remembrance is a process in which people begin to resolve their difficult emotions, where they begin to understand the past, and where they gain some perspective on their responsibilities and regrets. People often prefer to remember in a very safe place, so remembrance is often located among a common group of survivors or a second generation. In contrast, reconciliation must involve the reconciliation partners, those whose relationship is broken.

Restorative Justice

There can be little reconciliation among individuals without restorative justice because relationships cannot be repaired until power is balanced. Restorative justice repairs relationships between two people or groups who may be both targets and offenders. It means that people tell their stories to each other, acknowledge truths and facts, and agree to a different present and future.

Recall that restorative justice is quite different from conventional notions of retributive justice. Zehr (1990) says that in a process of restorative justice, the offenses violate people and relationships; justice aims at identifying needs and obligations so that things can be made right; justice encourages dialogue, acknowledgment, and mutual agreement; it gives targets and offenders central roles; it is judged by the extent to which responsibilities are assumed, needs are met, and healing (of individuals and relationships) is encouraged. Thus, restorative justice repairs reciprocity. Native American cultures, Japan, and the Maori in New Zealand have restorative justice procedures.

Restorative justice also requires a change in the way we view the accountability of offenders. For instance, retributive justice holds that offenses create guilt, that people are either guilty or not guilty, and that the guilt is indelible but can be paid by discharging a debt to society and taking punishment. In restorative justice, offenses create liabilities and obligations in which there are degrees of responsibility, and guilt is removable through repentance and reparation, through making the debt right to the target, and through taking responsibility.

The process of restorative justice empowers and transforms both the offender and the target. (And recall that in many cases the targets are also offenders and offenders are targets.) The target is the first concern of the process, followed by the target–offender relationship, followed by problem-solving about the present needs and future intentions. Targets are empowered because they become central to the process of justice and their needs and vulnerabilities are of primary concern. Offenders are empowered because they learn of their connection to others. They become aware that their attitudes and behaviors have repercussions that affect others and they learn empathy for others. They take responsibility for their actions and are accountable not to some impersonal state organization but to the very people who are potentially harmed.

Under most current systems, the state punishes offenders by putting them in prison, but this does not necessarily help them understand the damage that they have done to the target or accept their responsibility for what they did. The relationship between the target and offender must be concrete to the offender, who must be involved in a process of problem-solving to repair, insofar as possible, the relationship. Also, reconciliation sometimes involves people who have so far not offended but who belong to groups that do offend. They are offenders because of their membership in a sociocultural network that distributes guilt by association.

Zehr does not rule out the need for punishment in restorative justice, but he argues that it should not be central and normative. It should be fair and controlled and applied in an honest way; that is, without ulterior motives. In addition, Zehr notes that direct interactions between the targets of violence and their perpetrators may not be possible. In those cases, it works better to have targets and perpetrators of different offenses interact, so that they can understand each other better while avoiding severe emotional trauma and pain for the target. This is especially the case if remembrance has not paved the way for restorative justice and reconciliation.

Stages of Reconciliation

Peck (1987) describes stages of community in *The Different Drum: Community Making and Peace.* He outlines a sensitivity- or consciousness-raising process in which the members of the group give up their preconceived notions and expectations to meld together as one. When adapted to the classroom, the four stages Peck identifies also become relevant to reconciliation.

Pseudocommunity

Pseudocommunity describes a group in which members attempt to be pleasant to one another no matter what in order to smooth over conflict, rather than dealing with it. They keep their opinions, needs, and wants well hidden. People in pseudocommunity stay in denial about the reality of annoyances and conflicts; they respond to them by changing the subject and being polite. The members of a pseudocommunity are often minimizers and quitters, pretending that everyone's experiences, values, and motivations are the same and ignoring prejudice and privilege. The resulting culture can be superficially pleasant but also stagnating, repressive, and unable to change. Sometimes the conflicts are not avoided but rather stockpiled until an explosion occurs which cannot be smoothed over. Pseudocommunity does not describe an interdependent group where people anticipate conflicts and change their behavior to resolve them. It describes a group that avoids and ignores conflict and differences and does nothing to work through them.

Chaos

Chaos describes a group facing a conflict or crisis. Suddenly people are not the same as before; politeness no longer works. Some people struggle to go back to pseudocommunity, while others fight for change or to have their views accepted. According to Peck, a group in chaos is an improvement over pseudocommunity because there is a potential for authentic change as group members become aware of differences and injustices. They have gone through a process of conscientization. But a group in chaos is uncreative and even destructive because it cannot deal with conflict. Therefore, the conflict during chaos is tedious and frustrating as members argue about petty details and side issues or attack each other. They blame their leader because chaos must be the result of bad leadership. They come up with a new system of rules or a new structure to fix the problems. A group in chaos often slips back into pseudocommunity because it is safer and easier simply to hide the issue again in the hope that it will go away. As a result, communities sometimes move back and forth between chaos and pseudocommunity.

Emptiness and Healing

Emptiness comes about, according to Peck, when members empty themselves of such barriers to communication as feelings, assumptions, ideas, and motives. In dialogue, people give up their hidden expectations, prejudices, or the need to fix or control others. They voice their needs and others attend to them and acknowledge them. Truth, mercy, justice, and peace emerge during this third stage.

The last stage is a *healing* sense of community that transforms individuals in the group. Relationships are created or repaired so that people feel reciprocity and interdependence. Participants can envision the possibility of a different future.

The School for Peace

Neve Shalom/Wahat Al-Salam is a decades-old cooperative community in Israel where Jews and Palestinians have been living in peaceful coexistence. The town is a political, social, cultural, and emotional experiment in what dialogue and cooperation can do. In this town there is an elementary school for Christians, Jews, and Muslims to teach and learn together in a fully bilingual, bicultural, and binational setting. Since 1979, there has also been a "School for Peace," which brings together Jewish and Palestinian teenagers for workshops conducted by trained facilitators. By the year 2000, more than 20,000 teens had attended the workshops at the School for Peace (Feuerverger, 2001:xviii).

Grace Feuerverger describes a three-day reconciliation workshop for Israeli and Palestinian teenagers. Her discussion is somewhat marred by her thinking that it was a conflict resolution process instead of a reconciliation process. Nevertheless, her careful description is insightful. The participants came from a society so deeply divided that one cannot call it a single society. The teens knew little about each other and were understandably somewhat fearful of what the process would do. However, by the end of the three days, healing had begun to occur. An Israeli participant said: "We're both drowning in quicksand next to each other, but can we stretch out our hands to one another or will we sink in the mud with our raised fists?" (Feuerverger, 2001:111). A Palestinian participant said:

> Something in me has changed. We may not have solved the problem, but I come away with a real treasure—my heart is now filled with less hatred and instead there is a greater understanding of how complicated this conflict is. I saw what's behind the mask of my enemy. I think the process has to start from here.
>
> (Feuerverger, 2001:111)

The First Day

Feuerverger calls the first day "Narratives of Vulnerability." The morning began with icy silence; everyone was very nervous. At the same time there was a latency:

> It was a moment heavy with waiting, but open with infinite possibilities. There was so much meaning in this silence of brooding and pain . . . It was a sublime moment of perfect symmetry—a moment at which everything stood before us, where we could make or break anything. It was a moment of awe.
>
> (Feuerverger, 2001:96)

A facilitator went over the schedule and spoke reassuringly about what would happen. Students would receive information about each other and on the conflict between them. Some basic ground rules were that there were no expectations and that differences were to be acknowledged from the beginning. In the first discussions, many Jewish participants tried to avoid divisive political issues because they were painful and threatening. The participants were caught up in pseudocommunity. After a while, a Palestinian participant became a dissident, saying that if they did not talk about real issues, the workshop would be a waste of time. His complaint "opened a window onto an agenda for real dialogue about living in a state of war and terror" (Feuerverger 2001:97).

The group went into the chaos stage. The participants exhibited a lot of difficult feelings during this discussion. When one Jewish participant admitted to seeing people in terms of stereotypes, some of the other Jewish participants tried to make him feel like a traitor and silence him. There were other frustrations and power struggles between individuals and groups. People told their stories of war. The main issue that caused division came down to the Palestinians' need for legitimacy and recognition—they needed the Jews to admit that they were oppressing them. But that did not happen on the first day.

Throughout the day's discussion, the facilitators continually legitimized participants' anxieties and fears. They put a label on them and brought them into consciousness. They named the conversational strategies that participants used to silence one another or to stay in safe territory. They did not let any one person or group dominate and were careful to ask for comments from everyone. During the day, Feuerverger noted, although nothing was resolved, the participants began to socialize more freely with each other during the breaks and meals.

The Second Day

The next morning the participants did various cooperative activities to explore typical conflicts, like a Palestinian mother crying over her child killed by Israeli soldiers or an Israeli Jew on a bus in Jerusalem attacked by terrorists. Participants got into groups of four and each recounted a conflict they had had. One of these conflicts was selected to be dramatized in role play. After half an hour's preparation, the groups presented their plays. These served to highlight the complexity of the conflict between Palestinians and Jews. The raw wounds and fears were in plain view. This was part of the chaos. It was at this point that the facilitators began to model the reconciliation techniques that had been developed for their workshops. They explored the conflict through the experiences that came up in the discussion. The facilitators did not just teach reconciliation; they lived it in their context.

The facilitators came back often to the central question of the mutual failure to acknowledge the legitimacy of the other. The power struggles in the workshop mirrored the power struggles outside. As Feuerverger watched, she saw the process empower the participants individually and as members of a group, but they were also empowered "as a group of human beings whose purpose it is to examine the thorny issues that bar the road to peace" (Feuerverger, 2001:104).

The Third Day

When people's struggles are not acknowledged by the other, they feel like targets all over again. In Israel, two stories of victimization collide with each other. The Jews have been victims down through the centuries, including the Holocaust. Then they victimized and still victimize the Palestinians. At present Israeli Jews and Palestinians are locked in a deep conflict of reciprocal causation with many sociocultural, psychological, and emotional wounds on both sides. Feuerverger (2001:105) calls mutual victimization the hidden "ghost" that haunts each interaction between Jew and Arab. It accompanies the Jewish need for acknowledgment as a national identity and nation-state in the Middle East. It accompanies the Palestinian need for legitimization as a national minority in their homeland.

The third day brought more stories of victimhood. The Jewish and Palestinian teenagers slowly began to recognize the legitimacy of each other's nationality and political movements, and the possibility of equal dialogue began to emerge into actuality. Facilitators encouraged the teens to move beyond pain and into empathy for the other. It became a safer place for them to admit problematic emotions. Feuerverger (2001:106) notes that "In this site of authentic negotiation participants are encouraged to abandon any pretense to a fixed truth about their views of each other—

and the concrete structures of their mistrust and anxieties thus begin to crumble." The participants were moving from chaos to emptiness. The emptiness was soon filled with stories of injury, loss, and death, where both sides began to see that they had a common inheritance of exile, violence, displacement, and diaspora.

Through dialogue and journal-writing the participants began to understand their relationship with their past and their present, and the search for justice. They "inspected their individual, familial, and cultural differences to find that within these differences they actually have something in common" (Feuerverger, 2001:107). There was a great deal of critical reflection on identity, self-worth, and purpose. In sharing their journals, they heard the voice of the other so that they could retell their own stories from a different point of view. There were several organizational factors that made these workshops successful.

Organization

There were two well-trained and experienced facilitators, one Israeli and one Palestinian. They created a safe and nonjudgmental setting and attempted to build a sense of community and respect for others. Facilitators were careful to keep to an equal use of Arabic and Hebrew. Ordinarily, there is great asymmetry in language use. Feuerverger (2001:94) says,

> A great obstacle to meaningful contact continues to be the asymmetrical relationship between Hebrew and Arabic in Israel. Although both are considered to be official languages, Hebrew is, in fact, the dominant language in the country. Most Palestinians are bilingual, but many feel an emotional ambivalence toward Hebrew language competence because this may represent a sense of betrayal regarding their Arab national identity . . . Furthermore, most Jews in Israel do not have a strong command of Arabic.

Another way to achieve language equality is to use a third language, like English. Further, the participants were to develop "communication and negotiation skills to be used in interpersonal and intergroup situations within the teaching/learning environments of Israeli school" (Feuerverger, 2001:87).

There were three full days of encounters and participants stayed together at night in youth hostals. If there was one criticism of the reconciliation it was that it did not have enough follow-up afterwards. The process was created by the School for Peace along with psychology professors from an Israeli university. It was structured on American models of conflict resolution, including active listening, conversational strategies, reflection, role plays, and the like, and based on "intensive experiential knowledge in social and psychological intergroup processes, specifically designed for the Jewish–Palestinian workshop context" (Feuerverger, 2001:103).

The school received support from donations but the workshops themselves were supported by the Israeli Ministry of Education. Teachers who took part in these workshops received in-service training credits, which presumably translated into better pay or positions. There were varied formats for the reconciliation groups in the encounter. Some were uninational groups which met certain emotional needs and some were binational in which the numbers of each nation were equal and each group's needs were balanced.

Acknowledgment

Reconciliation is not conflict transformation even though the facilitators in this case had been trained to use independent conflict resolution methods and that is what they modeled and did. It is not conflict resolution because there can be no resolution of the conflict between Israeli Jew and Palestinian until the inequities of the systems and structures are resolved. What happened in the School for Peace was a process of reconciliation between (potential) targets and offenders, leading to a better understanding of the past and present in order to envision a different future. The crucial issue in reconciliation is the power of acknowledgment. After legitimacy is given to claims of suffering and injustice, relationships can be repaired and reconciled even when inequities are not yet addressed.

Pedagogies of Reconciliation

The School of Peace was a multi-ethnic reconciliation that used a process from the cultura franca, in this case conflict resolution procedures that were taught to both the Israeli and the Palestinian teenagers as a way for them to dialogue pro-socially during the meeting but also to be a resource for them in the future as pro-social communicative competence. The method had been adapted for local norms and situations. It followed a normative process that is adapted for teachers below.

Prescription

The English language teacher leads a three-part process using normative pro-social communication with students who wish to reconcile. In the first part, the teacher attempts to get the participants to recognize their part in injustice, offense, or violation and to take responsibility for it. Teachers encourage them to state the facts of what happened, how they felt about it, and the impact of the violation using I-statements. Others attend carefully and ask open-ended questions for clarification or for further information. In attending to each other, they realize the wrong that was done and how it had repercussions in the life of others. At some point, they accept responsibility for the violation. In the School of Peace, the offenses, injustice, and violations were (presumably) at some remove from the actual participants but both were involved because of their affiliations to groups. Their offenses were reciprocal. This type of process might work in the case of bullying, when conflict resolution is inappropriate.

In the next stage, the teacher assists the learners in finding a way to make the violation right. This may mean that the offenders apologize or pay certain damages or that they do something for the target in the form of work or help. The purpose is to restore equity in the relationship. In the School of Peace, equity was restored with the mutual acknowledgment of national status and rights.

In the third stage, learners make their future intentions explicit. They express their intentions in order to restore a sense of trust and to assure the targets that the offense will not occur again. The outcome is sometimes a written "contract" that states the conditions of the reconciliation. In the case of the School of Peace, there was no contract; however, participants did write and share journal entries that alluded to changes in their feelings and increased levels of understanding and trust.

Elicitation

Traditional methods of reconciliation and conflict transformation do not work everywhere. An elicitive approach uses various methods (observation, discussion, narrative analysis, role plays, word cards and storyboards) to get at local cultural resources and language for reconciliation. Teachers might start with these themes to elicit concepts, resources, and processes: relationship(s), preferred futures, repair, pro-social capitalists, resources, process, dialogue, attention, acknowledgment, apology, reparations, and commitment. Working with other teachers and learners, they explore additional local resources and themes for reconciliation. They may study a reconciliation that took place elsewhere to compare alternative processes of voicing, attention, and acknowledgment.

For instance, Farah (1993) discusses a Somali inter-clan reconciliation. Women were able to cross clan boundaries because they could travel freely from their clan of marriage to their clan of birth. Clan elders could also meet with elders from other clans. These cross-cutting relationships created a space in which inter-clan fighting could be stopped and discussions started. A series of intra-clan dialogues about grievances, issues, and reparations took place so that people could understand and acknowledge what was going on. Then numerous inter-clan consultations took place in which there was further dialogue but no decisions were reached. These meetings established a framework for a reconciliation process: a six-month-long peace forum marked by late night sessions with long speeches and poetry. At the end of the forum, the reparations were made.

Chapter 13

Forgiveness

> Whenever anger is about to come, you can train yourself to see the object of your anger in a different light. Any person or circumstance which causes anger is basically relative; seen from one angle it makes you angry, but seen from another perspective you may discover some good things in it. We lost our country, for example, and became refugees. If we look at our situation from that angle, we might feel frustration and sadness, yet the same event has created new opportunities—meeting with other people from different religious traditions, and so on. Developing a more flexible way of seeing things helps us cultivate a more balanced mental attitude.
>
> (Rinpoche, 2005:26)

Gyalwa Rinpoche, the Dalai Lama of Tibet, teaches Buddhist mind training in which people learn to discern whether their thoughts are positive or negative and reduce the negative thoughts of hate, anger, fear, vengefulness. When negative thoughts go away, a vacuum is created that positive thoughts of love, courage, and forgiveness can fill. In this quote, he explains how forgiveness works: before letting yourself get angry, change your thoughts. Becoming balanced and flexible makes people more forgiving.

Some people forgive and receive forgiveness by confessing the offense to a divine being or to a religious worker, perhaps doing some penance, and then they are made right and clean through forgiveness. Some faith groups have holidays or festivals of repentance and renewal which allow people to reflect on what they have done and vow to do better in the future. Some have prayers and meditations for sending out thoughts of loving-kindness to family, friends, enemies, and the world, ritual bathing or sprinkling of holy water or milk to symbolize the purity of forgiving and being forgiven.

The point is that spirituality often deals with repentance and forgiveness honestly and productively, but in the secular world there are few rituals or routines for it yet. There are not even many norms of communication having to do with forgiveness. The whens, whys, and hows of apology are quite different from place to place. Global civic culture should draw upon resources from forgiving cultures and develop innovative ways to help people forgive.

Choice

The Dalai Lama reminds us that when an offense has occurred between people, they have options. They can attempt to transform the conflict into a learning experience by using it as a basis for transformative dialogue of voice and attention. They can work through feelings of superiority and privilege or victimization and entitlement to reduce feelings of prejudice that may linger. They can remember the event so as to let it go, without incorporation. They can reconcile with others and repair the relationship through acknowledgment, recognition, and responsibility. They may, if they wish, forgive. All of these processes are related to each other, but they are not the same. It is possible, for instance, to reconcile and repair a relationship without complete forgiveness or to forgive without completely repairing the relationship. This chapter begins with a discussion of several different types, or perhaps degrees, of forgiveness. Later, we will look at the complex business of pedagogies of forgiveness.

Proactive Forgiveness

In the quote above, the Dalai Lama talks about *proactive forgiveness*, based on detachment and non-dissension because, when people manage their anger over time, they become slower and less prone to take offense. Insults and irritations are simply deflected away because they are not important. People notice slights and might remark on them, but they do not feel angry or hurt. Recall that this is a kind of interdependent agency where people adjust their emotions and behavior in order not to have a conflict with another.

> Forgiveness is a skill. The more you forgive, the easier it gets. Practice really does make perfect. Of course, forgiveness is more than a skill—it is an attitude of goodwill and a moral virtue that develops. It even becomes part of your identity, part of who you are, as you begin to incorporate it into your life. Forgiveness has a way of transforming your character and relationships as you understand it and practice it.
> (Enright and Fitzgibbons, 2000:74)

Responsive Forgiveness

The Dalai Lama discusses another kind of forgiveness, called *responsive forgiveness*. This is what people do after they have felt anger. When something bad happens to them, if, for example, they are evicted from their home and country, they try to see what good may have come from the experience. The Dalai Lama feels that this created opportunities to meet with others instead of staying isolated in Tibet. From the Western perspective, contact with the Dalai Lama himself and other Tibetans since the middle of the last century has allowed for greater understanding of Buddhism, nonviolence, and non-dissension in the West.

It is no coincidence that Western psychologists and doctors began studying meditation and mind training in the latter half of the twentieth century. In the 1980s, it even became permissible to research forgiveness. Researchers now tell us that forgiveness is good for people's mental and physical health and well-being. Tibetans have known that for centuries; it is their "national character, formed by cultural and religious values that stress the importance of mental peace through the generation of love and kindness to all other living sentient beings, both human and animal" (Rinpoche, 2005:18).

The Dalai Lama's strategy was to turn away from frustration over the loss of his homeland by seeing it from the perspective of the good that came from it. This is not easy for ordinary people to do once they have felt angry. Marietta Jaeger, whose daughter Susie was murdered, describes what happens if people let anger engulf them.

> Victim families have every right initially to the normal, valid, human response of rage, but those persons who retain a vindictive mind-set ultimately give the offender another victim. Embittered, tormented, enslaved by the past, their quality of life is diminished. However justified, our unforgiveness undoes us. Anger, hatred, resentment, bitterness, revenge—they are death-dealing spirits, and they will "take our lives" on some level as surely as Susie's life was taken. I believe that the only way we can be whole, healthy, happy persons is to learn to forgive.
> (Quoted in Enright and Fitzgibbons, 2000:14)

Unlike the Dalai Lama, and perhaps showing a more typically Western reaction, Jaeger says that when people suffer trauma, they have a right to react with anger. Then they have a choice to go through a process of mourning and remembering their loss, and either relinquishing it or incorporating it into their self-concept as melancholia. If they incorporate the wound, they become embittered. Sometimes, when they see how they were complicit in the abuse, they feel shame. Ultimately they revictimize themselves as they obsess about revenge and their need for acknowledgment or restitution.

However, because our resentment and anger give the offender power over us, letting go of resentment towards others leads to inner peace. If we continue to be wounded by the past, the incorporated wound festers and the offense takes over our lives. Forgiveness, on the other hand, is empowering, because we move from being a target to being a survivor. Zehr (1990:47) puts it like this: "Forgiveness . . . allows the experience to become part of one's life story, part of one's biography in an important way, but without letting it continue to control." The agency that it takes for people to maintain their anger and resentment can be redirected more productively. Seeking revenge and venting emotions are not good ways to heal.

Resentment and blame are obstacles to repairing a relationship. Forgiveness is a healing process for the individuals involved and also for the relationship. Forgiveness does not involve forgetting, letting people off the hook, or minimizing the offense. It does not eliminate responsibility for the future. In true forgiveness people recognize the damage to the relationship and commit to rebuilding it if possible. They remember the offense but do not incorporate it. They see offenders as fellow humans, without demonizing them. They mentally separate the person from the offense and imagine what the offenders were going through or what they may have felt.

Discipline

Forgiveness is hard because after people perceive something as a threat or offense, whether real or imagined, they feel afraid and angry. The sense of endangerment triggers a surge of chemicals that make people ready to react defensively or run away by providing a short-term rush of energy. At the same time, our nervous systems release long-lasting chemicals to keep our emotions aroused for quite a while after the first trigger. It is the combination of the trigger and the long-term arousal that makes people prone to anger when they have been provoked earlier. Stress and anxiety of any kind create a state of constant arousal. When people become enraged, one trigger sets the stage for the next in an escalating succession of chemical surges which overpower reason. People explode into violence because they are beyond all reasoning. Forgiving offenders in such cases is difficult because it is like closing the barn door after the cows have escaped. Anger and fear are already activated in the brain and people need to find a way to overcome them in order for healing to take place. The forgiving process must literally remove the effects of brain chemicals.

Marietta Jaeger gives a short but powerful account of how she was able to forgive the murderer, a serial killer, of her seven-year-old child, Susie. She writes about her experience with disciplined forgiveness:

I've heard people say that forgiveness is for wimps. Well, I say then that they must never have tried it. Forgiveness is hard work. It demands diligent self-discipline, constant corralling of our basest instincts, custody of the tongue, and a steadfast refusal not to get caught up in the mean-spiritedness of our times. It doesn't mean we forget, we condone, or we absolve responsibility. It does mean that we let go of the hate, that we try to separate the loss and the cost from the recompense or punishment we deem is due. This is what happened to me, all that I had been working for, as I heard, for the first time, this man's voice in my ear—and neither of us was expecting it.

(Quoted in Enright and North, 1998:12)

The killer had called Marietta on the phone, smug and taunting. As she communicated her forgiveness, he wept and lowered his defenses enough to give some clues to his identity, and as a result he was later caught and convicted. (It is paradoxical that one forgiving phone call accomplished what a year of criminal investigation could not.)

To forgive, people remember that they can choose to perceive what happened in a different way. Instead of blaming the other for offending them, they realize they have the choice to take offense or not. They try to control their negative emotions. They try to choose empathy for perpetrators rather than blaming them or demonizing them. They remember the emotional baggage that the others had. They see the perpetrator as a victim of a sick society; they feel pity for someone who was duped by a leader. They recast the event or behavior as something other than an attack. They find a new, important meaning or purpose in life. If people replace the anger and hurt of this particular offense with forgiveness, the offense is slowly erased and healing is complete. However, people need to be in the right emotional and mental space to be able to do this.

Forgiveness is always the same size. It seems as difficult for some people to forgive a slight insult as it is for others, like Marietta Jaeger, to forgive a daughter's murderer. In cases of genocide, letting go is not easy, but it is possible. Responsive forgiveness is possible no matter what the event or behavior is: from a slight miscommunication, to the murder of a woman's child, to racial oppression and genocide. Forgiveness is given with no strings attached. It does not matter if the offender knows about it, or accepts it, or forgives in return. Forgiveness means that the past no longer affects the present. People still remember the offense, but if they have truly forgiven someone, the offense has ceased to be an offense because its consequences have been removed. The hurt, the pain, the fear, and the anger are all gone. There is no sense of sacrifice in true forgiveness because what is being given up (revenge, suffering) is less than what is achieved (peace of mind). Forgiveness, both proactive and responsive, is the cornerstone of nonviolence.

Nonviolence

Ammon Hennacy, a pacifist social worker in the 1930s in the United States, described an occasion when the power of forgiveness and nonviolence overcame violence. He was being threatened by a violent man with a knife but he refused to fight back. Finally, after several hours, he was able to get the man to put away his knife. The man asked Hennacy why he had not fought him, and this was Hennacy's reply:

> What is your strongest weapon? It is your big fist with a big knife. What is my weakest weapon? It is a little fist without a knife. What is my strongest weapon? It is the fact that I do not get excited; I do not boil over; some people call it spiritual power. What is your weakest weapon? It is your getting excited and boiling over and your lack of spiritual power. I would be dumb if I used my weakest weapon, my small fist without a knife, against your strongest weapon, your large fist with a knife. I am smart, so I use my strongest weapon, my quiet spiritual power, against your weakest weapon, your excited manner, and I won, didn't I?
>
> (Hennacy, 1954:44)

Hennacy called forgiveness a spiritual power that was his best strategy to use to counteract his attacker. Gandhi called this spiritual power *satyagraha*, Sanskrit for "truth-strength."

Releasing the Past

Responsive forgiveness does not always address a recent personal offense. Sometimes responsive forgiveness neutralizes a past hurt which still affects the present; this is called *collective forgiveness*. Often this type of hurt is felt by group members who were the victims of a wrong perpetrated in the past by another group. Desmond Tutu's, F.W. de Klerk's, and Nelson Mandela's transformational leadership of South Africa demonstrated that a peaceful transition from oppression to freedom is possible if it occurs with collective forgiveness (Aikman, 2003:64).

There is a connection to Viktor Frankl's thesis in *Man's Search for Meaning* that people survive hardship mentally and spiritually intact if they can find meaning or purpose in their suffering (Frankl, 1985). Frankl's experience as a Jew in a Second World War death camp became "valuable" to him because of what he learned there about himself, human psychology, and the human search for purpose in life. Despite the fact that his wife and parents were killed, he was able to forgive. It has been pointed out that Frankl's work, although it is second only to *The Diary of Anne Frank* as a Holocaust book, cannot be found in the bookstore of

Washington's Holocaust Museum. The reason for this is that Frankl was, for his own complicated reasons, "too much of a reconciling spirit" (Scully, 1995:42). Perhaps he believed, as do other nonviolent leaders, that oppression and violence had important negative impacts on the perpetrators as well as the victims.

Still, it is clear that not everyone, no matter how wise and venerable, finds it possible to forgive. There is no shame in that. Elie Wiesel prayed for unforgiveness at a ceremony on the fiftieth anniversary of the liberation at the Auschwitz concentration camp: "God of forgiveness, do not forgive those who created this place. God of Mercy, have no mercy on those who killed here Jewish children" (quoted in Murphy, 2003:44). Eva Hoffman, a child of Holocaust survivors, in her book *After Such Knowledge: Memory, History, and the Aftermath of the Holocaust*, feels that it is not her place to forgive the past or to ask contemporary Germans for remorse:

> It is not my role or right, at this late stage, to forgive the perpetrators themselves. If some among the survivors find it in themselves to arrive at this most transcendent of ethical resolutions, then they cannot be gainsaid. But I, who have not been the direct object of persecution, am not entitled to dispense reprieve on behalf of those who were. Nor am I entitled to ask for responses from my German interlocutors which are not freely given. While we might hope that some genuine reparative remorse arises from a lived connection with the past, we have neither the right to ask for it, nor the power to absolve anyone from it.
>
> (Hoffman, 2004:109)

Acknowledgment

In the last chapter, we saw how important acknowledgment and recognition were in the School of Peace reconciliation process, but as Hoffman (2004) points out, we cannot demand acknowledgment or remorse. While it is not necessary to receive an apology or acknowledgment in order to forgive, some people find it easier to forgive the past if the offender acknowledges the offense and apologizes or offers restitution of some kind. The apology or restitution is an acknowledgment of a wrong that a people, or a people's ancestors or predecessors, committed. This is the basis for truth and reconciliation procedures that have occurred in Nicaragua and South Africa. Even though there is no way to undo the damages and pain of the past, the acknowledgment and apology help people to forgive and create a more peaceful present and future.

In 2008, the Australian Parliament apologized to the aboriginal population of Australia. There were one hundred aboriginal people present and many more watching on television. The apology acknowledged the mistreatment, indignity, degradation, and suffering of indigenous people, especially the "stolen generations," children who were removed from their homes for education elsewhere. The apology mentioned the people for whom it was intended: the descendants, the families and communities, honoring them and their culture. It stated an intention: that it be received as it was offered, in a spirit of healing and hope for a different future for all Australians. It resolved that the injustices of the past would never happen again and that current injustices (differences in life-expectancy, education, and economic opportunity) would be overcome. It specifically mentioned the "mutuality" of respect and responsibility for the future. Mutuality is another term for reciprocity.

The spokesman for the aboriginal peoples responded that the apology made their community feel a part of Australia for the first time in a long time. To them, it was about uniting, acknowledging the past, and moving on as brothers and sisters. If people believe that forgiveness is possible and practice it, there is hope for sustainable peace. If people can stop the past from affecting the present, they create a latency for preferred futures.

Pedagogies of Forgiveness

While it is, of course, impossible to make people forgive, it is possible to give people guidance and advice if they seek it out. If people want to forgive, they want to release themselves from the hurtful past and its effects on their present and future. They give up ideas of vengeance, punishment, and retribution. Forgiveness is unilateral and does not entail reconciliation. For sustainable peace, both partners in the conflict must want to forgive, resolve the conflict, and repair the relationship through reconciliation.

Elicitation

Enright and Fitzgibbons (2000) worked with victims of a variety of offenses. They described four phases in a therapeutic forgiving process when people want to forgive. However, the process seems inappropriate for the classroom. To make it more appropriate for a classroom dialogue or journaling experience, I suggest the themes of discovery, decision, discipline, and release to elicit cultural and personal resources for the process. The questions suggested for each phase are designed to help people reflect on their emotions and thoughts, and move on to the next phase, but they are flexible and must be adapted for each case. The process may take a long time, even years, as people reflect, remember, and recast the event. People who are trying to forgive should keep in mind Marietta Jaeger's advice to maintain diligent self-discipline, to corral the anger, fear and ego, to keep custody of the tongue, and to refuse to be mean-spirited.

- Discovery

  - What was the event or situation that injured you?
  - How did you perceive it or interpret it?
  - How did this perception or interpretation make you feel?
  - What are the effects of the injury on you and your life?
  - Have you incorporated the injury as a wound?
  - Do you feel angry, hurt, or disappointed?
  - Do you feel humiliated, guilty, or defensive?
  - What problems do you have related to the injury?
  - Do you want to be free of the past?

- Decision

  - Are you willing to free yourself from the past?
  - Why do you want to be free from the past?
  - Do you want to try to forgive?
  - Do you need to forgive? Why?
  - What cultural, social, or religious resources are there to take away your feelings of guilt or anger?
  - What would help take away the consequences of the injury?

- Discipline

  - What factors will increase your understanding of the other?
  - Can you feel sorry for the other?
  - Can you think of any reason why the offense might have happened?
  - Can you think of any way, no matter how remote or improbable, in which you may have contributed to the problem? (This question may not be appropriate for everyone.)
  - Can you take responsibility for your choice of attitude now?
  - Would you be willing to give the other a gift? What and when would you give?

- Release

  - Is there any meaning for your suffering?
  - Have you learned any positive lessons from what happened?
  - Who can help you or support you in this process?
  - Does this give you a purpose in life?
  - Do you feel freer from the effects of the past?

This process usually cycles through several iterations. However, if the negative feelings are not gone, if there is a sense of sacrifice, then it is false forgiveness in which the will to hold a grudge or to continue the effects of the offense has not gone away.

Prescription

I listened to a mind-training exercise like this from a female French lam (monk) at the Buddhist Meditation Center in Ulaanbaatar, Mongolia, where they teach meditation in English and Mongolian, run English classes and an internet café to attract people, and translate sacred texts from English and Tibetan to Mongolian. All this is being done after Buddhism was nearly obliterated under communism. Since this is a public-domain loving-kindness meditation, perhaps it is universal enough to be appropriate for people of other faiths and cultures.

> Let's begin by recognizing where we might feel guilt or blame. This helps us understand that others might feel guilt and blame also. Then we visualize those parts of us that are kind and loving. We will return to this awareness of our loving-kindness as an anchor for the rest of the meditation. Let each of us try to locate gentleness, warmth, and release within ourselves to create a context to which we can return again and again. It sometimes helps to accentuate those feelings by imagining a small baby. Once we have an awareness of that tenderness, we try to extend all the love and attention that we might extend to a baby to ourselves.
>
> Then we think about what we really need for ourselves and what we want and we say: "May I be happy. May I be peaceful. May I be free." We take all the time we need, exploring these feelings and letting loving-kindness grow and overwhelm us.
>
> Then we think about someone we love. Visualize that person and say, "Just as I want to be happy, may you be happy. Just as I want to be peaceful, may you be peaceful. Just as I want to be free, may you be free." Our feelings of loving-kindness should extend out and envelop this person. If this person you love has ever harmed you, extend your forgiveness to that person. Go through this procedure with other well-loved people.
>
> Then think about people in your family and repeat the visualization, saying, "Just as I want to be happy, may you all be happy. Just as I want to be peaceful, may you all be peaceful. Just as I want to be free, may all of you be free." The feelings of loving-kindness spread even further.
>
> Then we say to ourselves, "If I have harmed people knowingly or unknowingly, I ask their forgiveness." We visualize those people we have knowingly hurt and ask each one's forgiveness even if we have already been forgiven. Then we say to ourselves, "If people have

harmed me knowingly or unknowingly or even in the past, I freely forgive them." Let us visualize those who may have harmed us throughout our lives and without dwelling on the offense, we offer them our love and forgiveness again even if we have already forgiven them before. We return to our context of loving-kindness for ourselves, reaching for that part of us that seems most loving.

Now let us repeat the process for the person or people about whom there might still be hard feelings and grievances. There may still be resistance. Don't worry because healing always happens if you are sincere. Say: "Just as I want to be happy, may you be happy. Just as I want to be peaceful, may you be peaceful. Just as I want to be free, may you be free."

And for species identity, say: "Just as I want to be happy, may all people be happy. Just as I want to be peaceful, may all people be peaceful. Just as I want to be free, may all people be free."

Then let us open our feelings to all beings in the universe and wish them: "Just as I want to be happy, may all things be happy. Just as I want to be peaceful, may all things be peaceful. Just as I want to be free, may all beings be free."

Let each of us return all of this loving-kindness back to ourselves.

The Earth Charter

Preamble

We stand at a critical moment in Earth's history, a time when humanity must choose its future. As the world becomes increasingly interdependent and fragile, the future at once holds great peril and great promise. To move forward we must recognize that in the midst of a magnificent diversity of cultures and life forms we are one human family and one Earth community with a common destiny. We must join together to bring forth a sustainable global society founded on respect for nature, universal human rights, economic justice, and a culture of peace. Towards this end, it is imperative that we, the peoples of Earth, declare our responsibility to one another, to the greater community of life, and to future generations.

Earth, Our Home

Humanity is part of a vast evolving universe. Earth, our home, is alive with a unique community of life. The forces of nature make existence a demanding and uncertain adventure, but Earth has provided the conditions essential to life's evolution. The resilience of the community of life and the well-being of humanity depend upon preserving a healthy biosphere with all its ecological systems, a rich variety of plants and animals, fertile soils, pure waters, and clean air. The global environment with its finite resources is a common concern of all peoples. The protection of Earth's vitality, diversity, and beauty is a sacred trust.

The Global Situation

The dominant patterns of production and consumption are causing environmental devastation, the depletion of resources, and a massive extinction of species. Communities are being undermined. The benefits of development are not shared equitably and the gap between rich and poor is widening. Injustice, poverty, ignorance, and violent conflict are widespread and the cause of great suffering. An unprecedented rise in human population has overburdened ecological and social systems. The foundations of global security are threatened. These trends are perilous—but not inevitable.

The Challenges Ahead

The choice is ours: form a global partnership to care for Earth and one another or risk the destruction of ourselves and the diversity of life. Fundamental changes are needed in our values, institutions, and ways of living. We must realize that when basic needs have been met, human development is primarily about being more, not having more. We have the knowledge and technology to provide for all and to reduce our impacts on the environment. The emergence of a global civil society is creating new opportunities to build a democratic and humane world. Our environmental, economic, political, social, and spiritual challenges are interconnected, and together we can forge inclusive solutions.

Universal Responsibility

To realize these aspirations, we must decide to live with a sense of universal responsibility, identifying ourselves with the whole Earth community as well as our local communities. We are at once citizens of different nations and of one world in which the local and global are linked. Everyone shares responsibility for the present and future well-being of the human family and the larger living world. The spirit of human solidarity and kinship with all life is strengthened when we live with reverence for the mystery of being, gratitude for the gift of life, and humility regarding the human place in nature.

We urgently need a shared vision of basic values to provide an ethical foundation for the emerging world community. Therefore, together in hope we affirm the following interdependent principles for a sustainable way of life as a common standard by which the conduct of all individuals, organizations, businesses, governments, and transnational institutions is to be guided and assessed.

Principles

I.   RESPECT AND CARE FOR THE COMMUNITY OF LIFE

    1. Respect Earth and life in all its diversity.

        a.   Recognize that all beings are interdependent and every form of life has value regardless of its worth to human beings.

    b. Affirm faith in the inherent dignity of all human beings and in the intellectual, artistic, ethical, and spiritual potential of humanity.

2. Care for the community of life with understanding, compassion, and love.

    a. Accept that with the right to own, manage, and use natural resources comes the duty to prevent environmental harm and to protect the rights of people.

    b. Affirm that with increased freedom, knowledge, and power comes increased responsibility to promote the common good.

3. Build democratic societies that are just, participatory, sustainable, and peaceful.

    a. Ensure that communities at all levels guarantee human rights and fundamental freedoms and provide everyone an opportunity to realize his or her full potential.

    b. Promote social and economic justice, enabling all to achieve a secure and meaningful livelihood that is ecologically responsible.

4. Secure Earth's bounty and beauty for present and future generations.

    a. Recognize that the freedom of action of each generation is qualified by the needs of future generations.

    b. Transmit to future generations values, traditions, and institutions that support the long-term flourishing of Earth's human and ecological communities.

In order to fulfill these four broad commitments, it is necessary to:

II. ECOLOGICAL INTEGRITY

5. Protect and restore the integrity of Earth's ecological systems, with special concern for biological diversity and the natural processes that sustain life.

    a. Adopt at all levels sustainable development plans and regulations that make environmental conservation and rehabilitation integral to all development initiatives.

    b. Establish and safeguard viable nature and biosphere reserves, including wild lands and marine areas, to protect Earth's life support systems, maintain biodiversity, and preserve our natural heritage.

c. Promote the recovery of endangered species and ecosystems.

d. Control and eradicate non-native or genetically modified organisms harmful to native species and the environment, and prevent introduction of such harmful organisms.

e. Manage the use of renewable resources such as water, soil, forest products, and marine life in ways that do not exceed rates of regeneration and that protect the health of ecosystems.

f. Manage the extraction and use of non-renewable resources such as minerals and fossil fuels in ways that minimize depletion and cause no serious environmental damage.

6. Prevent harm as the best method of environmental protection and, when knowledge is limited, apply a precautionary approach.

a. Take action to avoid the possibility of serious or irreversible environmental harm even when scientific knowledge is incomplete or inconclusive.

b. Place the burden of proof on those who argue that a proposed activity will not cause significant harm, and make the responsible parties liable for environmental harm.

c. Ensure that decision-making addresses the cumulative, long-term, indirect, long-distance, and global consequences of human activities.

d. Prevent pollution of any part of the environment and allow no build-up of radioactive, toxic, or other hazardous substances.

e. Avoid military activities damaging to the environment.

7. Adopt patterns of production, consumption, and reproduction that safeguard Earth's regenerative capacities, human rights, and community well-being.

a. Reduce, reuse, and recycle the materials used in production and consumption systems, and ensure that residual waste can be assimilated by ecological systems.

b. Act with restraint and efficiency when using energy, and rely increasingly on renewable energy sources such as solar and wind.

c. Promote the development, adoption, and equitable transfer of environmentally sound technologies.

    d. Internalize the full environmental and social costs of goods and services in the selling price, and enable consumers to identify products that meet the highest social and environmental standards.

    e. Ensure universal access to healthcare that fosters reproductive health and responsible reproduction.

    f. Adopt lifestyles that emphasize the quality of life and material sufficiency in a finite world.

8. Advance the study of ecological sustainability and promote the open exchange and wide application of the knowledge acquired.

    a. Support international scientific and technical cooperation on sustainability, with special attention to the needs of developing nations.

    b. Recognize and preserve the traditional knowledge and spiritual wisdom in all cultures that contribute to environmental protection and human well-being.

    c. Ensure that information of vital importance to human health and environmental protection, including genetic information, remains available in the public domain.

III. SOCIAL AND ECONOMIC JUSTICE

9. Eradicate poverty as an ethical, social, and environmental imperative.

    a. Guarantee the right to potable water, clean air, food security, uncontaminated soil, shelter, and safe sanitation, allocating the national and international resources required.

    b. Empower every human being with the education and resources to secure a sustainable livelihood, and provide social security and safety nets for those who are unable to support themselves.

    c. Recognize the ignored, protect the vulnerable, serve those who suffer, and enable them to develop their capacities and to pursue their aspirations.

10. Ensure that economic activities and institutions at all levels promote human development in an equitable and sustainable manner.

    a. Promote the equitable distribution of wealth within nations and among nations.

b. Enhance the intellectual, financial, technical, and social resources of developing nations, and relieve them of onerous international debt.

c. Ensure that all trade supports sustainable resource use, environmental protection, and progressive labor standards.

d. Require multinational corporations and international financial organizations to act transparently in the public good, and hold them accountable for the consequences of their activities.

11. Affirm gender equality and equity as prerequisites to sustainable development and ensure universal access to education, healthcare, and economic opportunity.

a. Secure the human rights of women and girls and end all violence against them.

b. Promote the active participation of women in all aspects of economic, political, civil, social, and cultural life as full and equal partners, decision-makers, leaders, and beneficiaries.

c. Strengthen families and ensure the safety and loving nurture of all family members.

12. Uphold the right of all, without discrimination, to a natural and social environment supportive of human dignity, bodily health, and spiritual well-being, with special attention to the rights of indigenous peoples and minorities.

a. Eliminate discrimination in all its forms, such as that based on race, color, sex, sexual orientation, religion, language, and national, ethnic, or social origin.

b. Affirm the right of indigenous peoples to their spirituality, knowledge, lands, and resources and to their related practice of sustainable livelihoods.

c. Honor and support the young people of our communities, enabling them to fulfill their essential role in creating sustainable societies.

d. Protect and restore outstanding places of cultural and spiritual significance.

IV. DEMOCRACY, NONVIOLENCE, AND PEACE

13. Strengthen democratic institutions at all levels, and provide transparency and accountability in governance, inclusive participation in decision-making, and access to justice.

a. Uphold the right of everyone to receive clear and timely information on environmental matters and all development plans and activities which are likely to affect them or in which they have an interest.
b. Support local, regional and global civil society, and promote the meaningful participation of all interested individuals and organizations in decision-making.
c. Protect the rights to freedom of opinion, expression, peaceful assembly, association, and dissent.
d. Institute effective and efficient access to administrative and independent judicial procedures, including remedies and redress for environmental harm and the threat of such harm.
e. Eliminate corruption in all public and private institutions.
f. Strengthen local communities, enabling them to care for their environments, and assign environmental responsibilities to the levels of government where they can be carried out most effectively.

14. Integrate into formal education and life-long learning the knowledge, values, and skills needed for a sustainable way of life.

a. Provide all, especially children and youth, with educational opportunities that empower them to contribute actively to sustainable development.
b. Promote the contribution of the arts and humanities as well as the sciences in sustainability education.
c. Enhance the role of the mass media in raising awareness of ecological and social challenges.
d. Recognize the importance of moral and spiritual education for sustainable living.

15. Treat all living beings with respect and consideration.

a. Prevent cruelty to animals kept in human societies and protect them from suffering.
b. Protect wild animals from methods of hunting, trapping, and fishing that cause extreme, prolonged, or avoidable suffering.
c. Avoid or eliminate to the full extent possible the taking or destruction of non-targeted species.

16. Promote a culture of tolerance, nonviolence, and peace.

a. Encourage and support mutual understanding, solidarity, and cooperation among all peoples and within and among nations.

b. Implement comprehensive strategies to prevent violent conflict and use collaborative problem-solving to manage and resolve environmental conflicts and other disputes.

c. Demilitarize national security systems to the level of a non-provocative defense posture, and convert military resources to peaceful purposes, including ecological restoration.

d. Eliminate nuclear, biological, and toxic weapons and other weapons of mass destruction.

e. Ensure that the use of orbital and outer space supports environmental protection and peace.

f. Recognize that peace is the wholeness created by right relationships with oneself, other persons, other cultures, other life, Earth, and the larger whole of which all are a part.

The Way Forward

As never before in history, common destiny beckons us to seek a new beginning. Such renewal is the promise of these Earth Charter principles. To fulfill this promise, we must commit ourselves to adopt and promote the values and objectives of the Charter.

This requires a change of mind and heart. It requires a new sense of global interdependence and universal responsibility. We must imaginatively develop and apply the vision of a sustainable way of life locally, nationally, regionally, and globally. Our cultural diversity is a precious heritage and different cultures will find their own distinctive ways to realize the vision. We must deepen and expand the global dialogue that generated the Earth Charter, for we have much to learn from the ongoing collaborative search for truth and wisdom.

Life often involves tensions between important values. This can mean difficult choices. However, we must find ways to harmonize diversity with unity, the exercise of freedom with the common good, short-term objectives with long-term goals. Every individual, family, organization, and community has a vital role to play. The arts, sciences, religions, educational institutions, media, businesses, non-governmental organizations, and governments are all called to offer creative leadership. The partnership of government, civil society, and business is essential for effective governance.

In order to build a sustainable global community, the nations of the world must renew their commitment to the United Nations, fulfill their obligations under existing international agreements, and support the implementation of Earth Charter principles with an international, legally binding instrument on environment and development.

Let ours be a time remembered for the awakening of a new reverence for life, the firm resolve to achieve sustainability, the quickening of the struggle for justice and peace, and the joyful celebration of life.

Bibliography

Adler, P. (1976) "Beyond Cultural Identity: Reflections on Multicultural Man," in L.A. Samovar and R.E. Porter (eds) *Intercultural Communication: A Reader*, Belmont, CA: Wadsworth. 362–78.

Adorno, T., Frenkel-Brunswik, E., Levinson, D., and Sanford, R. (1950) *The Authoritarian Personality*, New York: Harper.

Aikman, D. (2003) *Great Souls: Six who Changed the Century*, Lanham, MD: Lexington.

Altemeyer, B. (2004) "The Other 'Authoritarian Personality,' " in J. Jost and J. Sidanius (eds) *Political Psychology*, New York: Psychology Press. 85–107.

Appiah, K. (2006) *Cosmopolitanism: Ethics in a World of Strangers*, New York: W.W. Norton & Company.

Arendt, H. (2003) "Eichmann in Jerusalem: A Report on the Banality of Evil," in P. Baehr (ed.) *The Portable Hannah Arendt*, New York: Penguin. 313–75.

Bar-On, D. (1989) *Legacy of Silence: Encounters with Children of the Third Reich*, Cambridge, MA: Harvard University Press.

Baum, R. (2000) "Never to Forget: Pedagogical Memory and Second-Generation Witness," in R. Simon, S. Rosenberg, and C. Eppert (eds) *Between Hope and Despair: Pedagogy and the Remembrance of Historical Trauma*, Lanham, MD: Rowman & Littlefield. 91–116.

Benedict, R. (1976) "Synergy," in B. Sanford (ed.) *Peacemaking: A Guide to Conflict Resolution*, New York: Bantam. 410–20.

Bennett, M. (1991) "Toward a Developmental Model of Intercultural Sensitivity," in M. Paige (ed.) *Education for the Intercultural Experience*, Yarmouth, ME: Intercultural Press.

Bettelheim, B. (1984) "Afterword," in C. Vegh (ed.), R. Schwartz (trans.) *I Didn't Say Goodbye*, New York: E.P. Dutton.

Birch, B. (1994) "Prosocial Communicative Competence in the ESL/EFL Classroom," *TESOL Journal* Winter: 13–16.

—— (1995) "Quaker Plain Speech: A Policy of Linguistic Divergence," *International Journal of the Sociology of Language* 116:39–59.

—— (2004) *Learning and Teaching English Grammar, K-12*, Columbus, OH: Merrill Education.

—— (2006) "Global Citizenship for (American) Dummies," unpublished manuscript.

Blatt, M. and Kohlberg, L. (1975) "The Effects of Classroom Moral Discussion upon Children's Moral Judgment," *Journal of Moral Education* 4:129–61.

Block, D. and Cameron, D. (2002) *Globalization and Language Teaching*, London: Routledge.

Bonanno, G.A. and Jost, J.T. (2006) "Conservative Shift among High-Exposure Survivors of the September 11th Terrorist Attacks," *Basic and Applied Social Psychology* 28:311–23.

Bond, M. (1986) *The Psychology of Chinese People*, New York: Oxford University Press.

Boulding, E. (1990) *Building a Global Civic Culture: Education for an Interdependent World*, Syracuse, NY: Syracuse University Press.

—— (2000) *Cultures of Peace: The Hidden Side of History*, Syracuse, NY: Syracuse University Press.

Boyle, D. (2005) "Youth Bullying: Incidence, Impact, and Interventions," *Journal of the New Jersey Psychological Association* 55(3):22–4.

Brenes-Castro, A. (2004) "An Integral Model of Peace Education," in A. Wenden (ed.) *Educating for a Culture of Social and Ecological Peace*, Albany: State University of New York Press. 77–98.

Brown, R. (2004) "The Authoritarian Personality and the Organization of Attitudes," in J. Jost and J. Sidanius (eds) *Political Psychology*, New York: Psychology Press. 39–68.

Bruner, J. (1986) *Actual Minds, Possible Worlds*, New York: Plenum Press.

Cameron, D. (1995) *Verbal Hygiene*, London: Routledge.

Canagarajah, A. (1999) *Resisting Linguistic Imperialism in English Teaching*, Oxford: Oxford University Press.

Center for Education and Research in Environmental Strategies (CERES) (2008) Available online: <http://www.ceres.org.au> (accessed July 1, 2008).

Collins, M. (1994) "Global Corporate Philanthropy and Relationship Marketing," *European Management Journal* 12: 226–33.

Davies, L. (2004) *Education and Conflict: Complexity and Chaos*, London: Routledge/Falmer.

de Tocqueville, A. (1945) *Democracy in America*, New York: Vintage, cited in M. Kaldor (2003) *Global Civil Society: An Answer to War*, Cambridge: Polity Press. 20.

Dicker, C. (2006) personal email communication, December 13.

Dower, N. (2005) "The Earth Charter and Global Citizenship: A Way Forward," in *Toward a Sustainable World: The Earth Charter in Action*. Available online: <http://www.earthcharterinaction.org/> (accessed April 18, 2008).

Earth Charter Initiative (2008) Available online: <http://www.earthcharter.org/> (accessed April 18, 2008).

Education Action (2008) Available online: <http://www.education-action.org/> (accessed June 21, 2008).

Education International (2008) Available online: <http://www.ei-ie.org/en/index.php> (accessed April 18, 2008).

Enright, R. and Fitzgibbons, R. (2000) *Helping Clients Forgive: An Empirical Guide for Resolving Anger and Restoring Hope*, Washington, DC: American Psychological Association.

Enright, R. and North, J. (1998) "Introducing Forgiveness," in R. Enright and

J. North (eds) *Exploring Forgiveness*, Madison: University of Wisconsin Press. 3–9.

Eron, L. (1997) "Theories of Aggression: From Drives to Cognitions," in L. Huesmann (ed.) *Aggressive Behavior: Current Perspectives*, New York: Plenum. 3–11.

Falk, R. (1999) *Predatory Globalization: A Critique*, Cambridge: Polity Press.

Farah, A. (1993) *The Roots of Reconciliation*, London: Action Aid.

Faruqi, I.R. (1986) *Toward Islamic English*, Herndon, VA: International Institute of Islamic Thought. Available online: <http://www.tesolislamia.org/ articles. html> (accessed April 18, 2008).

Feuerverger, G. (2001) *Oasis of Dreams: Teaching and Learning Peace in a Jewish–Palestinian Village in Israel*, London: Routledge/Falmer.

Fisher, R. and Brown, S. (1988) *Getting Together: Building Relationships as We Negotiate*, New York: Penguin.

Fisher, R., Ury, W., and Patton, B. (1991) *Getting to Yes: Negotiating Agreement without Giving in*, New York: Penguin.

Foundation for Universal Responsibility (2008) Available online: <http://www. furhhdl.org> (accessed February 15, 2008).

Frankl, V. (1985) *Man's Search for Meaning: An Introduction to Logotherapy*, New York: Pocket Books.

Gandhi, M. (1970) *Essential Writings*, R. Murti (ed.), New Delhi: Gandhi Peace Foundation.

Gee, J. (1994) "Orality and Literacy: From *The Savage Mind* to *Ways with Words*," in J. Maybin (ed.) *Language and Literacy in Social Practice*, Clevedon: Multilingual Matters. 168–92.

Geertz, C. (1974) "From the Native's Point of View: On the Nature of Anthropological Understanding," in K. Basso and H. Selby (eds) *Meaning in Anthropology*, Albuquerque: University of New Mexico Press. 221–37.

Gilligan, C. (1982) *In a Different Voice: Psychological Theory and Women's Development*, Cambridge, MA: Harvard University Press.

Glick, P. and Fiske, S. (2001) "Ambivalent Stereotypes as Legitimizing Ideologies," in J. Jost and B. Major (eds) *The Psychology of Legitimacy: Emerging Perspectives on Ideology, Justice, and Intergroup Relations*, Cambridge: Cambridge University Press. 278–306.

Glissant, E. (1997) *Poetics of Relation*, B. Wing (trans.), Ann Arbor: University of Michigan Press.

Global Compact (2008) Available online: <http://www.un.org/Depts/ptd/global. htm> (accessed April 18, 2008).

Global Reporting Initiative (2008) Available online: <http://www.globalreporting. org/Home> (accessed April 18, 2008).

Gray, J. (2002) "The Global Coursebook in English Language Teaching," in D. Block and D. Cameron (eds) *Globalization and Language Teaching*, London: Routledge. 151–67.

Great Transition Initiative (2008) Available online: <http://www.tellus.org/ activities/greattransition.html> (accessed April 18, 2008).

Greenpeace (2008) Available online: <http://www.greenpeace.org> (accessed April 18, 2008).

Hadley, G. (2004) "ELT and the New World Order: Nation Building or

Neo-colonial Reconstruction?" Available online: <http://www.tesolislamia.org/articles.html> (accessed April 18, 2008).

Hartley, A. (2003) *The Zanzibar Chest*, New York: Penguin.

Hennacy, A. (1954) *The Autobiography of a Catholic Anarchist*, New York: Catholic Worker Books.

Hoffman, E. (2004) *After Such Knowledge: Memory, History and the Aftermath of the Holocaust*, New York: Public Affairs.

hooks, b. (1995) *Killing Rage: Ending Racism*, New York: Henry Holt and Company.

Hsu, F. (1985) "The Self in Cross-Cultural Perspective," in A. Marsella, G. De Vos, and F. Hsu (eds) *Culture and Self*, London: Tavistock. 24–55.

Human Rights Watch (2008) Available online: <http://www.hrw.org> (accessed April 18, 2008).

International Association of Teachers of English as a Foreign Language (IATEFL) (2008) Available online: <http://www.iatefl.org/> (accessed July 21, 2008).

International Reading Association (IRA) (2008) Available online: <http://www.reading.org> (accessed February 20, 2008).

International Technology Education Association (ITEA) (2008) Available online: <http://www.iteaconnect.org/index.html> (accessed February 20, 2008).

Inter-Parliamentary Union (IPU) (2008) Available online: <http://www.ipu.org/english/home.htm> (accessed April 18, 2008).

Jaeger, M. (1998) "The Power and Reality of Forgiveness: Forgiving the Murderer of One's Child," in R. Enright and J. North (eds) *Exploring Forgiveness*, Madison: University of Wisconsin Press. 4–10.

Jaensch, E. (1938) *Der Gegentypus*, Leipzig: Barth, cited in R. Brown (2004) "The Authoritarian Personality and the Organization of Attitudes," in J. Jost and J. Sidanius (eds) *Political Psychology*, New York: Psychology Press.

Janowitz, M. (1985) *The Reconstruction of Patriotism: Education for Civic Consciousness*, Chicago: University of Chicago Press.

Johnston, B. (2003) *Values in English Language Teaching*, Mahwah, NJ: Lawrence Erlbaum Associates.

Jost, J., Glaser, J., Kruglanski, A., and Sulloway, F. (2003) "Political Conservatism as Motivated Social Cognition," *Psychological Bulletin* 129(3):339–75.

Jost, J. and Major, B. (eds) (2001) *The Psychology of Legitimacy: Emerging Perspectives on Ideology, Justice, and Intergroup Relations*, Cambridge: Cambridge University Press.

Kaldor, M. (2003) *Global Civil Society: An Answer to War*, Cambridge: Polity Press.

Karmani, S. (2005) "English, 'Terror,' and Islam," *Applied Linguistics* 26(2):262–7.

Kazmi, Y. (1997) "The Hidden Political Agenda of Teaching English as an International Language," *Muslim Education Quarterly* 15(1). Available online: <http://www.tesolislamia.org/articles.html> (accessed April 18, 2008).

Keane, J. (2001) "Global Civil Society?," in H. Anheier, M. Glasius, and M. Kaldor (eds) *Global Civil Society 2001*, Oxford: Oxford University Press. 23–47.

Kelman, H. and Hamilton, V. (1989) *Crimes of Obedience: Toward a Social Psychology of Authority and Responsibility*, New Haven, CT: Yale University Press.

King, M.L. (1964) "Letter from a Birmingham Jail." Available online: <http://www.africa.upenn.edu/Articles_Gen/Letter_Birmingham.html> (accessed December 7, 2008).

—— (1986) *A Testament of Hope: The Essential Writings and Speeches of Martin Luther King, Jr.*, J. Washington (ed.), New York: HarperCollins.

Kitayama, S. and Uchida, Y. (2004) "Interdependent Agency: An Alternative System for Action," in R. Sorrentino, D. Cohen, J. Olson, and M. Zanna, (eds) *Culture and Social Behavior: The Ontario Symposium (Vol. 10)*, Mahwah, NJ: Lawrence Erlbaum Associates. 137–64.

Kohlberg, L. (1981) *The Philosophy of Moral Development: Moral Stages and the Idea of Justice*, San Francisco, CA: Harper and Row.

—— (1984) *The Psychology of Moral Development: The Nature and Validity of Moral Stages*, New York: Harper and Row.

Kramsch, C. and Thorne, S. (2002) "Foreign Language Learning as Global Communicative Practice," in D. Block and D. Cameron (eds) *Globalization and Language Teaching*, London: Routledge. 83–100.

Kriegman, O. (2006) "Dawn of the Cosmopolitan: The Hope of a Global Citizens Movement." Available online: <http://www.gtinitiative.org> (accessed April 18, 2008).

Kumaravadivelu, B. (2008) *Cultural Globalization and Language Education*, New Haven, CT: Yale University Press.

Lederach, J.P. (1995) *Preparing for Peace: Conflict Transformation across Cultures*, Syracuse, NY: Syracuse University Press.

—— (2004) *Building Peace: Sustainable Reconciliation in Divided Societies*, Washington, DC: United States Institute of Peace Press.

—— (2005) *The Moral Imagination: The Art and Soul of Building Peace*, Oxford: Oxford University Press.

Lerner, M. (2003) *Healing Israel/Palestine*, Berkeley, CA: North Atlantic Books.

Lewis, D. (2002) "Civil Society in African Contexts: Reflections on the 'Usefulness' of a Concept," *Development and Change* 33(4):569–86.

Lipschutz, R. (2005) "Power, Politics and Global Civil Society," *Millennium: Journal of International Studies* 33(3):747–69.

Liss, A. (2000) "Artifactual Testimonies and the Stagings of Holocaust Memory," in R. Simon, S. Rosenberg, and C. Eppert (eds) (2000) *Between Hope and Despair: Pedagogy and the Remembrance of Historical Trauma*, Lanham, MD: Rowman & Littlefield. 117–34.

MachsomWatcher (2008) Available online: <http://www.machsomwatch.org/en> (accessed May 1, 2008).

Markus, H. and Kitayama, S. (1991) "Culture and the Self: Implications for Cognition, Emotion, and Motivation," *Psychological Bulletin* 98(2):224–53.

Martusewicz, R. (2001) *Seeking Passage: Post-structuralism, Pedagogy, Ethics*, New York: Teachers College Press.

McIntosh, P. (1992) "White Privilege: Unpacking the Invisible Knapsack," *Creation Spirituality*, January/February:33–5, 53.

McMillan, D. and Chavis, D. (1986) "Sense of Community: A Definition and Theory," *Journal of Community Psychology* 14(1):6–23.

Médecins Sans Frontières (MSF) (2008) *Doctors without Borders*. Available online: <http://www.doctorswithoutborders.org> (accessed April 19, 2008).

Michnik, A. (1998) "Why Post-totalitarian?," in *Letters from Freedom*, Berkeley: University of California Press, cited in M. Kaldor (2003) *Global Civil Society: An Answer to War*, Cambridge: Polity Press.

—— (1999) "The Rebirth of Civil Society," Ideas of 1989 Lecture Series, LSE, London, November, cited in M. Kaldor (2003) *Global Civil Society: An Answer to War*, Cambridge: Polity Press.

Miller, J., Bersoff, D., and Harwood, R. (1990) "Perceptions of Social Responsibilities in India and in the United States: Moral Imperatives or Personal Decisions?," *Journal of Personality and Social Psychology* 58:33–47.

Mino, T. (2006) "*Ijime* (Bullying) in Japanese Schools: A Product of Japanese Education Based on Group Conformity," paper presented at the Second Annual Re-Visioning Boundaries Conference of the School of Languages and Comparative Cultural Studies, University of Queensland, Brisbane, Australia, February 24–25.

Mohd-Asraf, R. (2005) "English and Islam: A Clash of Civilizations," in S. Karmani and S. Makoni (eds) *Islam and English in the Post-9/11 Era*, special issue of *Journal of Language, Identity, and Education* 4(2):103–18.

Moore, D. (2007) *The World Bank*, KwaZulu-Natal: University of KwaZulu-Natal Press.

Murphy, J. (2003) *Getting Even: Forgiveness and its Limits*, Oxford: Oxford University Press.

"Nehru, a 'Queer Mix of East and West,' Led the Struggle for a Modern India," *New York Times* May 28, 1964.

Neuffer, E. (2001) *The Key to my Neighbor's House: Seeking Justice in Bosnia and Rwanda*, New York: Picador.

Nussbaum, M. (1996) "Patriotism and Cosmopolitanism," in J. Cohen (ed.) *For Love of Country: Debating the Limits of Patriotism*, Boston, MA: Beacon Press.

Osborn, T. (2000) *Critical Reflection and the Foreign Language Classroom*, Westport, CT: Bergin and Garvey.

—— (2006) *Teaching World Languages for Social Justice: A Sourcebook of Principles and Practices*, Mahwah, NJ: Lawrence Erlbaum Associates.

Osland, J. and Osland, A. (2005) "Expatriate Paradoxes and Cultural Involvement," *International Studies of Management and Organization* 35(4):93–116.

Pax Christi Netherlands (2008) Available online: <http://www.paxchristi.nl/UK/index.htm> (accessed October 13, 2007).

Peace Brigades International (2008) Available online: <http://www.peacebrigades.org> (accessed April 18, 2008).

Peck, M.S. (1987) *The Different Drum: Community Making and Peace*, New York: Simon and Schuster.

Pennycook, A. (1994) *The Cultural Politics of English as an International Language*, London: Longman.

—— (2001) *Critical Applied Linguistics: A Critical Introduction*, Mahwah, NJ: Lawrence Erlbaum Associates.

Pennycook, A. and Makoni, S. (2005) "The Modern Mission: The Language Effects of Christianity," in S. Karmani and S. Makoni (eds) *Islam and English in the Post-9/11 Era*, special issue of *Journal of Language, Identity, and Education* 4(2):137–49.

Phillipson, R. (1992) *Linguistic Imperialism*, Oxford: Oxford University Press.

—— (2003) *English-Only Europe? Challenging Language Policy*, London: Routledge.

Poster, M. (1989) *Critical Theory and Poststructuralism: In Search of a Context*, Ithaca, NY: Cornell University Press.

Power, F., Higgins, A., and Kohlberg, L. (1989) *Lawrence Kohlberg's Approach to Moral Education*, New York: Columbia University Press.

Rahman, T. (2005) "The Muslim Response to English in South Asia: With Special Reference to Inequality, Intolerance, and Militancy in Pakistan," in S. Karmani and S. Makoni (eds) *Islam and English in the Post-9/11 Era*, special issue of *Journal of Language, Identity, and Education* 4(2):119–36.

Ranck, J. (2000) "Beyond Reconciliation: Memory and Alterity in Post-genocide Rwanda," in R. Simon, S. Rosenberg, and C. Eppert (eds) *Between Hope and Despair: Pedagogy and the Remembrance of Historical Trauma*, Lanham, MD: Rowman & Littlefield. 187–212.

Raskin, P., Banuri, T., Gallopín, G., Gutman, P., Hammond, A., Kates, R., and Swart, R. (2002) *Great Transition: The Promise and the Lure of the Times Ahead*, Boston, MA: Tellus Institute. Available online: <http://www.tellus.org> (accessed June 1, 2008).

Regehr, E. (1993) "War after the Cold War: Shaping a Canadian Response," Ploughshare Working Paper 93–3, Waterloo, Ontario: Project Ploughshares, cited in J.P. Lederach (2004) *Building Peace: Sustainable Reconciliation in Divided Societies*, Washington, DC: United States Institute of Peace Press.

Rinpoche, G. (2005) *The Essential Dalai Lama: His Important Teachings*, R. Mehrotra (ed.), New York: Viking.

Robertson, R. (1992) *Globalization, Social Theory, and Global Culture*, London: Sage.

Rosenberg, M. (2005) *Nonviolent Communication: A Language of Life*, Encinitas, CA: PuddleDancer Press.

Rosenberg, S. (2000) "Standing in a Circle of Stone: Rupturing the Binds of Emblematic Memory," in R. Simon, S. Rosenberg, and C. Eppert (eds) (2000) *Between Hope and Despair: Pedagogy and the Remembrance of Historical Trauma*, Lanham, MD: Rowman & Littlefield. 75–90.

Rothkopf, D. (2008) "What Power Looks Like," *Newsweek* 151(15), April 14. Available online: <http://www.newsweek.com/id/130637/output/print> (accessed April 14, 2008).

Russian Association of Indigenous Peoples of the North, Siberia, and Far East (RAIPON) (2008) Available online: <http://www.raipon.org/Default.aspx?alias=www.raipon.org/english> (accessed July 20, 2008).

Salverson, J. (2000) "Anxiety and Contact in Attending to a Play about Landmines," in R. Simon, S. Rosenberg, and C. Eppert (eds) (2000) *Between Hope and Despair: Pedagogy and the Remembrance of Historical Trauma*, Lanham, MD: Rowman & Littlefield. 59–74.

Schell, J. (2003) *The Unconquerable World: Power, Nonviolence, and the Will of the People*, New York: Henry Holt and Company.

Scully, M. (1995) "Viktor Frankl at Ninety: An Interview," *First Things* 52, April:39–43.

Servicio Paz y Justicia (SERPAJ) (2008) Available online: <http://www.serpajamericalatina.org/> (accessed April 18, 2008).

Simon, R., Rosenberg, S., and Eppert, C. (2000) "Introduction. Between Hope and Despair: The Pedagogical Encounter of Historical Remembrance," in R. Simon, S. Rosenberg, and C. Eppert (eds) *Between Hope and Despair: Pedagogy and the Remembrance of Historical Trauma*, Lanham, MD: Rowman & Littlefield. 1–8.

Solidarity Movement (2008) Available online: <http://www.palsolidarity.org> (accessed April 13, 2008).

Spring, J. (2004) *How Education Ideologies are Shaping Global Society: Intergovernmental Organizations, NGOs, and the Decline of the Nation-State*, Mahwah, NJ: Lawrence Erlbaum Associates.

—— (2007) *A New Paradigm for Global School Systems: Education for a Long and Happy Life*, Mahwah, NJ: Lawrence Erlbaum Associates.

Stabile, C. (2000) "Nike, Social Responsibility, and the Hidden Abode of Production," *Critical Studies in Media Communication* 17(2), June:186–204.

Staub, E. (1989) *The Roots of Evil: The Origins of Genocide and Other Group Violence*, Cambridge: Cambridge University Press.

—— (2003) *The Psychology of Good and Evil: Why Children, Adults, and Groups Help and Harm Others*, Cambridge: Cambridge University Press.

Staub, E. and Pearlman, L. (2003) "Healing, Forgiveness, and Reconciliation in Rwanda: Project Summary and Outcome," in E. Staub, *The Psychology of Good and Evil: Why Children, Adults, and Groups Help and Harm Others*, Cambridge: Cambridge University Press. 451–4.

Taki, M. (2001) "Japanese School Bullying: *Ijime*," paper presented to the Understanding and Preventing Bullying: An International Perspective Conference, October 19, Queen's University, Kingston, Ontario, Canada. Available online: <http://www.nier.go.jp/a000110/Toronto.pdf> (accessed June 1, 2008).

Taylor, H. (1969) "Toward a World University," *Saturday Review* 24:52.

Teachers of English to Speakers of Other Languages (TESOL) (2008) Available online: <http://www.tesol.org> (accessed April 15, 2008).

Tennant, A. (2002) "The Ultimate Language Lesson." Available online: <http://www.christianitytoday.com/ct/2002/december9/1.32.html?start=1> (accessed April 18, 2008).

TESOLers for Social Responsibility (2008) Available online: <http:///www.tesol.org/s_tesol/seccss.asp?CID=296&DID=1798> (accessed April 15, 2008).

TESOL Islamia (2008) Available online: <http://www.tesolislamia.org> (accessed April 15, 2008).

Tetreault, M. and Lipschutz, R. (2005) *Global Politics as if People Mattered*, Lanham, MD: Rowman & Littlefield.

Thakur [Tagore], R. (1916) *Sādhanā: The Realisation of Life*, New York: Macmillan.

—— (1917) *Gitanjali* [Song Offerings], New York: Macmillan.

Tikkun Community (2008) Available online: <http://www.tikkun.org> (accessed April 15, 2008).

Tohei, K. (1972) *Aikido in Everyday Life*, Tokyo: Rukugei.

Tutu, D. (2003) "Foreword," in *Truth and Reconciliation Commission of South Africa Report*. Available online: <http://www.info.gov.za/otherdocs/2003/trc/foreward.pdf> (accessed May 1, 2008).

United Nations Decade for Education for Sustainable Development (2008) Available online: <http://portal.unesco.org/education> (accessed April 18, 2008).

United Nations Universal Declaration of Human Rights (1948). Available online: <http://www.un.org/Overview/rights.html> (accessed April 18, 2008).

United States Peace Corps (2008) Available online: <http://www.peacecorps.gov> (accessed April 18, 2008).

Vilela, M. and Corcoran, P. (2005) "Building Consensus on Shared Values," in *Toward a Sustainable World: The Earth Charter in Action*. Available online: <http://www.earthcharterinaction.org/> (accessed April 18, 2008).

Walcott, R. (2000) "Pedagogy and Trauma: The Middle Passage, Slavery and the Problem of Creolization," in R. Simon, S. Rosenberg, and C. Eppert (eds) *Between Hope and Despair: Pedagogy and the Remembrance of Historical Trauma*, Lanham, MD: Rowman & Littlefield. 135–52.

Weisz, J. (1989) "Culture and the Development of Child Psychopathology: Lessons from Thailand," in D. Cicchetti (ed.) *The Emergence of a Discipline: Rochester Symposium on Developmental Psychopathology*, Vol. 1, Hillsdale, NJ: Lawrence Erlbaum. 89–117.

Wenden, A. (2004a) "Value-Based Perspective Development," in A. Wenden (ed.) *Educating for a Culture of Social and Ecological Peace*, Albany: State University of New York Press. 145–68.

—— (ed.) (2004b) *Educating for a Culture of Social and Ecological Peace*, Albany: State University of New York Press.

Werth, C. (2008) "Offshore English," *Newsweek* 151(18), May 5 (accessed online May 5, 2008; no longer available).

West, C. (1994) *Race Matters*, New York: Vintage.

White, M. and LeVine, R. (1986) "What is a Liko (Good Child)?," in H. Stevenson, H. Azuma, and K. Hakuta (eds) *Child Development and Education in Japan*, New York: Freeman. 55–62.

Wikimedia (2006) Available online: <http://www.wikimedia.org> (accessed November 29, 2006).

Wikipedia (2006) Available online: <http://www.wikipedia.org> (accessed November 29, 2006).

World Bank (2008) Available online: <http://go.worldbank.org/> (accessed April 18, 2008).

"World Peace" (2006) Available online: <http://en.wikipedia.org/w/index.php?title=World_peace&oldid=90372175> (accessed November 29, 2006).

Wurzel, J. (1998) "Teaching Reflective Thinking, Cultural Constraints and Cross Cultural Responses," *The Edge, the E-Journal of Intercultural Relations* 1(3), Summer (accessed November 12, 2006; no longer available).

Zehr, H. (1990) *Changing Lenses: A New Focus for Crime and Justice*, Scottdale, PA: Herald Press.

Zelditch, M. (2001) "Theories of Legitimacy," in J. Jost and B. Major (eds) *The Psychology of Legitimacy: Emerging Perspectives on Ideology, Justice, and Intergroup Relations*, Cambridge: Cambridge University Press. 33–54.

Index